Currently living in Brooklyn, STEWART LEE ALLEN has also called California, Kathmandu, Sydney, San Cristobel, Calcutta and San Francisco home. When not lounging about a café in a far-flung corner of the globe, he has worked as a grape-picker, theatrical director, bathroom attendant, grave-digger, punk musician, smuggler and, of course, a writer. He is the author of the award-winning fiction collection *The Art of Rape* as well as his acclaimed history of coffee, *The Devil's Cup*.

D0921223

By the same author

The Devil's Cup: Coffee, the Driving Force in History

In the
Devil's Garden

A SINFUL HISTORY OF
FORBIDDEN FOOD

STEWART LEE ALLEN

CANONGATE

First published in Great Britain in 2002 by
Canongate Books Ltd, 14 High Street,
Edinburgh EH1 1TE

This paperback edition first published in 2003 by Canongate Books Ltd

Originally published in the United States of America by The Ballantine
Publishing Group, a division of Random House, Inc., New York, and
simultaneously in Canada by Random House of Canada Limited, Toronto

This edition published by arrangement with The Ballantine Publishing Group,
a division of Random House, Inc.

10 9 8 7 6 5 4 3 2 1

British Library Cataloguing-in-Publication Data
A catalogue record for this book is available on
request from the British Library

ISBN 1 84195 405 5

Typeset in the United States of America
Printed and bound by Bookmarque Ltd, Croydon, Surrey

www.canongate.net

TO NINA J.

"The serpent poured upon the fruit the poison of his wickedness, which is Lust, for it is the beginning of every sin—and he bent the branch to the earth and I took of the fruit and I ate."

—Eve as an old woman describing humanity's last day in Eden
The Apocalypse of Moses
First century A.D.

"Too long, too late, I lost the taste for my own pleasure."

—Marguerite Duras
The Lover
1978

CONTENTS

Lust

Gluttony

Pride

Sloth

Greed

Blasphemy

Anger

Contents

Introduction:
ON SIN, SEX, AND FORBIDDEN FOOD

Jackson was lying on the kitchen counter allowing his father to change his diapers when a mysterious silver fountain rose up from between his thighs. Jackson's eyes popped open in amazement—did I do that? What a splendid effect! What a glorious sensation! The eighteen-inch geyser hung glittering for an instant. Then it collapsed, to break directly over his father's head and splash down his back. The crowd of relatives burst into applause. Jackson's mother, Paula, rushed over to give her boy a congratulatory kiss. Even Troy (his father) shook his hand. I mention all this because, while flapping his little arms in triumph Jackson came upon a pale green grape bouncing across the blue tile countertop. He immediately popped the fruit into his mouth. Paula's coo changed to a gasp of horror. No, Jackson! she screeched, No, no, no! You don't want to eat that! Bad! She yanked the forbidden fruit out of Jackson's maw and his jubilation was turned to grief.

The lesson my nephew learned that day was simple. Piss on your father, spit at your mother, but don't eat *that*. And *that* is the topic of this book, forbidden foods and their meaning, from chocolate to foie gras to the potato chip, from the Garden of Eden until today. It took Jackson's little adventure to bring home to me how profound our feelings are on this matter. Life, after all, is at heart an act of eating and so when we make a dish taboo, there is usually an interesting story to tell. The Bible used a tale of forbidden food to define all of human nature, and since then our religious and political leaders have been manipulating the notion so vigorously it has come to flavor every emotion we have about what we eat. We now judge a dish largely by how guilty we feel about eating it—at least judging from today's advertising—and if it is not considered "sinful" we find it less pleasant.

It's a situation that has led to the criminalizing of hundreds of common dishes throughout history, and, since we ban things because of their association with a particular sin, I've organized this book into sections corresponding with the famous Seven Deadly Sins: lust, gluttony, pride, sloth, greed, blasphemy, and anger. Within each section are the stories of delicacies tabooed for their association with a vice that the society in question found particularly abhorrent. The first chapter deals with lust, in honor of Eve's illicit snack and the ensuing roll in the hay. Food and sex are a heady combination; a quarter of all people who lose the ability to taste dinner also lose their sex drive, and Freud believed all humans experience their first sexual and culinary thrill simultaneously when they begin suckling on their mother's nipple. Our lust for aphrodisiac foods has led to the extermination of entire species and the fall of empires, per the curious tale of how hot chocolate became a risqué player in the French Revolution.

The book continues sin by sin to cover everything from how the first recorded image of God relates to certain taboos in Asia and the West, to how modern corporations manipulate our subliminal hunting/violent urges to make junk food more appealing. Since whom we invite for dinner can be as important as what we serve, there are stories on how these rules have played a part in events like the crucifixion of Jesus Christ. Disputes between "chefs," like the one that split Europe in half, make an appearance. There are also recipes. A plate of Joël Robuchon's famously sensual mashed potatoes (page 138) should give the flavor of the sloth-like ecstasy that led the English to try to ban the root in the 1800s. The ancient Roman dish on page 56 gives a taste of the gluttonous decadence that Caesar tried to stamp out when overindulgence was threatening the world's mightiest empire.

These food taboos were so important to our ancestors that they often starved to death rather than violate them, and at least half of the world's current population—from cow-crazy Hindus to kosher Jews to young Western vegetarians—still live with severe dietary restrictions on a daily basis. For many, these laws are crucial in defining themselves in relationship both to God and to their fellow humans, and fundamentally shape the societies in which they live. Even in the West, where outright bans are rare, food taboos still operate below the surface. Many scholars believe that psychological diseases like anorexia, which kills tens of thousands of people a year, stem in part from the complicated social psychosis left by ancient dietary laws. And sometimes when we ignore these rules, catastrophe has resulted; at least one of the greatest calamities of the twenty-first century is directly related to our violating deeply held taboos against cannibalistic activities.

What struck me while writing this book was the surprising extent to which people have judged, fought, and slaughtered others because of what they had for dinner. These laws about forbidden food give more than a unique perspective on history. They tell us quite a lot about the nature of pleasure and can turn the daily meal into a meditation on humanity's relationship to the delicious and the revolting, the sacred and the profane.

But getting back to that first apple . . .

IN THE DEVIL'S GARDEN

$\mathcal{L}$ UST

"And when Eve saw that the tree was good for food and that it was
pleasant to the eye, she took of the fruit thereof, and did eat, and gave
also unto her husband, and he did eat. And the eyes of them both
were opened, and they knew that they were naked. . . ."

Genesis, 3:8–12

L U S T   M E N U

A P É R I T I F
Blue Chocolate (recipe page 38)

S A L A D E
Salade de Jardin
Late-harvest Eden apples tossed with fig leaves.
Served with Paradise vinaigrette.

E N T R É E
Fruits des Homme
Cold, poached sea cucumber served with Sambian
mayonnaise.

P L A T   P R I N C I P A U X
Pâté aux Mon Petit Chou
Homemade lingamini smothered in
love apple and screaming basil.

D E S S E R T
Chocolat du Barry
Louis XV pastry topped with well-whipped cream.
Eaten with the left hand.

T H R E E   P E N I S   L I Q U E U R   W I L L   B E
S E R V E D   I N   T H E   L I B R A R Y .

First Bite

It was still dark out when we left the monastery. Dawn was breaking a midnight blue etched with icy rain. Ocean waves crashed against the cliffs below. To the left and farther up the trail loomed the solitary Mount Athos.

"Some Christmas," I grumbled when George and I finally found a sheltering cave. I handed him a soggy cracker. "It is the twenty-fifth, right?"

"Yes," he said. George was a Greek fellow I'd met in a refuge run by an exceptionally grumpy monk. "But don't wish any of the monks here a good Christmas! The people of Mount Athos believe Christmas doesn't come until January, and they don't like to be reminded that the rest of the world is celebrating it on the wrong day."

Mount Athos is a six-thousand-foot-tall mountain that stands at the tip of a peninsula near the Greek-Turkish border. Surrounded on three sides by the Aegean Sea and on the fourth by roadless forests, it's controlled and run by the Greek Orthodox Church, which has kept out almost all foreign and modern influences since the eleventh century. Military patrols search all visitors. Non-Greek males are allowed in on a strictly limited basis, and there have been no females, human or animal, allowed on the mountain for a thousand years. The only inhabitants are hundreds of robed monks who live in cliff-hugging monasteries exactly as their predecessors did twelve hundred years ago. There's no electricity, no roads, no cars. Foods not specifically mentioned in Christian writings are avoided. Even time is different on Mount Athos because the monks follow the ancient Julian calendar, which, among other things, places the birth of Christ in mid-January instead of on December 25. Aside from farming, which is done by hand, the main activities are chanting, prayer, and creating illuminated manuscripts.

It's a perfectly preserved slice of medieval Europe, the ideal place to find out how the apple came to grow in the Garden of Eden. The Old Testament does not reveal the exact identity of the Fruit of Forbidden Knowledge, and how the apple came to be identified with the evil fruit remains a mystery. George and I were trying to reach a monastery on the other side of the mountain where I'd been told there was a monk with opinions on the subject.

After our breakfast, George and I continued up and over the sea cliff, then headed toward the mountain. The rain turned to snow, and soon we found ourselves hiking through a landscape covered in silver ermine. Bunches of crimson holly berries encased in ice glittered on the leafless trees. It was like walking into a Noël fairy tale, so perfect and clean and clear, Christmas before all the lies. But as morning progressed, the snowfall turned into a blizzard. The trail disappeared, then the trees, then the mountain. All I could see were whirling flakes of snow, and even they dissolved into a surreal void as my glasses became encased in inch-thick ice. The snow was up to our knees. Then my head bumped into something. It was George. He was clawing at his face and shouting. It took awhile for me to real-ize he was saying that his eyes had frozen shut.

I defrosted them by cupping my hands over his sockets, but it was clear that the mountain did not want any visitors that day, and so we turned around and started back the way we had come. We were, of course, hopelessly lost, and it was only by chance that after some more wandering we discovered a run-down shack with a plume of smoke rising from its chimney. In a few minutes we were warming ourselves by a little coal stove and being clucked over by two grandpa monks with their beards tucked into their belts. They were hermits—the so-called "crazy of God"—who refuse the comfort of monastic life and live alone in the crudest of conditions. These two had "married" when they had grown too old to survive alone. I've never met a cuter couple. The quiet one prepared us a meal of raw onions, bread, and a homemade sherry while George ex-plained our quest. The other monk pulled out a tiny red apple.

All of nature, he said in Greek (George translating), reflects the intent of the Creator: the shape of the clouds, the sound of the leaves, the flavors of the fruit on the trees. The monk thrust a knife into the apple. He pointed to the green opalescent drops dotting the tarnished steel. Come, he said, please taste. George and I dabbed our fingers into the liquor and placed it on our tongues. The first flavor was a scintillating, honeylike sweet-ness, followed by a tongue-curling tartness. Sweet flavors are lures meant to distract the faithful from the word of God, said George. That's why every meal in Mount Athos is accompa-nied by a reading from the Bible, to keep the brothers from dwelling on the pleasures of the food before them, and treats like chocolate are avoided. So the apple's initial sweetness was a sign of seductive intent. The tart aftertaste indicated diabolic influence, because bitter flavors indicate poison, and all poisons were thought by medieval scholars to be the work of the Devil. Some view the apple's bittersweet savor as a literal allegory of the temptation of Eve; the sweet first bite represents the Serpent's "honeyed tongue" while the astringent aftertaste foreshadows humanity's ejection from paradise.

The monk sliced two thin wedges from the apple and handed them to George and myself. See how the skin is red like a woman's lips? he said. And the flesh, how white it is, like teeth and skin. He told us to take a bite. Crisp and delicious. This, too, was considered an evil sign, because most fruits soften as they grow ripe. The apple, however, actually grows harder, an "unnatural" behavior that alchemists like Vincent de Beauvais claimed was "a sign of great deviltry . . . and of an immoral, cruel and misleading nature." Our friend sliced the apple in half, vertically, and pointed to the seeds. You see? he said: There, within the heart of the fruit, is the sign of Eve. There was no doubt that from this angle the apple's core looked vaguely like female genitalia. Hardly compelling, I thought. But the monk was not finished. He pulled out another apple and cut it in half, this time horizontally. Do you see the star? he asked. Sliced this way, the seeds that had looked like a vagina now outlined a five-pointed star, the pentagram, the ultimate symbol of Satan. The design was no larger than a dime but unmistakable. Even more alarming, at least to a religious fanatic, was how the seed design was highlighted by minute cavities of browned, charred fruit surrounding each pip. This is simply the result of iron-containing chemicals reacting with the air, but it really did look as if someone had magically burned the sign of Lucifer into the apple's heart.

"In the fruit trees are hidden certain of God's secrets," wrote the famous medieval mystic St. Hildegard von Bingen, "which only the blessed among men can perceive." Hildegard was describing the scientific philosophy of the Dark Ages, a discipline derived from the Platonic belief that all earthly objects are shadows cast by the true beings in the World of Ideas. Plato had been speaking in abstractions when he laid out this scenario, but medieval Christians had assumed his World of Ideas referred to their Heaven. They reasoned, therefore, that all earthly objects were symbols sent by God to communicate His intent. The priests' job was similar to that of a Jungian psychiatrist: they interpreted God's hidden "messages" and explained them to the unenlightened masses. The apple's seductive colors, its two-faced flavor, its suggestively feminine core, and, above all, the hidden pentagram, were interpreted as signs that it was the fruit that had grown on the Tree of Forbidden Knowledge.

The hermit laughed after he had explained. But the Bible never identifies the evil fruit, he said; it was the Roman Catholics who put the apple there. The Greek Church sees the forbidden fruit only as a symbol of pride and carnal desire. He pointed; these are only apples, my friend, which by God's will are now divided into four pieces, one for each of us. He handed the wedges around with a smile.

Now *eat*.

Enveloped in Sweet Odor

For years after my Christmas on Mount Athos I puzzled over the hermit's comment that the naming of the apple as the forbidden fruit was a "lie of the Pope." I knew, of course, that the Greek Orthodox Church and the Roman Catholic Church had been bitter enemies for almost a thousand years. So his remark could have been just a spurious attack on an old enemy. But another possible explanation can be found in the maps of pre-Christian Europe. The Old World at that time can be roughly divided into two groups. South of the Italian-Austrian border lived the Mediterranean race, a dark-complexioned people who, among other things, were lovers of the grape. Worshipers, really, because the vine provided their preferred intoxicant, wine, which was used as a mystical tipple by everyone from the pagan Dionysian cults to the modern Roman Catholics. North of this imaginary border lived a bunch of barbarians often called the Celts. Since grapes did not thrive in their climate, they revered the apple. Instead of wine, their priests, the Druids, are believed to have used an alcoholic cider in their ceremonies. They even called their paradise Avalon, or Isle of the Apples, presumably with a cider press on the premises.

The Dionysian Mediterraneans merged their beliefs with Christianity to form the Roman Catholic Church. The Celts did the same with their Druid faith to create a brand of Christianity called the Celtic Church. Needless to say, the two groups loathed each other. Celtic monks would neither eat nor pray with Roman priests and considered utensils used by them to be contaminated. The Vatican, in turn, declared Celtic rituals to be heresy and threatened to execute the Celtic missionaries who were beginning to dominate western Europe. By the fourth century, the situation was threatening to split Christian Europe in half.

All of a sudden, the Tree of Forbidden Knowledge began sprouting apples.

> *One Apple down from all of those upon the fatal tree*
> *Enveloped in sweet odor, recommended it*
> *For pleasing sigh, and offered it to Eve.*

This description of Eve's first insidious bite was written by the Roman poet Avitus around A.D. 470, near the height of the Celtic/Roman conflict. It could have been coincidence that the Romans chose that particular moment to use the Celt's sacred fruit to epitomize all evil knowledge. But there are a number of things peculiar about their selection. First, biblical writings indicated that the forbidden fruit was a fig. Second, the Romans actually invented the word that Avitus used to describe the forbidden fruit. The word is *pomum*, based on Pomona, the pagan god of harvest. They could have stuck with the word the earlier Greek Bibles had used, *malum,* which meant both *evil* and *fruit*. Ideal, really. Why change it? We'll never know for sure, but the obvious allegory in naming the Forbidden Fruit after a pagan deity would have been to remind new Christians that the older, non-Christian religions were heresy, i.e., forbidden knowledge.

Christians are notorious for baptizing pagan deities to cash in on their good karma. This, however, does not appear to have been a typical case of assimilation, because the Romans turned the existing myths and emotions about the apple upside down. The Celts believed that apples contained the essence of a divine wisdom that transported the diner to a kind of paradise. Yet the Christian myth clearly stated that apple-inspired wisdom led straight to Hell. This wasn't assimilation, it was attack, and apparently so successful that they repeated the stunt one thousand years later in the New World. The Aztecs of Mexico believed humanity had once lived in a paradisiacal garden where people ate flowers. The *xochitlicacan* flowers in the original Aztec myths were thought to impart divine wisdom in the most positive sense, just as Celtic mythology had characterized the apple. When Spanish missionaries arrived in the 1500s, however, they began suppressing Aztec beliefs and teaching a new version of the fall of man that replaced Eden's apple with a flower. According to accounts from the time, the Indians said it was the destruction of these sacred flowers and plants, often used to make ritual beverages, that broke the heart of their culture.

Medieval Christians took their symbols much too seriously to have done all this while unaware of the repercussions. Particularly someone like Avitus. His poem, "The Fall of Man," was among the first dramatizations of the Bible aimed at the general population and was so popular it earned him the nickname of the "Christian Virgil." Since Avitus lived in the Celtic north, he would have realized with what fruit the word *pomum* would be identified. In fact, the Christians were so preoccupied with the hold the Celtic apple had on the popular imagination they created a bizarre series of myths that described the apple's power actually draining into the body of Christ. In these stories, probably created around the eighth century, Christ is crucified on an apple tree. Then a "wild apple," representing the Celtic faiths, is nailed into the same tree and its juices are allowed to seep into the Messiah. The end of the tale describes Christ growing out of the apple tree's foliage like a nature spirit. (This kind of propaganda was not that uncommon, and, in fact, some Islamic scholars did the same thing about five hundred years later when they identified the Catholic grape as the Fruit of Forbidden Knowledge.)

The Christian defamation of the apple did not end its consumption, but it did create a valuable tool to teach new converts in northern and western Europe of the dangers of heretic thought. Every peasant munching a McIntosh from then on received a visceral reminder of how the fruit worshiped by his grandfather had damned him to earthly purgatory. Its bittersweet flavor was a lesson in how sweet and tempting the teachings of non-Catholic churches might, at first, appear. It also changed the popular perception of the apple. The Celts had associated apples with the glorious wisdom from the sun (the Celtic word for apple, *abal,* is believed to derive from the name of the sun god Apollo). By the time the Christians were done, scholars had assigned it to "the jurisdiction of Venus" and lust. It became a low-class love charm sometimes associated with venereal disease.

The apple's most telling transformation can be seen in the story of King Arthur and Merlin, a myth cycle that is in many ways the aborted New Testament of Celtic Christianity. In the original version, Merlin's supernatural powers were consistently associated with the *abal.* He prophesied while standing beneath a tree dripping with crimson fruit, and his most famous writing, *The Apple Tree,* is an ode to the apple's crucial role in resurrecting the Druid faith after its destruction by the Romans. "The sweet apple tree loaded with the sweetest fruit," goes an early version of the poem, "growing in the lonely wilds of the woods of Cleyddon! All seek thee but in vain until Cadwaladr comes to oppose the Saxons. Then shall the Britons be again victorious, led by their graceful and majestic chief [Arthur]; then shall be restored to every one his own; then shall the founder of the trump of gladness proclaim the son of peace, the serene days of happiness." The apple orchard in Merlin's poem refers to Avalon, Isle of the Apples, where King Arthur is said to lie sleeping until his countrymen's hour of greatest need. The poem is thought to have been penned in the fifth century, around the time that the real King Arthur led a rebellion against the Romans and Avitus wrote his version of the tale of Eden. But when the official Christian version of the Arthur myth was put on paper seven hundred years later, the apple's role was again reversed. In this version, written in the twelfth century by the devout Geoffrey of Monmouth, the Druid priest/wizard Merlin is said to have been "driven mad and foaming at the mouth" by eating apples, which are described as being full of "the poisonous delights of women." Later versions tell of his being dragged into hell where his true father, Satan, awaited. The Vatican eventually banned the use of apple cider from its religious ceremonies.

In the end, however, it was the apple that had the last laugh. The Celts revered all trees—not just apples—and their priests used groves of oak and ash as places of meditation. It is these sacred groves that are the source of the trees we drag into our living rooms every Christmas, loving the forest smell that spreads through our homes, and admiring the globes that hang upon their branches: sacred *abals* every one of them, stylized, commercialized, but as red and green as any Pippin or McIntosh, our homage to an ancient vision of paradise.

Likeness of a Roasted Crab

All anyone can definitively say about the Celts' sacred apple juice is that it was probably similar to the tipple called Lamb's Wool. The name is a corruption of the Celtic *lama nbhal* or *la mas ubhal*, or Feast of the Apple Gathering, which was held in the fall, and the drink's curious wooly texture, which comes from using mashed roasted apples, toast, and sometimes eggs. It seems to be an attempt to re-create the texture of the original drink, which might have been an alcoholic porridge similar to the fruit beers still served in parts of Africa. These are as much food as drink and, like Lamb's Wool, are traditionally served in a bowl.

The drink's religious antecedents are clear from the accompanying rite known as "wassailing," a custom that may have once included the sacrifice of a young boy. It's still extant in parts of Great Britain, where people fling some of the drink on the roots of the oldest apple tree in the area while shooting guns and shouting, "Here's to thee, old Apple Tree/Whence thou may'st bud/and whence thou may'st blow/Hats full, Caps full/Bushel bags full!/And my pockets full too!/Huzzah!"

6 apples
2 quarts hard cider, or a mix of cider and ale
Up to ¼ cup honey or ½ cup brown sugar
⅛ teaspoon ground nutmeg
¼ teaspoon cinnamon
¼ teaspoon ground allspice

Core the apples and roast at 400° F for 45 minutes, or until they are soft and beginning to burst. Put the cider/ale into a large pot and dissolve the honey or sugar in small increments, tasting for desired sweetness. Add spices. Simmer for about ten minutes. Lightly mash apples and add one to each mug and pour hot cider on top. Sprinkle with cinnamon. Serves six.

Love Apple

The naming of the humble apple as the Fruit of Forbidden Knowledge is the most unlikely bit of propaganda the Christians have ever cooked up. Everyone knew that so sinful a fruit would be a voluptuous pearl glistening amid a tangle of tropical greenery, and that it would grow in a land far, far, far away where naked bodies and free sex were as common as flies. It would come from Eden, in short, which every educated person of the 1400s could find by looking at a map—there it was, right next to India. Christopher Columbus was so sure of Eden's location that he brought two crew members fluent in Chaldee and Hebrew, the languages thought most likely spoken by the Garden's inhabitants, just in case his ships wound up south of their destination in Asia. When he bumped into South America, Columbus mistakenly identified the Orinoco River in Venezuela as the gateway to Eden, but refused to sail up it lest the flaming cherubim God had hired as security guards attack his ships.

So when Columbus brought a particularly luscious newcomer back from the New World, everyone jumped to the obvious conclusion. We call it the tomato, but most Europeans originally dubbed it *poma amoris*, or the love apple. The Hungarians came straight out and named it *Paradice Appfel*, the Apple of Paradise. The tomato was everything the Forbidden Fruit ought to be—a slut-red fruit oozing lugubrious juices and exploding with electric flavors. Clearly an aphrodisiac. But what made it particularly terrifying to the Europeans was its similarity to a plant called the mandrake, also known as Satan's Apple or the Love Apple. It's basically the fruit from Hell and has the distinction of being the aphrodisiac with which Leah seduces Jacob in the Bible, saying, "Thou must come in unto me, for surely I have hired thee with thy son's mandrakes."

Herbalists in the fifteenth century were well aware that the mandrake had natural narcotic powers. No real problem there. What really earned the plant its ghastly reputation was the way its roots resembled a withered, shrunken human body (or penis, depending on your personal obsession). Medieval Europeans believed the roots were alive, demon sprits that whispered secrets in their owner's ear, and Joan of Arc's alleged possession of a mandrake root was one of the crimes that sent her to the stake. Witches claimed mandraks grew best beneath gallows trees, where the semen dripping down from executed criminals produced appropriate fertilizer, and that when cut the plant emitted bloodcurdling shrieks that drove bystanders insane. The only safe way to harvest a specimen was to tie a black dog to the stem, block your ears with wax, and lure Fido toward you with fresh donkey meat until the shrieking plant was torn from the soil. The dog, of course, expired in drooling agony.

Both the tomato and the mandrake belong to the nightshade family. Both have bright red or yellow fruit. But although people have bred them together to produce narcotic tomatoes, they're quite different from each other. The general population, however, considered them one and the same, and called both love apples for centuries. This confusion was reinforced by a maze of stories that seemed to connect the two plants to Eden. For instance, medieval writers believed that mandrakes were God's first attempt to make humans (hence those weird roots). This meant they originally came from Eden, which the popular imagination by the 1600s had firmly located in the tomato's native South America. This fit rather nicely with the belief that the Italian name for the tomato, *pomodoro* (literally, golden apple), referred to the golden apples that grew in the Pagan Greek Garden of the Hesperides. It seems Christian scholars had decided that The Garden of Hesperides—a walled enclosure guarded by spirits—was actually Eden,

Medieval people believed the mandrake root was the first attempt to create humanity and came from the Garden of Eden.

and that its magical fruit was actually Eve's famous snack. One popular tale even told how two elephants representing Adam and Eve were thrown out of paradise for eating mandrakes. Some people went so far as to claim that the tomato was actually Eden's *other* forbidden fruit: When an obscure Jewish-Portuguese immigrant named Dr. Siccaary brought tomatoes to North America in the early 1700s, he peddled them as being from Eden's Tree of Eternal Life, claiming that "a person who should eat a sufficient abundance of these apples would never die."

So cautious Christians snubbed the tomato for at least 150 years, and it wasn't until the early 1700s that it began to gain acceptance, mainly in Italy, as a decorative puree or garnish. But the rest of the West continued to drag its feet. They claimed tomatoes made your teeth fall out. Its smell was said to drive people insane. Many Yanks thought them just too ugly to eat. In the 1880s, the daughter of a well-known British botanist named Montague Alwood wrote that the highlight of an afternoon tea at her father's house had been the "introduction of this wonderful new fruit—or is it a vegetable?" As late as the twentieth century writers like Henri LeClerc still classed tomatoes with mandrakes as an "evil fruit . . . treacherous and deceitful."

Christian trepidation did not derive solely from the love apple's connection to the mandrake. The fruit's intrinsic morality was also in doubt. Consider the potato. Both it and the tomato arrived in Europe from the Americas at the same time. Both were associated with the mandrake. But what a different reception the potato received! Dull, brown, heavy-on-the-belly, the elite immediately fell in love with it—but only for the peasants. They spent the next two hundred years shoving it down the throat of every proletarian they could lay their white gloves on.

This was particularly true in Catholic countries, where the tuber seemed to have a halo floating over its scrubby little head, possibly because its Inca name, *papa*, is also the word for "pope" in Italian. Literally translated, *papa*, the potato, became "the pope's fruit," or the "pope-ato," and everybody sang its praises, like the Catholic officials who pleaded with the Vatican's morality czar to make the peasants "try and try again this delectable food."

Meanwhile, their brethren were putting the tomato on their lists of "disapproved dishes." "There is nothing more evil," wrote the well-known Catholic moralist Abbot Chiari during the tomato sauce *naissance* of the mid-1700s, "than [the growing habit] of foods that are covered in drugs [spices] from America." The fact that the tomato first gained wide acceptance as a sauce was another strike against the fruit. That it was often not meant to be eaten, but only to glorify a dish, was even worse. "Man is, by nature, not a sauce eater," wrote the influential St. Clement of Alexandria in the third century, and he wasn't referring to a lack of spoons. Sauces were considered insidiously Satanic because they glorified the act of eating, which led to gluttony, which in turn led to every one of the deadly sins of lust, pride, greed, etc. The tomato's unearthly brilliance, its zesty flavor, its lugubriously dripping succulence, were all anathema to the clergy. It "inflamed passions" in ways that the grubby brown potato could hardly be accused of doing. The potato's chaste nature was further proven by its method of asexual reproduction: it has no seeds but instead creates offspring directly from its body. Botanical Immaculate Conception. The Love Apple, dripping unctuous juices and seeds, soft and delicious, inviting the unwary to bite deep into its harlot-red flesh and let the juices flow, was an entirely different class of being: immoral,

lascivious, and decidedly un-Christian. This was serious stuff
back then. When a foreign princess introduced the fork to
Venice in the eleventh century, local religious leaders called divine wrath down upon her for the nicety. When she died of a
particularly vicious disease, prelates sermonized that it was the
"punishment of God" for the way she'd tried to glorify eating
by conveying "morsels to her lips by means of little golden
forks with two prongs."

Both forks and tomatoes eventually carried the day. Ironically, the last place to embrace the tomato was America, the
Land of Ketchup. The hero of the tomato was named Robert
Johnson, and when he announced in 1820 that he was publicly
going to eat one of the devilish fruits, people journeyed for hundreds of miles to his town in New Jersey to watch him drop
dead. He mounted the courtyard steps around noon and turned
to the throng. "What are you afraid of?" he snarled. "I'll show
you fools that these things are good to eat!" Then he bit into
the tomato. Seeds and juice splurted forth. Some spectators
fainted. But he survived and, according to local legend, set up a
tomato-canning factory.

The Ketchup with a Thousand Faces

Yes, people fell screaming in horror as Robert Johnson
bit into the bloodred tomato. There was panic in the
streets. Until a few years ago his derring-do was celebrated
every August in New Jersey with a reenactment of his
feat. The problem is that it never quite happened. Andrew
Smith is probably America's leading love apple historian

and in his opus *The Tomato in America* he documents over five hundred versions of the Hero Who Ate the Tomato fable. Thomas Jefferson saves the day in one version, a West African slave in another. The French, of course, have registered numerous claims. Not that Johnson's role is totally false; it's just suffered an awful lot of improvement.

Equally fallacious is the belief that tomatoes and ketchup are forever joined at the hip. To the ancient Romans, ketchup was a kind of fermented fish sauce called *garum* made by leaving salted fish intestines, heads, and blood in the sun to ferment for about two months. It was probably similar to contemporary Thai fish sauces and, in fact the word *ketchup* apparently derives from a Vietnamese version called *ketsiap*. In Europe *garum* evolved into a kind of pickle juice containing anchovies. It wasn't until the 1800s that someone tossed in a couple of tomatoes, but there were still lots of variations until the American government outlawed all fermented ketchup in 1906, thus inadvertently giving birth to the thick, supersweet goo with which the gullible now drown their dinners.

The true heyday of *ketsiap/kecap*/ketchup/catsup/catchup diversity was the 1800s. There were lobster-flavored ketchups, peach, walnut, beer, horseradish, and mushroom. There's a good sampling of these recipes in Smith's books, but the most divine version is still being made in the Caribbean out of bananas. This stuff is incredible: sweet, hot, and luscious. I learned the following recipe from a Senegalese cook in Paris who claimed it was native to his land, but it's more commonly associated with Jamaica. Follow the same sterilization procedures you would for making pickles or jams, and keep it refrigerated.

1 dried ancho chile
6 very ripe bananas, peeled and cut into chunks
1⅓ cups cider vinegar, divided
½ cup raisins, preferably golden
⅓ cup coarsely chopped onions
2 garlic cloves
⅔ cup tomato paste
2 cups water
¼ cup light corn syrup
½ cup dark brown sugar
½ teaspoon chili pepper
2 teaspoons ground allspice
½ teaspoon ground cinnamon
½ teaspoon grated nutmeg
Big pinch ground cloves
1½ teaspoons salt
Big pinch black pepper
6 tablespoons dark rum

Soak ancho chile in warm water for 15 minutes. Remove the stem and seeds. Puree the bananas with ½ cup vinegar and put into a heavy saucepan. Puree raisins, onions, garlic, ancho chile, tomato paste, and remaining vinegar in same processor (no need to wash) and add to saucepan. Add 2 cups water. Stir and bring mixture to simmer over medium heat, then reduce temperature to low and simmer uncovered for one hour. If mixture gets too thick, add water as necessary. Add the corn syrup and sugar and all the spices, including salt and pepper, and simmer for another thirty to forty minutes, or until it leaves a thick coating on the back of a spoon. Stir in the rum. Remove from heat and allow to cool. Puree again and strain it through a fine

sieve to remove solids. Store in an airtight container in the
refrigerator for up to two weeks.

Venomous Green

Some people like to grow flowers. Some like cacti. I grow
herbs. Right now I'm looking at my little basil bush. It stands
only about six inches tall, but it smells divine—sweet and deep
green. I water it carefully, and, when I pluck a few leaves for my
tagliatelle, I make sure to scream obscenities at its fuzzy little
head just like the Italians used to. It just tastes *soooo* much better
that way.

Basil was brought to Europe by Alexander the Great when
he returned from a war near India around the fourth century B.C. With the plant came a little tale about a girl named
Vrinda. It's a complicated story full of jealous gods and demons
and angelic seductions, but in the end our heroine, Vrinda, dis-
covers her husband has been killed. This so distresses her that
she throws herself on her husband's funeral pyre and is burned
alive. The Hindu gods commemorated this psychotic act of devotion by turning her charred hair into a sweet-smelling plant
named *tulsi*, or basil, which they order their priests to revere.
Some Indian courts still make people take the oath by placing
their hand over a basil bush, just as we swear by placing our
hand on the Bible, and millions of devout Hindus begin their
day with a prayerful circumambulation around the household
tulsi plant. In the evening they leave a sacred butter lamp burning by its side.

The basil bush Alexander the Great brought to Europe went
through a variety of genetic modifications. So did the story of
Vrinda. First the gods were lost. Then Vrinda's horrible suicide
was deleted. By the final version, Vrinda had become a girl

named Lisabetta who, unable to bear parting with the body of her dead lover, cuts off his head and buries it in a pot containing a basil bush. Lisabetta waters it faithfully with her tears until she dies of a broken heart. The plant, thanks to the nutrients afforded by its special fertilizer, grows so large that people make pilgrimages to visit it. It's the same basic story line—girl loves boy/boy gets killed/girl goes crazy/plant makes the headlines— only transformed by European values. While the Hindus focused on love and devotion, the Euro-Barbarians were more interested in madness and decapitation. This more morbid flavor is in tune with the Mediterranean view of true love as a "grave madness, a powerful force that knocked people off balance and caused them to do dangerous and terrible things," according to historian Margaret Visser. In his poem "Isabella," the poet Keats underlines this attitude by writing that the dead lover's rotting head gave the plant a particularly pleasant fragrance.

> *Whence thick, and green, and beautiful it grew,*
> *So that it smelt more balmy than its peers*
> *Of basil-tufts in Florence: for it drew (nourishment) . . .*
> *From the fast moldering head there shut from view*

This connection between basil and insanity led the Europeans to rename *tulsi* as *basilicum*, a reference to the mythical scorpion, the basilisk, which they claimed grew in the brain of those who had smelled the plant. Hence the curious Italian custom of "going mad" and screaming obscenities when plucking its leaves. They may have been on to something about the plant's unsettling effect. The oil lamp that Hindus light next to their basil plants represents not only Vrinda's undying love, but also her body writhing in the flames of her husband's pyre—a love sacrifice that started the tradition, called *sati*, of burning widows alive with their dead husbands. It's still practiced today in parts of India, not always voluntarily. Part of the tradition calls for the widow to die with a sprig of basil clasped in her hand.

Tulsi Ki Chai

Basil is considered too sacred to be used much in Indian cooking. There is, however, a fragrant tea called *tulsi ki chai* which is thought to ward off colds. The following recipe was given to me by Bhoopendr Singh, of the small town of Orchha in Madhya Pradesh.

To make:

Bring about two cups of fresh water to a rolling boil. Add a half cup of whole basil leaves. Lower heat and let brew for about four minutes. Add two teabags, or the equivalent in loose tea, and approximately 6 teaspoons of sugar. Bring to a quick boil and remove from heat. Crush one or two basil leaves and add to each cup. Pour tea over leaves and serve. This is usually served black, but if you want milk, you should add it with the tea and sugar. Please note that tea in India is usually lightly spiced with cloves, pepper, and nutmeg, so you could use one of the chai tea leaf blends now available in lieu of regular tea. Makes two cups.

The Ecstasy of Being Eaten

The first story about Adam and Eve consists of dinner followed by sex, and writers have been fixated on the combination ever since. Some studies claim that dinner precedes 98 percent of all literary seductions. If true, you'd expect the Chinese novel *Dream of the Red Chamber*, with its 971 dinner scenes, to be an outright orgy. You'd be disappointed (it's a rather stiff read), but that's because writers tend to sublimate. Nineteenth-century Russian author Nikolai Gogol wrote obsessively about food, but most agree he was really thinking about sex, which he never, ever, wrote about or, apparently, experienced. His story "The Fair at Sorochintsky" transforms a tryst between an unfaithful wife and a priest into a feast of lewdly shaped delights. "Here is my offering to you, Afansy Ivanovic," cries the woman, bouncing into the priest's chamber. "Here are curd donuts, wheaten dumplings and cakes!" The priest wolfs down the treats while eyeing her suggestively open blouse. "Though indeed, Kharonya Riniforovna," he leers, "my heart thirsts for a gift from you much sweeter than any buns or donuts!" In another story, a couple expresses their shared love by feeding each other night and day. There's smoked sturgeon and kasha and fruit jelly and stewed pears and sausage and pancakes and blinis and sour cream and mushrooms and sage tea and watermelon and, of course, fish head pie. They rack up eleven huge meals every day, and the husband's last words to his dying wife are, "Won't you like a little something to eat, Pulcheria Ivanovna?" After his wife's death, her favorite dishes make him cry.

Gogol obviously had food issues—he eventually starved himself to death—but his muddling of sex with eating is quite understandable because they're so damn similar. During both we allow a warm (or at least reheated) creature to enter our bodies. Before we begin a feast, our mouths produce thick saliva without which our taste buds would be unable to function, just as before beginning sex, a female produces a rush of mucus that facilitates her having, or at least enjoying, intercourse. During the act itself—of eating, that is—our lips flush and swell with blood in much the same way the clitoris and penis do during sex. All three, along with the tongue, are classified as "specific erogenous zones" because of their mucocutaneous nature and the density and sensitivity of their nerve endings.

So it's really no surprise that we're constantly muddling together the acts of sex and eating. What's interesting is the way the different genders go about it. Where Mr. Gogol makes the kitchen into an arena of bawdy adultery, Willa Cather makes it the "heart and center of the house" full of "the fragrance of old friendships, the glow of early memories." Kitchens, to Cather, are temples of domestic love, "like a tight little boat in a winter sea." Her famous novels set during the American pioneer era are fine examples of how female authors tend to write about eating as an act of sharing that is also quite sexual. In *One of Ours*, an old German widow feeds a man with an excitement that is deliciously lascivious.

> "I been lookin' for you every day," said Mrs. Voigt when she brought his plate. "I put plenty good gravy on dem sweet pertaters, ja."
>
> "Thank you. You must be popular with your boarders."
>
> She giggled. "Ja, all de train-men is friends mit me . . . I ain't got no boys mein own self, so I got to fix up liddle tings for dem boys, eh?"
>
> She stood nursing her stumpy hands under her apron, watching every mouthful he ate so eagerly that she might have been tasting it herself. . . .

Even when being raunchy most women authors have a different tone than their male peers. In Dorothy Allison's collection *Trash*, the writer remembers her lovers not only by what they ate, but also by the sex they performed using ingredients from the evening meal. Eggplants dominate this lewd yarn, but it's still all about soul love. "I remember women by what we ate together," she writes, "by what they dug out of the freezer after we'd made love for hours. I only had one lover who didn't want to eat at all. We didn't last long."

It seems a woman's take on eating is the same as sex—a shared experience that tends to fill you up. In a study comparing 489 food stories told by children between three and five years of age, sociologist Carole Counihan found that girls were twice as likely to describe eating in terms of a shared experience. Boys tended to see it as an act of killing and devouring. No wonder they later seem to find the whole thing less than satisfying when they grow up. In *The Gift of an Apple*, Tennessee Williams compares eating to "an act of love . . . draw out the final sweet moment. But it can't be held at that point . . . it has to be finished. And then you feel cheated somehow." Ernest Hemingway agreed. In *A Moveable Feast* the ultimate macho says writing reminds him of sex because both leave him "empty." His cure for this depletion, an aphrodisiacal plate of oysters washed down with a good white wine, helps. "As I drank their cold liquid from each shell and washed it down with the crisp taste of the wine, I lost the empty feeling and began to be happy and make plans."

This sense of emptiness Hemingway and Williams kvetch about might have something to do with the male tendency to eat one's mate. "No, on thy flesh I will feed," wrote one Elizabethan poet, setting the stage for centuries of skin-like-whipped-cream, cheeks-like-peaches, lips-like-cherries metaphors, a genre Margaret Atwood spoofed in *The Edible Woman* when she had the housewife character bake a cake shaped like her body so her husband could more conveniently consume her. The eighteenth-century author whose obsession with pain, love, and food gave us the word *sadist*, The Marquis de Sade, would have appreciated the thought. His *120 Days of Sodom* is the crown jewel of the let's-eat-the-girls genre and includes one scene in which two bound waifs are placed side by side in front of a succulent meal—since they can't get a bite, they wind up eating each other. Human flesh, we are told, is the ultimate aphrodisiac. But the marquis recommends a simple breakfast: a plain omelet served piping hot on the buttocks of a naked woman and eaten with "an exceedingly sharp fork."

The King's Chocolate

There were two items that the Marquis de Sade requested most fervently during his stay in the dungeons of the Bastille prison. The first were replacements for the mahogany dildos he kept breaking while amusing himself. The other was "chocolate . . . black like the Devil's ass." The eighteenth-century nobleman considered these items complementary because chocolate replenished his sexual fluids that, in consort with those superstrong dildos, enabled him to achieve his ten daily orgasms. Indeed, it was a chocolate-fueled sex-and-whips orgy that landed de Sade in prison in the first place. But his real sin, as we shall see, was to feed chocolate, called *Theobroma*, or the Food of the Gods, to the lower classes and women.

The first culture to fall down in awe before the bonbon was the Olmec people of Central America around 1500 B.C. It might have been the Mayans. We really don't know; hell, we don't really know if the "Olmecs" even existed. All we know for certain is that chocolate was revered by almost all early Central

American cultures. Cacao beans, the fruit from which chocolate is derived, were used as money. An egg cost three beans. A dalliance with a hooker set you back twelve. The Aztec ruler Montezuma kept a billion pods in his treasury, and archaeologists have discovered caches of counterfeit chocolate currency, porcelain cacao beans so artfully done that nobody realized they were fake until a scientist tried to cut one open. The pleasure of actually consuming chocolate, however, was restricted to the ruling classes, who enjoyed it with an after-dinner smoke much as we do liqueurs today. There were superexcellent *tlaquetzallis*, or blue-green chocolates. There were red chocolates flavored with anchiote, pink chocolates, orange ones, black and white chocolates. Many were flavored with wild honey or blue vanilla or "mad with flowers." There was also an alcoholic drink made from the sweet pulp surrounding the pod. None of this stuff resembled the dark, gleaming bodies we now so avidly devour. Back then, chocolate was a drink, served cold, honey-thick, and redolent of hot chili peppers. Milk and sugar were unknown.

The only time commoners were allowed a drop of this nectar was when they were about to die. Peasants marked for sacrifice took a tall glass of *itzpacalatl*, a chocolate drink mixed with human blood, just before the priests ripped out their still-beating hearts. The drink was said to render the victims docile, but it also had symbolic significance because the Aztecs believed that the cacao pod represented the human heart, and its liquor, blood. Its long-standing reputation as a powerful aphrodisiac made it particularly taboo for women and priests. Emperor Montezuma, on the other hand, apparently took fifty glasses a day and imbibed a special brew before braving his army of wives.

Although these early Americans believed cacao incited both violence and lust, it is the love connection that has stuck through time. "Chocolate," wrote the English poet Wadsworth "t'will make Old Women Young and Fresh/Create new Motions of the Flesh/and cause them to long for You-Know-What/If they but Taste CHO-CO-LATE!" Scientists say this is nonsense, because while chocolate contains stimulants like caffeine and theobromine, the amounts are too small to have any significant effect (aside from which, the only sexual enhancement attributed to caffeine is it tends to make sperm swim more vigorously). The euphoria-inducing compounds phenylethylamine and serotonin are present in even smaller amounts.

Despite this scandalous reputation, the cacao champagnes of the Aztecs first became popular with European ladies living in the New World, who liked to take a glass during Mass. When the local bishop realized what his followers were sipping, he condemned it as "a damned agent from the witch's brew." He then tried to throw them out of church, but a sword fight broke out, after which everybody decided to observe Mass at home until the priest came to his senses. Which he soon did, in a manner of speaking; someone poisoned him. Appropriately, it seems the poison was administered via the priest's own hot chocolate. According to the seventeenth-century traveler Thomas Gage, who was in the Mexican highland area of Chiapas where the scandal broke out, the lady suspected of being the killer claimed that since the priest was "clearly an enemy of chocolate in the church" it was really no surprise that it had not agreed with him. This femme fatale then set her sights on Gage, also a priest, and began sending *him* presents of chocolate. When Gage failed to respond to these blandishments, she sent him a more direct message—an oversized plantain (banana) in whose peel she'd carved a heart stuck with "two of blind cupid's arrows." Gage returned the plantain with his own message carved below, *Fruta tan fria, amor no cria,* which is to say, "Fruit so cold, takes no hold." The spurned woman then threatened to slip him a dose of "Chiapas chocolate," and Gage fled the area.

The battle lines were drawn. A few religious leaders urged all monks to abstain from the dreadful stuff. This irked the Franciscan order, by then making a pretty penny from exporting it to Spain, which then ruled that hot cocoa could even be enjoyed during the fast of Lent. They commissioned paintings of angels offering steaming mugs to fasting saints, urging them yes, yes, take a sip! "Oh Divine Chocolate!" the poets rhapsodized, "They grind thee kneeling/Beat thee with hands praying/and drink thee with eyes to Heaven!" When Marie-Thérèse of Austria (who was actually Spanish) introduced cocoa to the French royalty around 1661, everyone had a hissy fit. Her husband, Louis XIV, banned her from drinking it in public, lest it corrupt the morals of the French ladies, but this was soon overcome and *chocolat,* by now made with milk and sugar and scented with jasmine, became standard court rations. When the puritanical Madame Maintenon came into power, it was again briefly banned amid reports that habitués were giving birth to coal-black babies. The next Louis put his mistress, Madame de Pompadour, on a diet of creamy truffle soup and hot chocolate in order to "heat up" her amorous appetites. Pompadour, however, merely grew fat and was demoted to the King's "confidential adviser," a code for her increasingly desperate attempts to find women able to satisfy the king's peculiar sexual appetites—a quest that would end only with the entrance of the harlot-princess-slut divine, dominatrix bitch, Madame du Barry.

The Aztecs had been proven right: their sacred brew had

become the Food of the Gods, or at least the demagogue aristocrats who were the deities of eighteenth-century Europe. By the era of Madame du Barry, Europe had divided into three classes, each of which was identified with a particular brew. Peasants still preferred beer. The hardworking middle class had adopted stimulants like coffee and tea. The aristocrats, to whom work was a dirty word, doted on chocolate. "Chocolate appears as the status beverage of the *ancien regime*," wrote contemporary historian Wolfgang Schivelbush. It's a connection recorded in numerous paintings that depict marquises and marchionesses lounging in bed over a cup of cocoa, or in literary characters like Monsignor, whose fastidious chocolate ritual was used by Charles Dickens in *A Tale of Two Cities* to characterize the cruelty of the French aristocracy. There was Cosimo III, the last Medici, who was as famous for raping Tuscany to satisfy his appetite for extravagant delicacies as he was for his secret recipe for jasmine-scented chocolate. He especially enjoyed taking a cup of it while watching infidels being burned alive. The connection between the drink and aristocratic sadism eventually became the phrase "Sadean chocolate," which scholar Barbara Lekatsas explains was created to celebrate "chocolate as an aphrodisiac that symbolized power: the luxurious sacred beverage stolen from Indians who were massacred, both bitter and sweet."

At the top of this mountain of heartless luxury, sex, and fudge sits the aforementioned Madame du Barry. The last mistress of Louis XV, du Barry was a common streetwalker who'd gained entrance to the king's bed and the ultimate circle of power by her ability to sate his lecherous appetites. Her secret tool? Chocolate. In the popular eighteenth-century novelette *Anecdotes sur Mme. La Comtesse du Barry*, she helps the king get an erection with her special hot chocolate concoction and then uses techniques she picked up in the whorehouse to satisfy him. According to historian Robert Darnton, the reason du Barry is portrayed using cocoa to get the king erect was to convey that Louis was impotent as a man *and* as a king, "the scepter having become as feeble as the royal penis."

Certainly chocolate enjoyed a reputation as an aphrodisiac. There is, however, another possible meaning. Books like the *Anecdotes* were called *libelles*, illegal, politically motivated histories of the royalty's personal lives—sort of a cross between the *National Enquirer* and the Ken Starr reports—that often made their points via a series of elaborate codes. For instance, in another *libelle*, the king's earlier mistress, Madame de Pompadour, was lauded for spreading flowers everywhere she went, "but they are white flowers." According to Darnton, the "white flowers" were a reference to syphilis. The message is that France's first lady was a whore who was dripping syphilitic discharges upon the marble floors of Versailles. Likewise, when du Barry was repeatedly attacked for using chocolate to arouse unnatural passions in her lovers, it's worth remembering that Europeans had originally called chocolate *cacao* but had changed the name because *cacao* too closely resembled the word *caca*, slang for feces. So when French *libelles* like 1878's *La Comtesse du Barry* report that du Barry pulls chocolate out of her robe and "the decadent Parisians go crazy with a Roman orgy," one can reasonably wonder if this is a discreet reference to some form of anal sex. That is, after all, one of the acts classical Roman/Greek orgies were celebrated for back then. Was this constant harping on du Barry's insatiable appetite for chocolate a reference to some unusual techniques that the so-called Queen of the Left Hand had acquired at her famous brothel, the House of Gourdan? In the popular pamphlet *Drame en Cinq Actes*, the author writes that du Barry "honeyed the king's chocolate. . . . Then

the royalty consecrate a new verb for the French dictionary."
What was this "new act" they introduced into the French language? It's hard to believe it was really just a cup of hot cocoa
that got the most jaded emperor in Europe going.

Tlaquetzalli

Perhaps the most fabulous chocolate drink in history was the
one enjoyed by Aztec nobility. There appears to have been two
main types. The more sacred version involved a massive head
of foam, the precise nature of which has been debated for centuries. The only recipe I know of is in *The Food and Life of
Oaxaca* by Zarela Martínez, who claims that the secret is a
special kind of cocoa beans called *pataxtle* which are buried in
the ground for about half a year until it turns a chalky white.
The beans then go through an elaborate process that results in
an *espuma* or foam, akin to beaten egg whites, which is then
spooned cold atop a cup of a warm corn drink called *atole*. The
beans are impossible to obtain outside Oaxaca but according to
Martínez can be replaced with an equal amount of white orchid
flowers.

There was also a cold brew called *tlaquetzalli* ("precious
thing") which was heavily laced with chili peppers. The drink
seems to have become extinct and there are no recipes, but
some of the early European versions of chocolate appear to be
closely related. The following is adapted from a 1652 recipe
attributed to Captain John Wadsworth of London. Purists
will be furious—for one thing, I use skim milk instead of the
water—but the combination of sweet/spicy/cold is surprisingly
refreshing.

2 dried ancho chilies
4 cups very cold skim milk
1 teaspoon fennel seed
8 wedges of Ibarra or other Mexican chocolate containing
   sugar and cinnamon

Soak the ancho in warm water until softened, about 20 minutes. Remove stem and seeds. Cut into smaller pieces. Put them and all the other ingredients into a food processor or blender and blend on highest setting until all ingredients are completely pulverized. Spoon off the particulate matter floating on top into a large bowl and pour the remaining liquid into it from a height to create a bubbly, frothy surface. Drink immediately. Alternately, strain and discard the solids. Whip to create a froth. Makes three cups if strained. Serve in chilled, gold-lined tortoise shells.

Gay Gourmand

In her prize-winning essay *How to Eat, Drink, and Sleep as a Good Christian Should*, Margaret Sidney tells the heartbreaking tale of a family watching their young boy turn into a homosexual at the dinner table. "Father often looks up from his own dinner in concern, or thinks it over during his hard day's work at the office. He wonders if 'Mother' is on the right track," she wrote in the 1886 piece for *Good Housekeeping* magazine. "Both parents know that little Tom should be helped up into a sturdy boyhood and not have all his girlish fancies indulged. But how can they make him love the rare, juicy tender roast beef, the hot baked potato that he now turns away from?"

Real Men, the moral goes, eat only meat. That's Man with a

capital *M*: Man the Magnificent, Man the Macho, the Meat-Killer and Lord of the Jungle who thrives on "hero sandwiches" and Manhandler beef stews. No queers need apply. But if men like meat, then why shouldn't men like men? Greek heroes like Milos of Croton boasted of eating a whole bull in one sitting and then a young boy for dessert, because the classical Greek cultures considered both dishes excellent ways to fortify one's machismo. This was particularly true for the warrior nation of Sparta. "A seventh-century Dorian (Spartan) nobleman through his phallus transferred to a boy the essence of his abilities as a man," writes historian Thorkil Vanggard. "Through the pederastic act the grown man's valuable qualities, which were incorporated as these people saw it in his phallus, were transferred to the boy. . . ."

The Spartans did this anally (preferably in Apollo's temple), but other cultures believe that true masculinity was best ingested orally. At the age of eight or so, Sambian boys in Papua New Guinea are forced into all-male households similar to those of the Spartans, where they eat only "men's food" in order to counteract the effect of all those years of "women's food." The food in question is sperm, which they get fresh by giving older men fellatio as often as possible. The Sambians consider this a form of breast-feeding, and when the boys reach the age of fifteen they in turn "nurse" the younger boys toward manhood. It's a carefully controlled process, according to field psychoanalyst Robert Stiller, and if an older boy attempted to give head to a younger boy it would be "a perversion, shocking; it would be, in our terms, homosexuality." When they get married, the men refill their manly juices by drinking the white sap from a certain type of tree.

There's actually a long history of banning foods that provoke not only lust but the "wrong" kind of lust. An early version of the New Testament banned eating rabbit because it was believed that they grew a new rectum every year and that eating their flesh would fill the diner with an urge to sodomize. The same text claimed eating a weasel instilled an insatiable urge to perform oral sex because the animal procreates through its oral cavities. Hyena sandwiches were a complete no-no because the beast's well-known habit of changing its sex at the full moon inevitably induced bisexual impulses in the unsuspecting gourmand.

The most shamelessly homosexual of dishes, however, is freshwater fish. It seems the Egyptian deity Osiris lost his penis during one of those cosmic battles way back when. It fell into the Nile, and a fish called *oxyrhynchus* gobbled it down, an act that the heterosexual patriarchy found so appalling they made the fish shape the hieroglyph for loathing. They even used to encourage fish bashing by beating the aforementioned guppies to death at religious ceremonies, crying, "Horus [a.k.a. Osiris] of Edfu triumphs over all evil ones." The saying "Don't speak to me with that mouth that eats fish" is still used to call someone sexually false and a liar in neighboring Somalia. Even so-called modern cultures still view fish as a more feminine food than meat.

The same is true for foods thought to threaten a woman's "feminine" nature. Women today explain their passion for green salads as a way to achieve a slimmer figure. In fact, the association between leafy greens and the feminine gender goes back to a muddled series of Greek myths that connected green lettuce with a lessening of animal desire; since women were not supposed to feel these kinds of emotions, salad became the most feminine of dishes. In nineteenth-century America, when slenderness was definitely not in vogue, girls routinely suffered a nutritional imbalance called "green sickness" that came from living on nothing but sweets and salads. Lectures on feminine foods began with fish and salads and moved straight on to dessert, and newspapers still report studies that "prove" expectant mothers who go vegetarian are more likely to have a baby girl, while meat-eating Moms, of course, tend to produce boys. In one case a teenage American girl was put on a diet of two green salads a day by her psychiatrist to "cure" her lesbianism. "I was on a schedule of green salads interspersed with prayer," wrote "Whitey" in the collection *Word Is Out: Stories of Some of Our Lives*. "I was full of expectations that . . . it would solve all my problems and make my mother happy." When this prescription failed, her parents locked her up in an insane asylum for four years. It was while in the asylum that she had her first lesbian experience.

Beijing Libido

The Chinese are the world's reigning omnivores. They eat cats. They eat dogs. They eat monkey brains, fish bladders, and gorilla paws. They gulp down Tibetan lamas, and it seems just a matter of time before the running dogs of Taiwan slide down the national gullet. But their appetite for what Western minds might perceive as socially unacceptable shines most bright when it comes to aphrodisiacs. It's almost as if someone had run down a list of protected species and ticked them off one by one. The recent stability of the world's tiger population, for instance, is now threatened by a Chinese demand for the animal's penis. You can get tiger penis in capsule form or in the ever-popular "three penis" wine (actually more like a whiskey). Some fifty thousand seals have the same bit of their anatomy hacked off every year for similar reasons, making their little man 500 percent more valuable than the rest of the animal's carcass combined. The horn of the rhino now sells for $54,000 a kilogram in China. The eggs of the endangered leatherneck sea turtle also rate high on the list.

But the lust for exotic erotica is universal. Seafood of any kind rates high, but whale mucus is particularly popular in the Middle East. Malaysians suck blood from a freshly decapitated rattlesnake to get going. Japanese mix the testes of the poisonous puffer fish with hot sake, and the Romans once fancied the feet of the skink lizard. Everything from cockroaches to leeches to jackal bile to asses' milk has been vainly rubbed on weary members for so long, it's a wonder the damn things haven't been rubbed right off. The only men who considered the ladies' feelings appear to be the Mongolians, who once used goat's eyelids as a sexual enchancer; apparently those wiry eyelashes drove the girls crazy. But it's the English who win the prize for perverse quirks—Elizabethan men found prunes so titillating that brothels kept jars of them on the bedside table. How most of these items came to be considered love engines is anyone's guess, although many bear a vague resemblance to genitals, particularly the ever-popular sea cucumber, which squirts out white threads when alarmed. None of these aphrodisiacs are particularly effective, which is perhaps their sole virtue; scientists now hope that the proven effectiveness and relative cheapness of the drug Viagra will decimate the market for tiger penii. One species has already made a comeback. Thought to have been exterminated by China's libidinous appetite for its antlers years ago, a small herd of Tibetan red deer was recently spotted two hundred miles from the Dalai Lama's former home in Lhasa. Perhaps some of Tibet's other endangered species will stage a similar comeback.

The Rainbow Egg

The Australian Aborigines say that long ago during The Dream-time a fisherman found an egg lying on the beach. He was hungry and put it in the fire to cook. As soon as he put the egg in the flames, a terrible storm broke out. Rain fell and fell. Then the egg cracked open and out of it poured more water—oceans and rivers—and mountains and rainbows and suns and moons and stars, all gushing out like a roaring river and washing The Dreamtime away. And so the world was born. But still the rain fell, and more water came from the Rainbow Egg until the world was drowned. So the fisherman had to change himself into an angry duck.

Minus the irate duck, this Australian Aborigine tale of the creation of the universe exists in almost every culture. The Egyptians said the universe was once an egg, which they called the "essence of the divine apes," and that the yolk was the sun and the egg white the galactic emptiness in which we drift. The pre-Buddhist Bon cult of Tibet believed the world was nothing more than an egg with eighteen layers, an idea embedded in the egg-shaped Buddhist temples throughout the Himalayas. The Orphic cult of Greece, which banned the eating of eggs around 600 B.C., celebrated the omelet most eloquently:

> *O mighty first begotten, hear my prayer*
> *Two-fold, egg-born, and wandering through the air.*
> *Bull-roarer, glorying in thy golden wings*
> *From whom the race of gods and mortals springs.*

All this praising of an egg might seem a bit much to Western-ers, but there's a universal series of beliefs that cast the egg as the Viagra of the gods. Near the Chinese/Indian border a woman who offered a man an egg was proposing marriage. Listless Filipino men eat *balut*, an egg in which a young duck has developed, to restore sexual vigor. For maximum potency you should feel the embryo's bones and feathers as you chew. German farmers once smeared eggs on their plows to ensure fertile fields. Colored eggs, especially red, are considered particularly powerful from Greece to China, where they are tossed into the laps of women desiring pregnancy. The Koreans claim their first king emerged from a mysterious red egg left by a flying horse. Christianity's multicolored Easter Egg hunt no doubt relates to all of this, though where the giant rabbit came from is anybody's guess.

These egg/fertility beliefs have led to rather eccentric behavior. Nineteenth-century German explorer Eduard Vogel was murdered in Chad in part because he "gave general offence by his egg-eating, for no decent person could live on such food." Many African cultures had profound taboos against egg eating, especially by a woman. Ethiopian ladies were once enslaved for the act, while the Yaka people of the Congo believed that a woman who ate an omelet would lose her mind. If she indulged while pregnant, her children would be born pink and bald, like those egg-eating Europeans, a fate generally conceded to be worse than death.

There's a very old folktale that explains all this nonsense. Once upon a time, it goes, all women were barren. The girls complained to the goddess of Heaven, sometimes called Eka Abassi, saying how could they have children if they had no eggs? So Eka Abassi went to the hen and asked if it could spare one of her beautiful eggs for the humans. The hen reluctantly agreed, and ever since the women have borne children. But it would be bad manners if the women were to steal another egg from so generous a hen, so bad that the people think Eka Abassi would take back the original egg and leave the world barren once again. Those stories of women going mad and having pink babies? They were just made up by the elders to frighten the uneducated into leaving the hen's eggs alone. It worked. One study from 1974 showed that 3 percent of the women in rural South Carolina believed that it is bad luck for a pregnant woman to eat an egg.

I believe that the West's bizarre propensity for painting its eggs in spring relates to the true meaning of that old Aboriginal tale. When I first heard the Australian story, I'd imagined the Rainbow Egg as a kind of tie-dye superball floating in space. But one evening while standing on the roof of my building in New York after a summer rain shower, I turned around and found a huge rainbow arching across the sky. It was The Egg, I realized. The Aborigine storyteller had been saying that the rainbow's arch was the upper half of a huge, cosmic egg, with the rest of it hidden below the horizon. The sun was setting and there on the horizon, right in the middle of the arch, was a yolk-colored sun fading away. The Rainbow Egg. Europeans had merely memorialized the same concept with an annual rite of rebirth in which eggs are dyed the colors of the rainbow—red, blue, green, and yellow. At least that's what I thought as I watched the rainbow fade that day, staring at it so long the world seemed to be rushing toward me, the clouds and the sky and the city and the sun's golden light.

$\mathcal{G}$LUTTONY

"Oh Son, come back!
Why should you go so far away?
All kinds of good food are ready.
Ribs of the fatted ox cooked tender and succulent;
Sour and bitter blended in the soup of Wu;
Stewed turtle and roast kid, served up with yam sauce,
Geese cooked in sour sauce, casseroled duck, fried flesh of the
*   great crane;*
Braised chicken, seethed tortoise highly seasoned, but not to
*   spoil the taste;*
Fried honey cakes of rice flour and sugar-malt sweetmeats;
Jadelike wine, honey flavored, fills the winged cups;
Here are laid out the patterned ladles
And here is the sparkling wine . . ."

"The Summons of the Dead"
China, 221 B.C.

GLUTTONY
MENU

Dinner at Trimalchio's, April 1, 0076

APERTIVO

Roman Honeyed Wine

ANTIPASTO

Ovis Apalis

Soft-poached eggs served with a Roman pignola sauce.

(Recipe on page 56)

CONTORINI

Salami Esotici

Exotic salami: pickled rabbit fetuses, milk-fed snails, ostrich
brains, flamingo tongues, and other cold cuts.

PRIMO

Ortolan au Mitterrand

Wild songbird; blinded and then drowned in Armagnac.
Eaten whole.

Dolia

Force-fed dormice raised in enclosed container and killed
without seeing daylight. Dipped in poppy seeds.

SEGUNDO

Porcus Troianu

The famous "Trojan Pig": an entire steer gutted and
stuffed with a lamb, which is stuffed with a pig,
which is stuffed with a chicken.
Sauce au jus.

DOLCI

Rutab Mu'assal

Poached Khustawi dates stuffed with almonds and
served in a honey-saffron sauce.

(Recipe on page 61)

VOMITORIUM FOR CUSTOMERS ONLY!

Original Sin

Most of us think it was the vice of lust that got us thrown out of the Garden. Not so. Gluttony was the villain, according to theologians, who say that Eve's true sin was simply a love of good food. That's the true paradox of gluttony; the evil lies not in *over*indulging during dinner but merely *enjoying* it, because the latter indicates the diner is focusing on earthly pleasures instead of the will of God. The seeming innocuousness of the sin makes it one of Lucifer's favorites for luring the naive deeper into hell. Take the story of Gervais the Washerwoman, the main character of Émile Zola's classic novel *L'Assommoir*. Gervais dragged herself out of the gutter to set up a modest little laundering service. She helped her neighbors. She even talked her hubby into giving up the bottle. The perfect Christian. Then she developed a taste for good food and went straight down to Hell via the seven sins, from *steak frites* to a little sloth, then adultery, theft, drunkenness, envy, and prostitution. When she's at her lowest, begging from the people she once employed, the author shoves his point down the reader's throat by writing "It showed where love of food can land you. To the rubbish heap with all gluttons." He then let poor Gervais starve to death in a closet under the staircase.

That as late as the twentieth century a so-called "scientific" writer like Zola (who was French to boot) still portrayed gluttony as the most pernicious of sins indicates how deep runs the antieating sentiment. Legislation intended to curtail the enjoyment of dinner dates back to the early Spartan cultures and was among the first laws in Western culture. The Romans took the opposite course and considered it acceptable for dinner guests to visit the vomitorium to vomit out the preceding courses in order to make room for more food, a custom that caused the great poet Seneca to grumble "they eat to vomit, and vomit to eat." Disgusting? Perhaps, but hardly more so than the high-tech emetics like olestra and liposuction that we employ today. Roman lawmakers eventually changed their tune and banned the most excessive of dishes, but it was the Christians who really went to war. They passed legislation limiting everything from which vegetables could be enjoyed in which season, to what kind of wine could be served with dinner. Their pathological preaching on the evils of a good meal made starvation a veritable virtue and helped set the stage for modern psychological conditions like anorexia and bulimia.

Porcus Troianu

The first thing the waiter does is trim your toenails. Then a glass of Falernian wine from a century-old Opimian vintage is served. A servant singing a poem written by your host, Trimalchio, brings out a heaping platter of cold cuts: spiced sow udders, rooster combs, winged rabbits, testicles, flamingo tongues, and ostrich brains. Finally dinner begins. Milk-fed snails the size of tennis balls served in a sweet-and-sour sauce gets things rolling, followed by an *amuse-gueule* of dormice, eaten whole after being dipped in honey and poppy seeds. Fish are killed *à table* by pouring scalding hot sauce onto them. They're still moving as you dig in. The fowl course begins with a pastry "egg" containing a minuscule bird called *beccafio*, or fig-pecker, covered in raw yolk and pepper. You eat it in one mouthful, bones and all. Whole roast geese and swans are brought out, but when you take a bite, surprise! They're made of pork. Finally, the main course: cow-stuffed-with-lamb-stuffed-with-pig-stuffed-with-rooster-stuffed-with-chicken-stuffed-with-thrush. Dessert comes in the form of cakes that descend from the ceiling and squirt saffron-scented juice in your face. For those guests still peckish, there are pickled rabbit fetuses to nibble while Trimalchio stages his own funeral and has his obituary, praising his good taste and generosity, read out loud.

Trimalchio was the kind of arriviste that caused the Roman Senate to ban hundreds of dishes around the first century B.C., a former slave turned multimillionaire who blew his fortune on the most obscene luxuries money could buy. Almost everything he served at that famous dinner—described in the anonymous first-century book *The Satyricon*—was criminal contraband at one point or another. During one course, a whole roast pig is carried triumphantly into the dining room, only to have Trimalchio go berserk when he "realizes" that his chef has neglected to gut the beast. The cook is about to be strangled in front of the guests for his incompetence, but Trimalchio decides that his last act on Earth should be to gut the animal with everyone watching. When the chef, weeping, begging for his life, plunges a knife into the carcass, a sea of sausages gushes out. Ha! Ha! It was all a joke. The cook receives a gold crown, and the guests all make a quick visit to the vomitorium to empty their stomachs before digging in. This kind of dish was called *porcus Troianu*, or Trojan pork, because like its namesake, the Trojan Horse, it was stuffed with piquant surprises. It was banned so often that the dish must have figured on the Top Ten Most Wanted list of the Roman police.

Equally illegal were those poppy seed–crusted dormice. The dormouse was a long-tailed rodent that Romans kept from birth in ventilated clay jars called *dolia*, where their inability to move, combined with intensive force-feeding, ensured they would become a ball of butter-soft flesh. These potbellied rats were apparently so delicious, the government feared it would turn their army into a bunch of spineless, rat-eating gluttons. Guards were posted at the markets with orders to seize any specimens offered for sale. When dormice grew scarce, the elite simply "crammed" (force-fed) chickens and pigs until they reached unnatural size and tenderness. Clerks recorded the animals' weight at the dinner table, before oohing guests. Moralists like Cato the Elder then required that people dine with their doors open so everyone could see exactly what was being eaten. He then limited the number of dinner parties per week. He punished guests as well as hosts. Cato was such a prude, he even campaigned against the civilized fad of building statues to chefs instead of generals.

Roman excess eventually ate the empire alive by making it overreliant on foreign imports. (Unless you subscribe to the theory that their lead-lined wine flagons caused their downfall via brain damage, in which case they drank their empire to death.) During the ensuing Dark Ages, when there was nothing to eat, much less overeat, laws restricting gluttony disappeared, only to pop up again in sixteenth-century Florence, which sternly restricted cardinals to a mere nine dishes per meal. Japan's nineteenth-century royal family allowed only certain produce to be sold in designated seasons, thus ensuring no merchant ever got a better *matsutake* mushroom than the Emperor. Wild fowl was banned for similar reasons, as were new cake designs and, of course, "thick green tea." The number of courses served at dinner was determined by one's social class. Peasant farmers were allowed only one plate per course, as compared to the Samurai's nine, and were not allowed to drink sake. Peasant parties also had to end by sunset. The message was clear—farmers were meant to grow food for the emperor's dinner, not enjoy it.

All these laws were in vain, thank God, for what is civilization if not an eternal quest for a new sensation? Some call it moral rot, but, of course, one man's rot is another man's wine. So the eleventh-century Indian king Shrenika threw vegetarian orgies whose courses were defined not by the dish served, but how it was consumed; the first course consisted of fruits that were chewed, then a course of the sucked, then the licked, and so forth. Turn-of-the-century American millionaire Diamond Jim Brady would put away twelve dozen oysters in a sitting and hired naked girls to feed them to him by hand. England's King James I threw a memorable party in 1606, at which noble ladies playing the Seven Virtues ended up so sodden with food and drink they were unable to play their parts. "Faith was left sick and spewing in the lower hall," wrote one correspondent describing the scene, "and Victory slept off the ill effects." The most notable modern effort was a series of secret meals in the 1990s that featured endangered species like the *ortolan*, woodcock, and, presumably, dolphin and whale (all denied by the participants, of course).

But it's the normally abstentious Greeks who have the last word. Literally, because the longest single word in their language was a dish recorded by Aristophanes in his work *Ecclesiazusae*.

> Now must the spindleshanks, lanky and lean,
> trip to the banquet, for soon will, I wean,
> high on the table be smoking a dish,
> Brimming with game and with fowl and with fish.
> (called)
> Plattero-filleto-mulelto-turboto-cranio-morselo-pickleo-acido-silphio-
>   honeyo-poureontehtopo-ouzelo-thrusheo-cushatao-culvero-cutleto-
>   roastingo-marrowo-dippero-leveret-syrupo-gibleto-wings
> So now ye have heard these tidings true,
> get hold of a plate and an omelet too!

Ovis Apalis

While not as tasty as potbellied rats, the following recipe for eggs with pignoli sauce gives a hint of Roman hedonism. Served with honeyed wine (made by adding half a cup of heated clear honey to a bottle of white wine and chilling), it would be a fun way to start off a dinner party. The recipe is from the West's oldest cookbook, *Apicius de re Coquinaria,* written by Apicius sometime in the first century.

2 ounces pine nuts
3 tablespoons vinegar, preferably red-wine vinegar
1 teaspoon honey
A pinch of pepper
A pinch of lovage (celery leaf)
4 medium boiled eggs (about four minutes)

Soak the pine nuts in the vinegar for four hours. Puree with all other ingredients (except eggs) in a blender. Serve sauce separate from eggs, and allow guests to add according to taste. The sauce will stay good for days.

Cocktails with the Devil

The gravity with which Christian moralists viewed Rome's gluttonous frolics is best measured by the exquisite horrors assigned food lovers in Hell. One medieval Irish manuscript leaves them to float forever in the Lake of Pain, a single drop of which "would destroy all the creatures on the face of the Earth by the bitterness of its chill." Others have them lounging before a dinner table groaning with delicacies that they can never quite sink their forks into. But the most popular torture is to have a demon shove frogs and snakes down their jaded gullets. Hardly prestigious, but more telling was the man who administered the punishment, none other than Satan's right-hand man, Beelzebub. Other cultures mete out similar unpleasantness. The Buddhists devote not one, but two levels of their eight-story inferno to chastising gourmets. On the first floor is *Samjive*, where meat eaters relax in a pit full of dung that is a-crawl with maggots that gnaw the gourmand's tongues. Three levels down is *Raurave*, also known as the "Screaming Hell," where restaurant critics bob helplessly in a river. Every now and then a solicitous demon fishes one of them out to ask if he'd care for refreshment. "Oh please, just water and bread," cries the epicure. "I'm not fussy!" Ha! Ha! laughs the one rogue devil. Then he pries open the critic's mouth and pours down a goblet of molten lead.

The real punishment for these bon vivants, however, must

be to watch the feasting upstairs in Heaven because, in the typically topsy-turvy logic of all religions, those who disdained dinner on Earth are rewarded with a celestial smorgasbord that would have left Trimalchio drooling. Most religions mention rivers of milk and delicious wine and clear-run honey, but Islam arguably provides the most details. Early Muslim scholars reported that chickens the size of young camels fell freshly fried at your feet. Fish liver seemed popular, as well as boiled and salted camel. Later, theologians decided that every palace in Heaven had "seventy tables in every house and on every table seventy different types of food." That comes to forty-nine hundred courses per meal, dessert included. Al-Haythami, the medieval scholar who did the preceding math, however, failed to describe the exact dishes in his writings. For this we have to examine the menus served in Islam's famous Paradise Gardens, designed to re-create the "Garden of Delights" where faithful Muslims spent eternity. The Koran describes heaven as a walled garden full of fountains and trees (the word *paradise* comes from an ancient Persian word that means "walled garden"). Some of these earthly gardens had fountains every 50 yards. Others featured declawed tigers to reflect the belief that men and animals lived harmoniously in Heaven. One turned the caliph's entourage into weightless spirits by constructing elevated footpaths in a sea of flowering trees; from the palace, it appeared that the viziers were actually floating among the treetops.

This obsessive re-creation of the afterlife went beyond mere landscaping. "Truly, the companions of the garden that day will be busy and merry," claims the Koran, an innocent-sounding passage that was somehow interpreted as meaning that the faithful would be "busy and merry" deflowering virgins. The question is, how many? Our friend al-Haythami again provides the math. "A palace in paradise is made from a pearl; within are 70 courts of ruby and in every court, 70 houses of green emerald; in every house is 70 bedrooms, and in every bedroom, 70 sleeping mats; and on every mat, a woman." This adds up to roughly 23 million lubricious nymphets for every man. Truly devout caliphs gathered the hugest of harems in order to prepare for the labor to come. Some went as far as to adorn their gardens with structures named the Hall of Mirrors, which were nothing but gargantuan domed bedrooms devoted exclusively to Allah's labor.

The caliphs were equally fastidious in re-creating the heavenly diet. Tenth-century Egyptian caliph al-Aziz had fresh cherries from Lebanon flown in, tied to the feet of carrier pigeons. His predecessor Khumarawayh preferred dates stuffed with almonds because that was the fruit most often mentioned as heavenly provender. He was particularly partial to consuming them while floating atop a pool of quicksilver set in the midst of his garden. Another popular dish was the sweet *judhaba*:

> *Judhaba made of choicest rice,*
> *as shining as a lover's eyes;*
> *How marvelous in hue it stands,*
> *beneath the cook's accomplished hands!*

Poetry like this would be recited as each dish arrived at the caliph's table. When the guests were too stuffed to take another bite, the poets would extol the virtues of coming delights in order to revive their appetites.

> *Here capers grace a sauce vermilion*
> *whose fragrant odor to the soul are blown,*
> *here pungent garlic meets the eager sight*

and whets with savor sharp the appetite,
while olives turn to shadowed night the day,
and salted fish in slices rims the tray.

Lamb appeared frequently on the menu, and flavors like saffron, rosewater, and cardamom dominated. Specific dishes would have included fried eggplant dressed in a saffron/sesame sauce (served cold), lamb covered in poppy seeds, fish stuffed with walnuts, cod in a sweet-and-sour raisin sauce, and chicken with dried pears and peaches, to name a few. People slaked their thirst with date wine and afterward nibbled on a multitude of refreshing sherbets and the sweet jellies called *rahat lokum* ("giving rest to the throat"), which we Westerners call Turkish Delight. Then steaming black coffee served in jeweled *zarfs*, scented with ambergris and cardamom and presented by Heaven-sent virgins. Then, ah yes, back to that "work."

But better than the endless food and sex, dinner in Heaven would never be interrupted by a trip to the bathroom. A mere belch takes care of all unpleasantness, an emission producing a divine odor "like that of musk," which would be of itself an act of praise to Allah.

The Sultan's Date

There are said to be eight hundred separate uses for dates in Arabic cuisine, including wine; the naturally alcoholic juice from the tree is Islam's sole "legal" source of alcohol (it tastes a bit like peanut butter), and is so popular that the Egyptian government had to ban the cutting down of date trees. The following recipe for Rutab Mu' ass al (dates in saffron) comes from the classic eighth-century Baghdad cookbook *Kitab al-Tabikh*, as adapted in

David Waines's *In a Caliph's Kitchen*. The
script was written by a member of a royal
male slave and is Islam's earliest culinary tex

1 pound fresh dates, preferably *Khustawi* variety
Blanched almonds, one per date
3 tablespoons rosewater
1/4 teaspoon saffron
2 tablespoons honey
2 tablespoons superfine sugar, plus more to cover
2 teaspoons cinnamon

Slit and remove the stone from each date and replace with one blanched almond. Squeeze closed. Bring the rosewater, saffron, and honey to a boil and simmer for three to four minutes. Let cool and pour over the dates. Make sure every date is coated. Let them sit for a couple of hours or overnight. Mix sugar and cinnamon together. Remove dates from the syrup and roll in the sugar/cinnamon mixture (see endnotes for more elaborate recipe). Store in a cool place, covered with more sugar. Dates (frozen) are available year round but are best in the fall, when you can get them fresh.

Angel Food Cake

The diet enjoyed by human souls in the afterlife seems relatively clear. But what about the angels? The nature of angelic cuisine has been debated for centuries. Islamic scholar Ibn Majah said the Heavenly Host dines exclusively upon the "Glory of God," washed down by "Proclaiming His Holiness." Mark Twain felt certain that the heavenly food must be watermelons.

ε preponderance of evidence, however, suggests angels prefer toast. Psalm 78 of the Bible states that these spirits (we're talking Judeo-Christian-Islamic here) live on "the wheat of heaven," or manna. The former suggests bread, but manna? In the biblical language of Aramaic, manna is said to mean, "What is this?" Hardly definitive. Fortunately, the Bible contains some interesting clues, particularly in the bit where the Jews fleeing Egypt run out of grub, and, boom!, this manna stuff starts falling from the sky. Moses immediately tells everyone to grab it up because "this is the bread which the LORD hath given you to eat." Everybody gathered the stuff up and baked it into something that tasted "like wafers made with honey." It turns out there's a mosslike lichen, *Lecanora esculenta,* that clings to cliffs in the Middle East. High desert winds will sometimes scatter this stuff throughout the desert until it falls like rain on Bedouin settlements. It has a naturally sweet flavor. The locals call it the "fat of the Earth" and use it to make a kind of bread that is sometimes flavored with anise and honey called *Panakarpian* (popular in Alexandria). Bread made from manna, the ideal food of the angels. It's best enjoyed fresh from the oven or toasted. It also makes a nice jam.

Should Jehovah ever offer you a slice, however, don't be as greedy as the Jews, who, after forty days of nothing but manna, started kvetching. "We remember the fish, which we did eat in Egypt," they whined, "the cucumbers and the melons, and the leeks and the garlic. But now our soul is dried away: there is nothing at all, besides this manna, before our eyes." So Jehovah obligingly sent over some delicious little chickadees, actually quails, which, just like the manna, fell from the sky at their feet and waited to be eaten. Fires were kindled, wine decanted, and everybody set to. But it was a trick. The LORD, it seems, was "most wroth" at their display of gluttonous ingratitude—what if all his angelic employees started complaining about manna?—and "while the flesh was yet between their teeth . . . the LORD smote them with a very great plague." Food poisoning, in other words. It turns out that this tale is also likely true because quails traditionally migrate through the area en route to Africa. It's a long flight, and by all accounts the birds arrive completely exhausted, hence the bit about their flopping down at the Israelis' feet. The Heaven-sent "plague" stems from the fact that quails eat the herbs hellebore and henbane, both of which contain toxins. This is not normally a problem, but when the birds are seriously dehydrated, the poisons can get dangerously concentrated in musculature. The Greeks knew about this, but the Jews did not, and the quails gave the entire Nation of Israel one serious stomachache. Those who'd complained loudest about the manna were buried on the spot.

Saints and Supermodels

Medieval saints and modern fashion models may seem to strive for very different types of perfection—one strictly spiritual, the other physical—but both have traditionally chosen extreme dieting as the surest means to express their divine natures. The current vogue for skeletal beauty is too well known to require comment. But they were closely paralleled by medieval holy women, half of whom engaged in compulsive dieting, often to death, and who were twice as likely as their male equivalents to engage in starvation fasts. In his book *Holy Anorexia*, Rudolph Bell postulates that the two ages' shared obsession stems from outbreaks of anorexia nervosa, a psychological condition in which women starve themselves under the delusion that any eating is an act of gluttony. Others suggest it stems from women's unique relationship to food and motherhood. Whatever the reason, the menus put together by both are enough to take away the appetite of even the most devout sinner. St. Veronica spent most of her life eating spiders and cat vomit, but eventually settled into a regime consisting of vegetable soup and two ounces of fruit for breakfast. Dinner was a few grapes. Margaret of Cortona in the 1200s lived on nothing but dry bread and minuscule amounts of raw vegetables. Modern models often follow remarkably similar regimes, especially in the weeks before a major shoot or show, during which they eat nothing but cabbage soup in order to reduce their body fat to an absolute minimum. One famous ballerina reportedly survived for years on an apple a day, while others have deliberately induced starvation by drinking enormous quantities of water to kill off their appetite. A number of well-known actresses follow more modern versions of the saints' regimes by replacing the stale bread breakfast with a fat-free muffin and the raw vegetable dinner with a lightly dressed arugula salad.

What's interesting about the female saints' fasting is their motivation. Food deprivation among Judeo-Christians originated as a form of penance and as a reaction to the indulgence of pagan Rome. These female Christian mystics, however, used it primarily to alter their consciousness, a technique summed up by Margaret of Cortona's comment that she fasted obsessively "in order to be more light headed and allow her soul to be fervent." True starvation can lead to a complete absence of daydreams—or even dreams—but controlled deprivation tends to leave the subject prone to suggestion and hallucination. And trip out these ladies did. The most popular "vision" among the medieval Twiggies consisted of sexual encounters with Christ. "At first she kissed Christ's breasts," recounted Angela of Foligno's confessor/biographer in the 1300s. "And then she kissed his mouth from which, she said, an admirable and sweet fragrance emanated . . . then she placed her cheek on Christ's cheek and Christ placed his hand on her other cheek, and drew her close to him." St. Teresa of Avila described how angels plunging "burning spears into my entrails" made her moan with desire. At times this supercelestial foreplay gets positively coquettish. The patron saint of Italy, Catherine of Siena, described how Christ teased her by "showing me His most sacred side (the open wound) from afar and I cried from the intensity of my longing to put my lips to the sacred wound. After He had laughed for a little while at my tears—at least that is what He seemed to do—He came up to me . . . and put my mouth to where His most sacred wound was." In other passages she rhapsodizes about how Christ inserted a "red and gleaming" organ (a heart) into her body.

This has striking parallels with the modern dilemma. Models, of course, do not diet in order to have sexual hallucinations involving the Son of God. At least, not exactly. Bear in mind that the fantasies of the medieval saints described above were not private affairs. They were made for public consumption and usually told to a male confessor who shared the vision with the public via pamphlets like the incredibly popular fourteenth-century biography written by St. Catherine of Siena's confessor. In lieu of achieving sainthood via priests, the modern "saint" creates otherworldly fantasies with fashion designers and photographers, who then share them with the public via an endless stream of magazines. That these tabloid visions are as sexual and paradisaical as those of the saints is beyond question. Perfect women drift through surreal settings of bucolic perfection and insane wealth. They lounge beside swimming pools shimmering with celestial light. To the reader, these are images of an unobtainable Heaven—only slender and perfect goddesses are allowed in these pages! The male models in these tableaus tend to have the same asexual look medieval artists used in portraying Christ: hairless, beautiful, and slender. The women are pictured touching the male model's body reverently, almost in worship, and many of the photos are done in the "soft focus" look now associated with romance but which was originally connected to the diffused light shed by a halo. When St. Veronica died, her followers tore her body to pieces and then sold the various limbs as religious relics. Italian churches are filled with similar ghoulish trophies, and some have compared this practice to the experience of the runway model being torn asunder in an explosion of paparazzi flashbulbs to create "relics" for worldwide distribution.

In both industries women who have "purified" themselves through extreme fasting are working with or being manipulated by men—priests or fashion designers—who are in the business of selling illusory perfection and who are reputedly largely either gay or sexually inactive. Even the stereotype of the misogynous male fashion designer has an early Christian archetype. St. Jerome, a fourth-century monk, originated the waif look by urging his followers to dress their daughters in rags and make them fast without cessation in order to cool "their hot little bodies." His definition of a true lady was "one I never saw eat," and his followers forced their girls to dine alone in a darkened room so no one could see their shameful behavior. That Jerome's theories should prove so sympathetic to Western fashion moguls isn't really surprising when you consider that both come from a culture that considers the sexiest sin in history to be the gluttony of a woman named Eve. Jerome ended up in some hot water when one of his female followers, Blaesilla, starved to death under his regime. Likewise, reports indicating that the fashion industry's obsession with emaciated femininity is creating a generation of women riddled with psychological problems relating to food—currently 84 percent of all American women are on a diet and one in two hundred female college students have been diagnosed with an eating disorder—has led nations like Denmark to hold tentative discussions on outlawing unhealthy media images.

Bitter Herbs

Christina the Astonishing fed on milk from her own miraculously swelling breasts, but the preferred nosh of saints worldwide is a weed so noxious that its touch burns. It is called stinging nettles and makes a nice soup. The twelfth-century Tibetan saint Milarepa lived on the nettle soup *satuk* for so long that his hair turned green. St. Columba of Ireland followed a similar regime until he developed a mysterious weight problem. When the saint confronted his cook with the situation, he discovered she'd been using a hollow spoon to surreptitiously add milk to his broth.

Wear rubber gloves while cutting the nettles, and only use the tender tips. Serves four.

1 heaping cup young nettle leaves
Sliced leeks (for extra flavor)
2 cups combination of boiling milk and stock (or water)
1 ounce butter
2 ounces rolled oats (or rice)
Salt
Pepper
Parsley

Sweat the nettles and leeks without browning for two to three minutes. Add boiling milk and stock combination, the butter, and then the oats (or rice) and salt and pepper to taste. Simmer thirty to forty-five minutes. Taste and correct seasoning. Toss in some parsley and serve forth.

Red Lady

John pointed to a watermelon-sized pair of nipples hanging over our heads.

"These are for her milk, they say," he explained doubtfully. A pair of worshipers paused to anoint themselves with the milky-looking water dripping from the concrete teats. "They say it is holy."

We were in Amritsar's House of the Red Lady. Amritsar is a city in the northwest of India, best known for the Golden Temple belonging to the Sikh religion. Like dutiful tourists, Nina and I had visited the temple and sat by the Holy Pool ("Please to keep your legs crossed . . ."). We'd watched the screaming, sword-waving worshipers make their pilgrimage. We'd gazed at the Sikhs' Holy Book, which is surrounded night and day by chanting priests. As we left, our rickshaw driver (John) had asked us if we wanted to visit the "ladies museum." A ladies museum? Our heads immediately filled with visions of some weird tribute to the women's liberation movement, and we agreed, only to find ourselves at the house of a woman who'd achieved sainthood by intense dieting. That's an understatement; the general belief is that she lived almost her entire life without eating a single mouthful. Though this is typical behavior in the West, it's relatively rare in Hindu culture, where female saints, or gurus, tend to be plumpkins who dispense blessings via distinctly maternal hugs. It's the men who go for the waif look in India. The Red Lady was almost Christian in her love of misery, spending most of her life alone in a little house where she eventually died in the mid-1980s. Word of her ability to survive on air, however, soon spread, and by the time we visited in late 1999 her house had grown into a temple complex with about twenty rooms.

The main room, accessed through a filthy alleyway, contained a brightly painted statue of the Red Lady wearing a pair of hornrim glasses. She looked suspiciously well fed. Dozens of older women snoozed on the floor at the base of the statue. The real action was upstairs, which blurred the boundary between a carnival madhouse and a church. You enter by crawling through a minuscule hallway meant to replicate a fetus's passage through its mother's uterus. Once "reborn," one proceeds through a maze of odd-shaped rooms that wind their way up to the roof and then back down again. There were bright red rooms shaped like a tube. Others were covered in fake stalactites. There were painfully narrow hallways lined with pictures of the Red Lady and Hindu deities like Hanuman the Ape God, elephant-headed Ganesha, and the goddess Kali, her tongue lolling out bloodred and with a severed head in one hand. One room was covered floor to ceiling with beautiful orange and white flowers. The scent of incense was so strong it made one dizzy, and people were singing and praying in every corner. Children—reacting to the fun-house effect of the place—were screaming and running about in a frenzy. The last chamber was a pitch-black room full of water through which you waded in order to reach chanting priests, who led the faithful in a call-response routine before handing out magic coins guaranteed to make their real rupees multiply like jackrabbits.

John explained all the details with a skeptical grin and continually reminded us that he, a former Untouchable who'd become Christian, did not believe in such stuff. He also cast some doubts on the Red Lady's claims to absolute abstention. Like her Western sisters, who'd had a distinct weakness for communion wafers, the Red Lady had been rumored to enjoy an occasional cup of milk from the sacred cow.

The Joy of Fat

"You are so fat!" exclaims a member of Canada's Ojibwa people, meaning "looking good": healthy, wealthy, and oh so fine. Most of the world still thinks fat is beautiful, and as little as a century ago, B. Johnston, the American author of the famous *Eat and Grow Fat*, was making a bundle by advising frantic maidens (and men) who "are prepared to go to any reasonable length to acquire a few extra layers of fat." Books like these were by no means directed at anorexic types. "Every woman who is thin likes to be stouter," wrote French dietician Brillat-Savarin. "It is a wish we have heard a thousand times." Savarin's remedy was to feast on sponge cakes, macaroni, and grapes, combined with hot baths and "lots of naps." Those lacking the willpower to stick to the Savarin Regime cheated by padding their clothes. In fact, the word *diet* as we know it—referring to an interminable Hell on Earth—didn't even exist. The closest thing were nineteenth-century cults like Fletcherism, whose American devotees prided themselves on chewing each morsel thirty times before swallowing.

This passion for cellulite extended beyond the human form. Ancient Egyptians wore discs of scented animal fat on their heads that would create lovely perfumes as they melted during

dinner. But the big demand was on the dinner table itself.
"Some persons," wrote John Trusler in his eighteenth-century
The Honors of the Table, "prefer the soft, the other the firm, and
each should be asked what [fat] he likes." He advised that while
pork had delicious marrowlike flab, there was also a "nice,
gristly fat to be pared off about the ear" of a calf. Because veni-
son fat was "very apt to cool," Trusler urged thoughtful hosts to
provide heated dishes to keep it nice and runny, "a sight which
never fails to give pleasure to your company." Carvers distributed these delicacies by holding the carcass aloft with one hand
and artfully slicing with the other, so that the juicy translucent
gems drifted down like rose petals to fall in perfectly overlapping patterns onto the guest's waiting plate.

Fat, in fact, is Jehovah's preferred dish, and the Bible specifies
that the "fat of the beast" should be burned in the temple for
His consumption. We mere mortals had to make do with the
lean cuts. It was often used as a kind of sauce, and every roast
came with a side of grease. Roast lamb was best served with
bits of quivering tail fat, which Trusler says "may be readily divided into several pieces" to accommodate the salivating hordes.
Middle Eastern cultures had a particular fondness for sheep-tail
fat and bred animals with tails so gargantuan—up to eighteen
inches across—that mini carriages were harnessed to their be-
hinds to keep the precious appendage safe from bruising. Tail
fat is essential for delicacies like *qawarma* (lamb confit), and was
once the secret ingredient in the best baklava. The Dutch doted
on the marine-flavored fat of young herons, which was obtained by shaking fledglings out of their nest. When a foreign
dignitary visited Holland's Zevenjuizen Forest in the early 1600s,
more than five hundred birds were shaken from their nests for
lunch. Perhaps the most famous French fat (excluding Norman

butter) is the *sots-l'y-laisse*, which translates as "only idiots don't eat it," found near a chicken's buttock. When *New York Times* critic Craig Claiborne took his famous thirty-two-course, $4,000 meal in 1975, one dish consisted of dozens of the gelatinous morsels.

Truly fat-free foods, like people, tend to lack personality. Fat is comparable to the volume knob, because without it our taste buds are incapable of distinguishing flavors but in and of itself it is almost flavorless. How then did it become the food taboo of the modern world? It isn't, of course. It's only the *idea* of fat we loathe. Westerners, particularly Americans, love it to death, and they spend enormous amounts of money to create artificial replacements that give them a thrillingly opulent mouthful without the caloric penalties. For the true fat haters, we have to go back to the Native Americans. When asked in the 1600s what were the three greatest evils Europeans had introduced to the New World, the Mayans first mentioned torture and genocide. But third on the list was the conquistadors' propensity for "basting with lard."

Fat-tailed sheep, seventeenth-century engraving.

Mitterrand's Last Supper

When French president François Mitterrand realized he was about to die of cancer, he invited his friends over for a final New Year's Eve dinner: December 31, 1995. The first course was oysters. Then came foie gras. Then roast capon. But no dessert course, no cheese: the last flavor Mitterrand wished to savor belonged to the flesh of the endangered *ortolan*, a songbird the size of a human toe that is a crime to buy or hunt, and is certainly illegal to eat. Mitterrand devoured it in the traditional manner, first covering his head with an embroidered cloth, then inserting the entire bird into his mouth.

If guilt is a flavor, and it definitely is, then *l'ortolan* is one of the world's greatest dishes. The lemon-colored songbirds, called buntings in English, originally appeared in French chansons as symbols of innocence and of the love of Jesus. Then a tribe near Bordeaux began trapping them as they migrated south to Africa, pulling them out of the sky with little wooden traps called *matoles* hidden high in the treetops. The birds must be taken alive; once captured they are either blinded or kept in a lightless box for a month to gorge on millet, grapes, and figs, a technique apparently taken from the decadent cooks of Imperial Rome who called the birds *beccafico*, or "fig-pecker." When they've reached four times their normal size, they're drowned alive in a snifter of Armagnac. This sadistic *mise en scène* has transformed the bird from a symbol of innocence to an act of gluttony symbolic of the fall from grace. In Colette's novel *Gigi*, for instance, the tomboyish main character prepares for her entry into polite society with lessons in the correct way to eat lobsters and boiled eggs. When she begins training to be a courtesan, however, she is said to be "learning how to eat the *ortolan*." Not that it was only courtesans who indulged. The tradition of covering one's head while eating the bird was supposedly started by a soft-bellied priest trying to hide his sadistic gluttony from God.

Cooking *l'ortolan* is simplicity itself. Simply pop them in a high oven for six to eight minutes and serve. The secret is entirely in the eating. First you cover your head with a traditional embroidered cloth. Then place the entire four-ounce bird into your mouth. Only its head should dangle out from between your lips. Bite off the head and discard. *L'ortolan* should be served immediately; it is meant to be so hot that you must rest it on your tongue while inhaling rapidly through your mouth. This cools the bird, but its real purpose is to force you to allow its ambrosial fat to cascade freely down your throat. When cool, begin to chew. It should take about fifteen minutes to work your way through the breast and wings, the delicately crackling bones, and onto the inner organs. Devotees claim they can taste the bird's entire life as they chew in the darkness: the wheat of Morocco, the salt air of the Mediterranean, the lavender of Provence. The pea-sized lungs and heart, saturated with Armagnac from its drowning, are said to burst in a liqueur-scented flower on the diner's tongue. Enjoy with a good Bordeaux.

What could be more delicious? Nothing, according to initiates, who compare the banning of the *ortolan* to the death of French culture and continue to eat them despite fines of up to $2,000. "It is the most incredible thing—delicious!" says Jean-Louis Palladin, a French chef who once smuggled four hundred *ortolans* into the United States for a dinner at his restaurant in Washington's Watergate Hotel (he hid them from customs in a box of diapers). Palladin sneers at the idea that the covering of the diner's head is to hide their shame from God. "Shame? *Mais non!* It is for concentrating on the fat going down the throat. It is really like you are praying, see? Like when you take the Mass (communion wafer) into your mouth from the priest's hand in church and you think about God. Now that is what eating *l'ortolan* is really most like."

President Mitterrand appears to have agreed. Although so ill that he was passing out between courses, France's last truly great leader broke the traditional limit of one bird per diner that night in 1995. He ate two. It was the last thing he tasted. The next morning Mitterrand began refusing food. He died within the week.

$\mathcal{P}$RIDE

"Poor white trash I am for sure/I eat shit food and am not worthy."

Dorothy Allison,
Trash: Stories

PRIDE MENU

COCKTAIL HOUR
The Dirt Eater
Traditional Southern Champagne cocktail with chocolate
overtones. Served with disdain.

FOR STARTERS
Crostini di Fegato
Traditional Tuscan crostini covered with a lily-livered pâté.
(Recipe on page 100)

THE BREAD BASKET
Pane de Indio
Bread basket of native baked goods like blue someviki and
psychedelic blinis. Served with wildflower jams.
(Recipe on page 106)

VEGGIES
Dead Man's Lima Beans
Fresh lima beans tossed with butter and bacon fat. Served
with a Judas sop.

THE BLUE PLATE SPECIAL

Humble Pie

A traditional Batalia pie filled with chitterlings, sweetbreads,
and sots-l'y-laisse. Served with a Florentine sauce.

FOR THE SWEET TOOTH

Galette des Rois

Traditional New Orleans epiphany cake.

(Recipe on page 111)

WE FOLLOW A SEGREGATED

SEATING POLICY.

The Egotist at Dinner

What I found surprising while researching the sin of pride was how wrong I was. I mean, I'm usually right about everything. The idea of my being wrong is absurd. I am *always* right and invariably superior in every way to my peers, above whom I reign in a cloud of jasmine-scented perfection constantly flickering with the lightning flashes of my creativity and insight. Did I say *peers*? How tellingly indicative of my modest inclination and my desire to bestow credit on even the most undeserving. But for many, I think, pride is a constant pitfall. Particularly when it comes to dinner. That's why I anticipated that this section would be a tale of boorish snobs who openly sneer at other cultures' cuisine and insist on choosing the wine. A history of France, in other words. Instead, it turns out to be a tale of racism and hatred.

Take the term *beaner*. The original expression was *bean eater*, a reference to the Mexicans' beloved *frijoles*, but used as a derogatory label by white racists to suggest Mexicans' supposed laziness and ignorance. Modern English is littered with similar expressions. African Americans deride whites as "crackers," presumably referring to a uniquely Caucasian love of Nabisco baked goods. Whites slander blacks for their alleged addiction to watermelons. The English are "limeys" because their sailors sucked on limes (to avoid scurvy). The French are "frogs" because of their national dish of frogs' legs. At the height of World War II, with all sorts of vicious and absolutely applicable insults available to hurl at the Nazis, the allies expressed their horror by focusing on Germany's unnatural appetite for pickled cabbage and defamed them with "krauts" (for sauer-*kraut*). The National Socialists, however, were unapologetic. "Also our noble sauerkraut," intoned a Nazi-era cookbook called *Homeland Cooking*:

> We should not forget it
> A German created it
> Therefore it's a German dish
> If such a little piece of meat, white and mild
> Lies in a kraut, that is a picture
> As like Venus in Roses.

The meaning is obvious: You are what you eat, and if you don't eat like me—or like what I eat—you're my enemy. In some cultures the word for enemy translates literally as "those with different mouth." Does this mean world peace could be achieved by implementing a Universal Menu? Those humanitarians at the McDonald's corporation seem to think so, which makes one wonder if there are not worse things than an occasional war. At any rate, behaviorists explain the rampant food abuse of hatemongers to the fact that eating among animals is generally a single-species activity, and hence a key definer of group identity. Psychologists have reported cases of clinical depression among expatriates that were cured only when the patient went on a steady diet of his or her native food. It's a pretty good indication of how important a role cuisine plays in our sense of self, hence the keen interest in forcing conquered peoples to lose their native dishes, particularly in the United States, where the idea of the "melting pot" demands that immigrants lose their cultural identity and become "white bread" Americans both in their hearts and at the dinner table.

The Dirt Eaters

The dirt eater is the ultimate scum of American society. He or she is the outcast, the loser, the one who has not only admitted defeat but made it his daily bread, the lowest of the low, the sucker up of the ground upon which we walk, on which dogs piss and garbage is tossed. "Technically, I'd rather eat dirt than food," Georgia's Rena Bronson told the media in 1999. "If I could eat dirt for breakfast, dirt for lunch, dirt for dinner and a little iced tea, I'd be fine." Bronson is a registered nurse who eats three small bags of clay a week. Not just any old dirt. She's an epicure who dines exclusively on creamy white kaolin clay, the flavor of which has been described in truffle-ian raptures. Dirt eaters like Ms. Bronson have been around for centuries and, contrary to current American attitudes, generally have been considered quite respectable. Some African Americans still send bags of clay to expectant mothers, and over a million Mexicans every year participate in a Christian/Mayan Eucharist ceremony in which clay tablets are eaten in lieu of the traditional wheaten wafer. As in much clay cookery, the Mexicans bake their mud to get rid of excess moisture and concentrate flavors, a craft perfected by the Australian Aborigines who make a white organic loaf that is kneaded and sun-dried before being wrapped in leaves and baked. Women in northern India used to buy a clay pot that imparted a pleasant odor to their water. When their thirst was slaked, they would consume the cup itself. The Kai people of Papua New Guinea string small balls of clay on a stick and grill them like Middle Eastern kebabs; one would imagine this would go rather nicely with the original potato-chip dip the Peruvian Incas created out of a special riverside mud patch. *Mise en scène* aside, there are three basic dirt varieties: red (rustic), white (creamy and light), and black (comparable to bitter chocolate). The best, though, are the rare "blue earths" which are full of coal-tar air bubbles that tickle the palate with champagne sensations.

Tasty and cheap, these foods are rich in minerals; they often played an essential role in diets worldwide. The extreme denigration of dirt eating is primarily a North American attitude, and it probably developed because the food's popularity among African slaves led to its being associated with laziness, perhaps because prisoners tend to be undermotivated, or because dirt coating the stomach lining slows absorption of vitamins and can cause lethargy and sometimes death. Some slave owners actually made workers wear iron gags to keep them from excessive snacking. But what makes the American loathing of dirt eating so interesting is that although the habit was heavily associated with Africans, the first literary dirt eater was a white man. His name was Ransy Sniffle, and he appeared in an 1833 magazine story called "The Fight" by Augustus Baldwin Longstreet. The writer describes Sniffle as a flat-headed monstrosity with oversize joints, withered limbs, and a complexion a "corpse would have disdained to own." The archetypal white trash, in other words; a "clay-eater, his bloated watery countenance illuminated by the exhilarating qualities of rum." Mr. Sniffle, however, was more than a mere fancy. He was a caricature created as part of a campaign against the Populist democratic movement of Andrew Jackson. There was a whole cadre of writers and magazines involved in this effort, and their primary mission was to portray poor whites as animals whose habits not only made them unsuitable dinner guests but, by association, inappropriate participants in the political arena. By making Sniffle a "dirt eater" like the disenfranchised Africans, Longstreet was indulging in the hallowed tradition of manipulating food habits to exclude a group from political power.

A Dinner Party in Kishan Garhi

The use of food to disempower has a long tradition in the American South. "The commonest of these [social] taboos," wrote John Dollard in his study of southern racial segregation, "are those against eating at a table with Negroes." Interracial eating was second only to interracial sex among the taboos of the old South, and a disproportionate number of civil rights battles were fought over segregated lunch counters. The American system of culinary segregation, however, is pretty weak stuff compared to the system devised by India's Hindus, who, at over 1 billion, now constitute about one-fifth of the world's population. Hindu society is divided into four rigidly segregated classes called castes. At the top are the Brahmins, or the priest class. Then come the Kshatriyas, warriors. Next the Vaisyas, merchants. At the bottom is the servant class of Sudras. Within these four *über*-castes are also thousands of subcastes (many based on profession), all of which maintain their social standing by snubbing one another's dinner parties. Sociologist McKin Marriott showed what a soap opera this can become in a 1968 study that focused on the tiny village of Kishan Garhi, which, despite containing only 166 families, boasts a whopping thirty-six individual castes. The trouble began when the local goatherds decided to force the village barbers to accept a dinner invitation. Under Hindu social rules, this would have put the barbers below the goat boys. The barbers didn't seem to care—more free grub for us seems to have been their admirably pragmatic attitude—but it put the top-dog Brahmins in a bind. If the barbers lost caste it meant they would no longer be able to trim the Brahmins' hair because, as priests, the Brahmins must follow strict regulations not only about what they eat—and with whom—but also which castes are allowed to touch or even breathe on them.

The village elders conferred. A compromise was worked out. They ruled that the barbers could have dinner with the goatherds but could eat only non-*kacca*, or unsacred, dishes. This left the hair stylists just enough social rank to continue as the Brahmins' barbers. The goatherds, however, were furious. They fired their local Brahmin priest and replaced him with one from a distant village. Then the plot thickened: a *local* Brahmin was seen eating with the goatherds. The village was scandalized. What they didn't know, however, was that the Brahmin in question was blackmailed into accepting the dinner invite to get a money loan from the goatherds. The village eventually found out, and all hell broke loose. The Brahmins wouldn't eat with the Brahmins, the barbers were out of work, and the goatherds' position was so confused that they were virtually (gasp!) without caste.

The caste system is not just fun and food fights, of course. Beneath the four main castes are the so-called Untouchables, or

Dalits, a group of about 250 million people who are completely *without* caste, and so . . . well, untouchable. They get to clean the latrines, but that's about it. If they take water from the communal well, they are sometimes killed. If they try to eat with caste members, the food is pushed off their plates until they leave in tears. This horrific repression (now illegal) is said to stem directly from the sense of separation caused by the dietary rules enshrined in the ancient laws of Hindu society. "The feelings of Untouchability in the caste system," writes Sundar La Sar in *Hindu Culture and Caste System*, "had their roots in the compulsory separation of food-habits among the people." The upside for the Untouchables is that they can eat anything they want without losing social status—beef, caviar, foie gras, even truffles. Compare that to the menu of poor, pitiful Brahmins, who not only must follow a strict vegetarian diet, but also must abstain from things like garlic and onions. No booze, of course. Some are not even allowed carrots or tomatoes because their origin in foreign lands means they have no caste and are therefore "untouchable." Nor is the conversation at dinner likely to make amends for the cuisine. "One should take one's food alone and not in the company of even one's relatives," suggests the three-thousand-year-old Laws of Manu, "since who can know the secret sins of a person in whose company one eats?" Some high-caste Brahmins dine in a room devoted exclusively to that purpose, or at least set up screens to keep impure influences at bay while eating. True blue bloods purify the dinner table with cow dung or, better yet, eat straight off the karma-enhancing excrement by "pouring water over a spot and plastering [leaves] with cow dung."

The only other major group with a comparably strict dining etiquette are ultra-Orthodox Jews, some of whom will not use a plate that a nonbeliever has touched. The similarity of the two groups' food obsessions, plus the fact that the Jews have been called "the Sons of Abraham" (read "A Brahmin"), have led to speculation that both sprang from some prehistoric super-priesthood. While this thought might have some historical basis, what the two really share is a profound awareness of the connection between food, purity, and morality. "The dietary rules [of the Jews] merely developed the metaphor for holiness," wrote scholar Mary Douglas in her book *Purity and Danger*, by "keeping distinct the categories of creation." In her view, kosher dietary law forbids the eating of animals like the salamander because the Lord created the world to be in three separate categories: earth, sky, and water. The amphibious salamander violates this organization by living both on earth and in water. Hence, it is a creature created by the Devil and unclean. The Hindu prohibition against castes sharing meals stems from the same concept. Just as God created separate categories of matter, He created separate groups of humans. It would be as immoral to breach the latter as it would the former. This is particularly true about breaking bread together, because eating is so intimately tied to tribal identity and religious worship. Moreover, this concept of "sacred separation," or boundaries, is the underlying principle of almost all morality, according to Douglas. A lie is only wrong because it pretends to be true, i.e., it mingles two separate categories of nature: falsehood and truth. In Douglas's point of view, the peculiar dietary laws of the Hebrews and the Brahmins were created to force believers into ritualized daily meditations on these great questions—truth, purity, holiness—and return dinner to its roots "as a meaningful part of the great liturgical act of worship, which culminates in the sacrifice [meal] in The Temple."

The Last Supper

The New Testament is littered with tales of Jesus' lousy table manners. He forgets to wash his hands before eating. He takes dinner with hookers. He does lunch with unbelievers. These were more than mere breaches of etiquette; like the Hindu caste code, these rules upheld the society of the time and were taken extremely seriously. Members of the Essenes, a cult that Christ probably studied with, starved to death rather than eat food touched by non-Essenes.

Christ's déclassé dinner parties were tolerated as long as he held them out in the boonies. But dining out in the big city, Jerusalem, was another matter. In *The Scrolls and Christian Origins: Studies in the Jewish Background of the New Testament*, religious scholar Matthew Black notes a number of odd circumstances surrounding Christ's Last Supper. First, it appears to have been kept a secret. Christ refused to tell even his apostles where it was to be held, instead making them meet with a stranger who led them to the dinner party's location. Black believes this indicates that the meal was probably an illegal ceremony of some kind. He then reconstructs the calendar of Jesus' time and concludes that, although the Last Supper occurred around Jewish Passover, it did not fall on the officially sanctioned holiday. Black then looks at the circumstances leading to the arrest of Jesus, particularly the behavior of the traitor Judas during the meal. The New Testament notes that "having received the sop he [Judas] immediately went out: and it was night." A curiously bleak turn of phrase, especially when you realize that a sop is just a piece of bread used to soak up gravy. Couldn't Judas just have wanted something to snack on? Hardly. "In carrying off the sop he took evidence with him to the priests and the Pharisees that an illegal feast had been celebrated," Black concludes, "[and] that Jesus was challenging Pharisaic law in its stronghold, Jerusalem itself." Judas took the gravy-soaked crust to prove that Christ was holding an illegal feast—a satanic passover— and that if the police acted immediately they could catch this charlatan Messiah red-handed. In this light, the copious amount of biblical ink spilled on the Last Supper appears quite reasonable. Christ's reason for coming to Jerusalem seems to have been to provoke a confrontation with the authorities, but he gets arrested before anything happens. Perhaps the Last Supper *was* the planned confrontation. During dinner, he predicts the imminent arrival of the cops. If the soirée had been a deliberate affront, his prophesy is no more clairvoyant than a protester foreseeing jail time after staging a sit-in at the mayor's office.

Christianity is unique among the major religions for its almost complete lack of food taboos. This was no accident. The New Testament specifically quotes Matthew as saying, "Know and understand; it is not what goes into the mouth that defiles a man, but that which comes out." Christ's choice of a dinner party to take a theological stand makes sense if you consider that his years of training with the food-obsessed Essene cult would have left him preternaturally aware of the connection between pride and dietary taboos. After all, how can people be truly equal if they can't all eat the same food at the same table? His manipulation of the Passover feast for political gain, however, was to prove catastrophic; in the ensuing two millenniums, ignorant Christians mourning Christ's death during Easter routinely massacred Jews because their simultaneous Passover feast—a joyous event commemorating their release from Egyptian bondage—was mistaken as celebration of Christ's death on the cross.

Humble Pie

So here I am in some subterranean dive in Manhattan's East Village. Everywhere you look, there are Japanese hipsters in horn-rim glasses sucking on Sapporo beers and munching omelets covered in writhing bonito flakes that look like barf monsters from a bad sci-fi flick. I take a mouthful of my *motsu yakitori*. *Motsu* means cow intestines. I love 'em, which is just as well, since each *yakitori*—a kind of Japanese shish-kebab—is only three inches long, and I am determined to choke down an entire cow intestine. There's approximately 150 feet of digestive tract per animal, which means I have another six hundred *yakitori* to go. The divine Nina J. is my companion in this adventure. She looks as if she's going to throw up. She's a dainty one, that Nina, who doesn't eat meat, and is restricting herself to a shrimp.

"That," I say defensively, pointing to the pink body on her spear, "is a bottom feeder. Do you know what *it* eats?" Happily, I remember her brother Jerry certifies kosher restaurants for his synagogue. "Jerry would rather be strangled than put one of those in his mouth."

Nina ignores me and continues eating. I change tactics. Sure, I say to her, few self-respecting Americans would be caught dead eating cow intestine or heart or liver—at least not publicly—but organ meats like these were once the sacrament of the world's most powerful priesthood, the Etruscan haruspex. The Etruscans were the original inhabitants of Italy's Tuscany region. They taught Imperial Rome not only how to read and write but how to foretell future events, and no Roman emperor worth his salt made a political decision without ordering an Etruscan haruspex to read the future in a sheep's entrails. I describe the scene to Nina: the bleating animals, the incense, the priests pulling the organs out of the beast's still-steaming body to examine it for prophetic markings. Then, if the lower intestine gave the go-ahead, the politicians would send an army out to conquer, say, Asia Minor and the haruspex priests would sit back to enjoy a snack very much like the one before me now. Charred heart and liver shish-kebab, salted and eaten with the grill's ashes still sticking to it.

But that was all a long time ago. Ancient history.

Or so I thought.

The guinea pig took another sip of his beer and rolled his eyes in exasperation—was this never going to end?

"He works better when he's drunk," Señor Villanova explained. "You'll see, señor."

My personal journey into the mystic realm of variety meats began in the village of Husao high in the Peruvian Andes. Peru is probably the last place in the world to continue a Tuscan-like reverence for entrails. The only real difference is that the Etruscan priests used sheep. The Peruvian priests, *curandernos,* prefer guinea pigs.

Villanova poured another mouthful of beer into his pet's maw. Not all *curandernos* get their guinea pigs drunk, but Villanova had been highly recommended. And that was good, because I was beginning to feel skeptical. For one thing, his pants didn't fit. He also seemed tipsy, at least judging by the incomprehensible mix of Quecha (the native Inca language) and Spanish that he mumbled out of the corner of his crooked mouth. In fact, his whole face looked vaguely out of kilter. Nor did his office décor help—nothing but two rickety wooden stools and a table covered with dirty leaves. Every other witch doctor I'd visited had displayed a healthy supply of gods and talismans.

Hell, I thought, if the walls had been painted white instead of raw cement I could have been in the office of a Western doctor, God forbid. The most impressive thing about Villanova was how he got his pet to drink the beer. He held the animal by the skin around its shoulders and, when it was time to administer a chug, pulled back on the skin to force its little mouth open. Then he dunked its head straight into the mug. The guinea pig had a helluva foam mustache, but in minutes they'd gone through half a large bottle of *Cuzco cerveza*, although I couldn't say whether Señor Villanova or the pig had done most of the drinking.

He explained tomorrow's procedure to me. First, he would enchant his pig and rub it over my naked body so it could absorb my illness. This normally kills the beast; then, amid prayers and chanting, Villanova would cut it in half to examine the inner organs for signs indicating the best way to heal me. Villanova compared it to taking an X ray without the dangers of radiation.

Very Etruscan, I thought. Straight out of *Bella Tuscany*. I asked Villanova if he'd ever heard of Tuscany. Frances Mayes? Risotto? He didn't seem to understand, so I pulled out a picture of the Piacenza liver, a two-hundred-pound, three-dimensional bronze reproduction of a sheep's liver made by the Romans around the second century B.C. to teach priests how to prophesize in the Tuscan way. It shows forty-four sections, each of which is sacred to a particular divinity. The idea was to look for prophetic polyps. A distended gallbladder, for instance, was considered propitious for war because martial gods like Hercle (Hercules) dominated the area. I presume that's why we used to say, "she's got a lotta gall" about someone with an unusually fiery temperament, but I could be mistaken.

I told Señor Villanova all about the Etruscans. I waved my

Xerox of the Piacenza liver at him and asked if *curandernos* had similar learning aids. But my Spanish must not have been up to the task, because he just gave me a pitying look.

"Please stay calm, *señor*." He patted me on the shoulder. "When you come back tomorrow you will see my wife. She specializes in these kinds of conditions." Then he poured us both out a glass of the beer. "I suggest you drink this," he said, gulping his down. "It will make you feel much better."

The Romans came to depend on the Etruscan prophets in much the same way we depend on tabloid journalists. It was a haruspex named Spurinna who came up with the famous "Beware the Ides of March!" headline, and Caesar's personal priests warned him to stay home the day Brutus struck because they had disemboweled an animal without a heart. The flavor of these rites is captured nicely by the Roman chronicler Silicus Italicus in a scene in which the great general Hannibal consults a *haruspice* (a female haruspex) prior to declaring war on Rome. The divination takes place in a blood-splattered cave full of hissing gases and wailing spirits. "Then a black victim was sacrificed to the goddess of triple shape; and the priestess, seeking an oracle, quickly opened the still-breathing body and questioned the spirit, as it fled from the inward parts that she had laid bare in haste." Consulting the entrails she plops on the table, the priestess prophesies, "I see the Aetolian field covered far and wide with soldiers' corpses, and lakes red with Trojan blood . . . the river Po runs blood." She was describing the events of the Second Punic War, the most significant conflict in Roman history.

The abrupt disappearance of Etruscan culture around the fourth century B.C. has long baffled some historians, but some now think that when their priests divined their culture's demise in a sheep's liver, the race simply merged with the Romans rather than fight the inevitable. Tuscany's love of chopped-liver, however, seems to have lived on in Europe. The ancient Irish *Vision of Mac Conglinne* tells in great detail how the king could be satisfied only with "son of fat, son of kidney, son of slender tripe," and how the tribute to the royal ladies consisted of sweet-breads and pig hearts. Organ meats fetched significantly higher prices than chops in the markets of seventeenth-century Paris. The French called these delicacies *parties nobles*, and every hunter carried a ritual set of knives with which to remove them. He would then present them, on a forked stick, called *la fourchie*, to the most powerful person present and they would be grilled on the spot in a little ceremony meant to honor the nobleman's bravery. We still say a brave man has "guts" or "pluck" (a kind of intestine). Cowards, of course, are "gutless" or "lily-livered."

In fact, the entire world seems to be riddled with a perverse reverence for variety meats. The Scottish have made entrails wrapped in entrails (stomach), called haggis, a national dish, which they eat in a ceremony filled with pomp and bagpipes. The Tongans believed the liver was the finest part of the meal because it was where the animal's courage resided, which is why they gave it to the chief. The heads of the African Masai eat nothing but milk, honey, and roasted livers, for similar reasons. The Turkish high holiday Kurban Bayrami, the Day of Sacrifice, culminates in the ritual eating of a bowl of tripe stew called *iskembe corbasi*. The ancient Greeks claimed Achilles' courage came from a diet of lion intestines. The nomad tribes of Sudan make a delicious dish from giraffe innards that they claim allows them to communicate telepathically with their revered giraffe.

And then, of course, there was the Inca empire of Peru and their sacred guinea pigs.

* * *

Señora Villanova was waiting for me when I returned to the *curanderno's* house the next day. She was about four feet tall, a hundred years old, and wearing a massive pleated skirt and foot-tall white top hat. Braids to her waist. Now here, I thought, was a witch doctor who knew how to dress the part! She should give her husband some tips. We began the session with some prayers to a pile of coca leaves (the base for cocaine, and considered sacred). These were then laid on a piece of gift-wrapping paper and covered with dried moss, pink cookies, a couple of marbles, the hand off of a Barbie doll, mattress stuffing, and some confetti. This was my symbolic "body." My mind began to wander. I was already feeling rather spacy from the three days I'd spent sitting in Husao's single dirt street begging the Villanovas to see me. They actually had quite a following, and I often found myself in a crowd of patients outside—men shaking with palsy, ominously limp infants, boys with purple mold covering their faces. Serious stuff. And not just dirt-poor peasants. Some of these suckers were rich. One even arrived in a BMW. You would think with that kind of money coming in, the Villanovas would spruce up their operation, but no. Roosters wandered in during my séance. A hunchbacked boy stuck his head in the door for a stare. By the single naked lightbulb I could make out some decorative touches. A pink-and-yellow plastic reindeer head. Donald Duck statues covered in muck. Not as grand as the gory altars of the Roman haruspex but an Etruscan priestess would probably find a Day-Glo pink reindeer pretty damn impressive. Only a truly powerful deity, they might reason, would possess such an otherworldly color. That strangely dressed duck was obviously a lesser wood spirit.

I suppose it was sometime during my little daydream that two other women, identical to Señora Villanova in every respect, sneaked into the room. Before I knew it, they were all jabbering away with one another and throwing golden flower petals at me. I felt as if I was on Mars—three sisters bent double with age, their wrinkled faces glowing a bright parchment yellow and dressed in matching white top hats and blue velour dinner jackets. *Blue velour dinner jackets.* Where, I wondered, did they get outfits like that? One of them pulled out a jet-black guinea pig and started pouring beer down its gullet. Another tied a mass of pink and green ribbons to each of its paws. Then a bundle of pink ribbons was knotted about its waist.

Then they told me to take off all my clothes.

> *"Mr. Leopold Bloom ate with Relish the inner organs of beasts and fowl. He liked thick giblet soup, nutty gizzards, a stuffed roast heart, liver slices fried with crustcrumbs. . . ."*
>
> James Joyce
> *Ulysses*, 1922.

It was at some point during the late 1700s that the sacred meats of Tuscany began their long journey into disgrace. The most logical explanation for this demotion was Europe's increasing urbanization and the propensity of organ meats to spoil. Where in the past the European elite had enjoyed them deep in the forest after a kill, they now became the dish of people who lived near the cities' enormous slaughterhouses in 'hoods called "shambles," mazelike arrondisements puddled with coagulating blood and the stench of death. Hearts, kidneys, liver, udders, spleens, and blood pudding became Europe's soul food, both loved and hated. There were curious remnants of its former glory—it was considered an honored dish on St. Patrick's Day in parts of Ireland, where butchers would celebrate the holiday by decorating pigs' heads with top hats and placing a tobacco pipe in their mouths. "I'd bring [it] over and I'd eat it like chocolate. I'd eat it like chocolate," told one elderly resident of Cork to historian Regina Sexton. "With a hot potato and the cabbage and as for the pig's tail, I'd eat every bit of the fat on the pig's tail and I didn't eat a pig's tail now for ten years." Younger generations developed an aversion to their grandpa's "chocolate," and some households began serving two separate dinners, one with offal for the elders and another offal-free for the youngsters. The popular seventeenth-century delicacy Batalia pie took its name from *béatillae*, a reference to the small precious things hidden under the crust—cockscombs, sweet-breads, and such. By the late 1800s an identical dish was called 'umble pie, *'umbles*, or *numbles*, being English slang for various organ meats. This treat soon became the symbolic "humble pie" we all enjoy from time to time when abjectly humiliated before large crowds of gloating spectators. Organ meat cuisine today verges on the extinct, at least in the English-speaking world. Americans are so terrified of eating "humble pie" they consume its ingredients only via the alarmingly pink anonymity known as the hot dog. Followers of America's Nation of Islam have banned this kind of food because of its association with the diet once forced on slaves in the South.

I've never had a pet guinea pig, but I must say I quite enjoyed having one give me a massage. The warm fur felt absolutely di-vine as they ran it over my legs, my chest, the small of my back. Behind my ears. Not only did it feel good, but as the three witches from Husao rubbed the tipsy beast over my body, I felt all bad energies depart and my inner organs fill with a radiant light that sang like a thousand angels. The air above their top hats began to crackle and glow with electrical discharges. The Earth shook. And then it was done. The guinea pig was dead.

The ladies laid it reverently on the table and prepared to cut it open to examine its entrails. I grew terribly excited as they whetted an evil-looking knife. Finally I would experience the same thrill of Hannibal, of Caesar, of Nero! Then I looked down at the doll-size body lying still upon the table. Poor little guinea pig, I thought; you have died for my sins. I noticed it seemed to look back at me.

"He's not dead," I said.

One of the ladies picked him up.

"I thought they absorbed the disease and it killed them," I said. "That's part of what makes me better, no?"

The ladies conferred. It seemed that my illness had been so mild that the packet containing the coca leaves and pink cookies had ameliorated it. This would be burned and since the pig had survived the ordeal (save for a possible hangover), it would be released into the wild. Or so they said. When I indicated I wanted to escort it to freedom, I noticed some hesitation. Indeed, I suspect they were secretly planning to recycle my pig on the next patient. A special fee took care of the problem, however, and I was soon walking with the hunchback boy to the fields beyond the village. We watched the pig stagger off, its colorful ribbons flashing bravely in the brown stubble. He seemed headed for the snowy mountains that ringed the valley. Won't all those ribbons about make him easy prey for hunters? I asked. Peruvians consider guinea pig a delicacy and eat about 60 million a year.

"No, señor, he is safe," the boy replied. "Any person who sees those ribbons will know he is possessed by bad spirits. He will live to be the oldest guinea pig in Peru."

A Prophetic Chicken

One of the more popular snacks in Tuscany is called *Crostini di Fegato*, made of chicken livers, a dish that is believed to have evolved from the Etruscan method of divination. Religious chicken livers might seem like a stretch, but it turns out Imperial Romans had whole cadres of prophetic roosters. Before every major battle they'd offer some poultry a bowl of grain. If the birds ate with good appetite, victory was assured; if not, defeat was inevitable. Before one famous battle a couple of chicken oracles who'd lost their appetite were thrown into the sea to drown by P. Claudius Pulcher, an irate general who remarked, "May they drink if they won't eat." Pulcher went down to defeat.

The following recipe comes from the grandmother of writer Giuseppina Oneto of Rome, who writes:

"My grandmother, Faustina Ciampolini, was born in a little Tuscan town south of Florence, Certaldo—Etruscan area. Truthfully she didn't look like an Etruscan, and looking like an Etruscan in Italy means that you are not very beautiful, and probably she didn't know much about them either. She was afraid of mysteries and ancient tombs. But she did like mummies. Anyhow, she taught her daughter this recipe and added, 'You cook this only during Christmastime!' No explanation about that, but in Italy modern sacrifices appear to happen only at Christmastime. She had her own chickens, and she used to add their precious livers to the ones bought at the local butcher's—'a malicious man,' she used to add."

2 tablespoons olive oil
2 bay leaves
1 clove of garlic, crushed (optional)
7 ounces (200 grams) chicken liver
3.4 ounces (⅒ liter) red wine
2 cloves (optional)
Black pepper
Salt

Put olive oil and bay leaves (and garlic, if you like it) in a clay pot and heat. Add the chicken liver cut in pieces, and salt and pepper. Heat. Add the red wine (and the cloves, if using) and let mixture cook at high flame for four to five minutes. Take the bay leaves out (and garlic and cloves, if added). Crush the rest with a fork; while still warm, spread on a *crostino* (small slice of bread dried in the oven). *Buon appetito!*

Impure Indian Corn

Native Americans revered corn above almost anything on Earth. They believed the first humans were made from the plant and considered it so sacred that when the first Europeans fed it to their horrible monsters (horses), they almost attacked them for blasphemy. Not that the white men were being consciously disrespectful. In fact, Columbus quite liked corn, although he believed it was a curiously large ear of wheat. That changed as Europeans went from being guests to invaders and felt compelled to demonize the enemy's favorite snack. "The barbarous Indians which know no better are constrained to make a vertue of a necessitie, and think it a good food," wrote the author of the influential Gerard's *Herbal* of 1597, "whereas we may easily judge that it nourisheth but little and is of hard and evil digestion." Others claimed "Indian wheat" caused scabs and burned the blood. When they grew bored with blaming those red-skinned barbarians for the stuff, Europeans renamed it "Turkish wheat" after their archenemies in Istanbul and many nineteenth-century Irish preferred starvation to eating "brimstone yellow" corn bread.

European colonials in America were too reliant on corn to completely snub it, so they assigned it to the lower classes. "Gentlemen's houses," noted Robert Beverley in 1705, "usually had bread made of wheat," while corn bread was "mostly reserved for the servants," an observation borne out by the African-American adage, "we grow the wheat and they give us the corn." It was so déclassé that no American cookbook bothered to print a single corn recipe until the eve of the nineteenth century. It's an attitude still reflected in corn's relative scarcity at the dinner table. Maize's primary solo role is as "junk food," like popcorn and chips, or as animal feed. The prejudice against it is so pervasive that we've made "corny" synonymous with "trite." The message seems clear enough. Pig food, junk food. This is hardly food at all. It's garbage.

It is impossible to definitively identify the cause of social attitudes and taboos. But psychologists generally agree that parents identify "bad food" to their children based not so much on nutrition but on class associations, which in the United States is usually coded by race. In this regard, it's interesting to note the very different fate of New World foods like chocolate and tomatoes. Both were first adopted by the European elite who then reintroduced them to North America, where they quickly became among our most popular foods. Corn and turkey, introduced directly from Native American cuisine, remain in many ways marginalized.

"Not assimilated yet—still eating pasta," a New York social worker wrote in 1920 about the dangerously un-American dinners enjoyed by a family of Italian immigrants. Just as the early Jews had used dietary taboos to give their far-flung people a cohesive identity, white Americans intent on creating an ethnic melting pot have tried to eliminate alien foods that threatened their social construct. All non-European cultures received similar treatment—the current governor of Washington State, Chinese-American Gary Locke, still reminisces about a third-grade teacher who beat him for eating un-American breakfasts like rice porridge and dried shrimp—but the Native Americans bore the brunt of this intolerance. The most appalling example was how big business and the government deliberately reduced the original 100 million American buffalo to a mere 21 animals during the 1800s. The buffalo was more than just food to the Native Americans, it was a crucial symbol of cultural identity. The Cherokee leader Black Elk described his famous Ghost Dance as a racial prayer for "the return of the buffalo" and the culture it represented, a movement that ended when American soldiers gunned down hundreds of women and children in the Wounded Knee Massacre of 1890. "A peoples' dream died then. It was a beautiful dream," he wrote. "And I, to whom so great a vision was given in my youth—you see me now a pitiful old man who has done nothing, for the nation's hoop is broken and scattered, and the sacred tree is dead."

Once the government forced Indians onto reservations, they began banning their feasts and traditional foods. "These dances or feasts, as they are called, ought to be discontinued," wrote Secretary of the Interior Henry Teller to the Commission on Indian Affairs in 1882, referring to events like the green corn dance of the Cherokee tribe. When Smithsonian anthropologist Frank Cushing "went native" among the Zuni in the early 1900s, he found an entire culture/cuisine based on corn. There were hot-pink corn cakes and green ones and blue and white. The latter were made extra pale by adding kaolin clay, but the most prized were the purple-colored pastries called *he-wi* or *piki*, a kind of *mille-feuille* made of layers of thin blue corn crepes. There was a vast array of dumplings and biscuits and even "ice cream" breads made by freezing rather than baking. There were creamy corn biscuits laced with lamb's milk and "salted buried bread" called *k'os-he-pa-lo-kia* made of the best white corn cooked in corn leaves and flavored with licorice or wild honey. There was even a psychedelic pancake, which was made by pouring red, green, white, yellow, blue, and purple corn batters into a design on a hot stone and then frying it as an enormous flapjack. People expressed themselves in ideas and language directly derived from their beloved cuisine. Just as we say a woman has creamy smooth skin, the highest compliment a Zuni girl could receive was to be told her cheeks were "smooth and silky as the *piki* stone" used for cooking maize crepes.

When the American government made the Hopi language illegal in 1910 and began pushing "American" foods like white flour and potatoes and roast beef and sugar, it not only spelled an end to a historic cuisine, it undermined an entire way of life. Ironically, corn-based cuisine of the Southwest survived, only to have the Europeans actually make the plant itself almost inedible. Scientists in the area now believe that the high-sugar corn hybrids introduced in the 1950s have helped cause a massive outbreak in diabetes and other diseases because the Native American's digestive system has trouble breaking down sugar. Prior to 1950 diabetes was unknown among native populations of the American Southwest. It now has among the highest rates in the world.

The Butterfly People

They first appeared among poor Spanish shepherds in the eighteenth century. But it didn't stop there, and the so-called "butterfly people" were soon seen everywhere: dazed peasants marked on the bridge of the nose with a curious butterfly design, which soon spread to the rest of their body in huge throbbing scabs. Some drowned themselves to stop the itching. Others went slowly insane. By 1881 an estimated one hundred thousand people in Italy were affected, and corn, which had become a staple among the poorest of the poor, was fingered as the cause. Some said the vegetable's "impure Indian" nature lay at the root of the horrible disease. Others claimed moldy kernels were the culprit. In America, where the disease was rampant among the poorer people in the South, South Carolina actually put the vegetable on trial. "Corn stands indicted!" wrote the state's agricultural commissioner in 1909, "the original wild grass of Aztecs and given to us by the Indian. You are here assembled to try the case and render a verdict . . . for the charge of murder. . . ." It wasn't until the mid-1900s that Nobel nominee Joseph Goldberger proved that the disease, now called pellagra (rough skin), was caused by the absence of the vitamin niacin in corn. The mystery, however, was why there were no cases of pellagra among the Indians, who for centuries had been relying so heavily on the stuff. The answer lay in how the plant was processed. Indians always soaked the kernels overnight in a bath made of water and lime or wood ashes before grinding it into meal. The European invaders had assumed this was merely to make the maize easier to grind and had taken it as an exam-

ple of "Indian laziness." It turned out that the step of soaking
the grain with ash, called nixtamalization, was what released
the niacin "bound up" inside corn and turned the plant into a
kind of universal superfood that met almost all nutritional re-
quirements. The Indians were well aware of this—they used a
similar process with coca (cocaine) leaves to activate its chemical stimulants—but the European invaders were apparently so
arrogant they hadn't bothered to ask.

Sky Blue Corn Flakes

The greatest exception to Euro-American contempt for
corn is, of course, cornflakes. Not that the cereal didn't
meet initial resistance; it was called "horse food" when
introduced in the late 1800s by John Harvey Kellogg
(brother to Will Kellogg of Kellogg's cereal fame). Food
writer Margaret Visser credits the cereal's triumph to the
fact that it was served submerged in milk, because "in
North American culture, nothing bathed in fresh milk can
be threatening or bad." The original cornflakes, however,
were sky blue and invented by the people of the American
Southwest, who took the leftover crumbs of their blue *piki*
bread (a kind of crepe) and dried them to a crunchy texture. Traditional *piki* is rather difficult to make—for one
thing, you need to polish a four-hundred-pound stone to a
silky smoothness without speaking—so you might try this
recipe for *someviki* dumplings. Some tribes served it with
fermented fruit pastes called *tsu'-pi-a-we*, but it's good
with blueberry preserves.

2 cups blue corn flour
24 teaspoons of honey

1½ cups boiling water
36 corn husks soaked overnight in water and shaken dry

Combine corn flour with honey and mix well. Add the hot water slowly and mix. Knead until very thick. Place two tablespoons dough in a corn husk and wrap it up tight, using rubber bands if necessary. Drop in simmering water and cook for 45 minutes.

To test for doneness, slice a dumpling in half; if you can see dry or uncooked flour, cook further.

Ghost at the Dinner Table!

I was writing a magazine piece on the political alliances between white supremacists and the environmental movement ("A Pure Environment for the Pure White Race" is one of the more catchy slogans) when I heard my first antibean sentiment in many, many years. It was on a prerecorded message from San Diego's White Aryan Resistance (W.A.R.). Recorded messages are quite popular among hate groups and W.A.R.'s was the typical five minutes of brain-dead racist drivel followed by a pitch for contributions. Its only memorable feature was that most of the abuse was directed at Mexican immigrants. Mexicans, the tape informed me, were lazy and criminal. They were drug dealers. They bred like rabbits. They were, moreover, "beaners." As soon as the twangy voice on the tape said these words, I felt a wave of nostalgia sweep over me—the stereotype of a do-nothing man snoring on the couch while engulfed in a miasma of bean-inspired flatulence was standard fare during my California youth. I'd never actually considered calling someone a bean eater to be particularly insulting, or at least no more so than calling a Frenchman a frog or a Brit a limey. So

I was puzzled at W.A.R.'s belief that Mexico's supposed predilection for beans was seriously defamatory. The Mexicans themselves, the original ones, had a very high opinion of the legumes. The Mayans called them their "little blackbirds."

Bean baiting, however, has an ancient pedigree among European types. It all began with Pythagoras. Everybody knows Mr. P from high school geometry where his self-named theorem about triangles is taught ad nauseam. But the Greek philosopher was also the founder of a religious cult that espoused sexual equality, vegetarianism, reincarnation, and the well-tempered musical scale millenniums before it was fashionable to do so. He was also the first to publicly theorize that humans reproduce through "seeds," which I suppose makes him the discoverer of sex. His most controversial belief, however, was that no one, under any circumstances, should ever eat a bean. There are a variety of theories explaining this curious taboo—it was about politics, or some peculiar disease—but the generally accepted reason was the one given by his near peer, Diogenes Laertius. "One should abstain from eating beans," wrote the Roman scholar around the first century B.C., "because they are full of the material which contains the largest portion of that animated matter of which our souls are made." The key words in this explanation are "animated matter" and "soul." The Greek word for soul is *anemos*, which also means "wind." The "animated matter" Diogenes refers to is the intestinal ululation associated with bean eating. Thus the reasoning behind the Pythagorean ban becomes clear. The buried dead were thought to release their souls in the form of gases or winds that, drifting up through the soil, got sucked into delicious little fava beans and frozen. When these beans were eaten and processed by a human's intestine, these soul winds were released and—eager to resume their ascension to Heaven—headed straight for the nearest opening, from which they exited with a cry of joy.

This belief puts our horror of flatulence in a new light—does it derive from the same "horror" we feel when we see (or hear or smell) a ghost? A number of our rules of etiquette make it seem rather likely. We think it merely good manners to cover our mouths when yawning, but the gesture was originally meant to prevent evil spirits from slipping inside. Likewise, we say "Gesundheit!" when someone sneezes to prevent devils from jumping into the breach. At any rate, Pythagoras' peers viewed the situation with the utmost gravity. The philosopher himself compared eating beans to biting off the head of one's mother, and he apparently allowed himself to be beaten to death rather than escape by walking across a field of fava beans. Historian Reay Tannahill seems to believe that the Greeks let their fields go fallow rather than plant the haunting vegetable.

Equally interesting is how the rise of Christianity shaped the culinary treatment of the bean. Early Christian Romans cooked fava or broad beans with sage and then tossed them in olive oil on the Day of the Dead (November 2). A distinctly adult, serious dish and quite delicious. But as the pagan gods became the stuff of fairy tales this dish morphed into a sweet called *Fava alla Romana o dei morti* because sweets, like fairy tales, are the provender most associated with childhood. It was traditional to leave a bowl of these *morti* out overnight for the spirits, with the children inheriting whatever the ghosts left. Not that there weren't more adult manifestations. Romans continued to spit out black beans at midnight ceremonies while chanting "Deliver me from evil, protect me and mine from death, oh ye beans!" As late as the sixteenth century, Cardinal Gabriele Paleotti called the practice of giving beans to a dead person's relatives heresy. Even the "bean-fests" British employers still throw for departing employees are said to derive from the Celts' traditional funerary food called Beano. And while it's hard to believe they're related, there are similar practices in Buddhist countries, and many Japanese still scatter beans around the house to drive out bad spirits during their Setsubun winter festival—*"Oniwa-soto, Fukuwa-uchi!"* shouts Dad as he tosses red beans about (Devils outside, good luck inside!).

So this, I thought, was the context of W.A.R.'s "beaner" remark about Mexican immigrants. What I'd taken to be teenage racism was actually a richly allusive analogy with multiple interpretations; W.A.R. was obviously a group of erudite Classicists whose obscure pre-Christian allusions had been disgracefully misrepresented by the popular press. But when I called their headquarters to inquire, there was no answer. It appears the White Aryan Resistance has gone out of business.

King's Cake

Le gâteau de roi, or the King's Cake, has the most convoluted, scandal-ridden history in the Annals of European pastry. The trouble comes from the tradition of hiding a

Spirit in the Bean porcelain fava in a fin de siècle Paris catalog.

bean in the cake. The child who gets the slice with the hidden legume is crowned king for a day. It sounds innocuous, but the attendant rituals are loaded with references to Pythagorean beliefs, like addressing the child as Apollo (Pythagoras was known as the Thigh of Apollo) and treating him or her as an oracle. Christians sanitized these pagan overtones by restricting the cake's consumption to the Epiphany celebration following Christmas. The bean was then replaced with a porcelain figurine that showed a ghostly face emerging from the tip of a fava bean. When this failed to appease the priests, the bean figurine was changed to a crowned head in honor of the biblical three kings. This made the priests happy, but the politicians began to raise a fuss during the French Revolution when a king's head, whether in a cake or on the guillotine, became controversial. In 1794 the mayor of Paris urged the people to end the holiday and "discover and arrest the criminal *patissiers* and their filthy orgies which dare to honor the shades of the tyrants!" The French, to their credit, ignored him, and he had to settle for renaming the cake *le Gâteau des Sans-Culottes* or "the Cake of the Men-Without-Pants," in honor of the illustrious beggars of Paris.

Almost every European country has a version of the cake, from the port-flavored *bolo rei* of the Portuguese to the fruitcake preferred by the English. The following recipe is from *La Bonne Cuisine de Madame E. Saint-Ange,* who claimed it came from "a good old cookery book from the time of Louis XV."

1¾ cups (550 grams) flour
1 teaspoon (10 grams) salt
2 tablespoons sugar (optional)
7 ounces (250 grams) unsalted butter
1 egg yolk for dough (optional)
2 egg yolks, beaten with 2 tablespoons water for glazing
About 1 cup water
1 dried fava, broad, or lima bean

Mix flour, salt, and sugar in a slightly chilled bowl. Make a well in the flour and put the slightly softened butter into it with the egg yolk (optional). With your fingers, roughly mix the butter and flour, adding water as needed, gradually incorporating the flour until you have a firm dough. If it is too wet, add more flour. Do not knead. Gather into a ball, flour lightly, wrap, and let rest in a cool place for forty-five minutes.

On a floured surface roll out the dough into a rectangle about 24″ × 8″. Fold in thirds, putting the top third on the middle, and then the bottom third on top of that. Let rest in a cool place ten minutes. Then turn it 90 degrees (like turning a book sideways), roll it out again and fold in the same manner. Again, let rest ten minutes and repeat. Now (it should be folded into thirds at this point) fold the corners up over the dough to form a round pad. Roll out to a disc about ¾ inch thick. Notch rim with knife, and trim to a circle. With the point of the knife make a slit in the edge and insert the bean and reseal. Place on an ungreased, unfloured baking sheet. Brush the top with an egg glaze and score with grillwork or other design (the royal fleur-de-lis would be most appropriate). Prick through in several places.

Bake in an oven at 450°F for thirty to thirty-five minutes. For a sweeter glaze, dust with powdered sugar a few minutes before removing. Cool on a rack and make sure to eat it while warm.

S LOTH

"It is not in the least surprising that when ancestors are forgotten, fathers eliminated and mothers absent, young people frequent snack bars to find that food of orphans, adventurers, and travelers, the sandwich. . . . the tombstone of taste. When the fire dies in the hearth, the funereal delights of cold snacks come into their own."

Piero Camporesi,
The Magic Harvest

SLOTH MENU

Le Fée Vert
Absinthe mixed with champagne.

POTAGE
Consommé Spartacus
The traditional soup of ancient Sparta: a demitasse of intensely concentrated broth drizzled with fresh boar blood and Xeres vinegar. Garnished with fleur de sel.

with

Pain au Turgot
A basket of specialty breads including the bien brun *croutons of Philippe Cordelois.*
The famous green breads of Anne-Robert Turgot are available with twenty-four hours notice.

PREMIER PLAT
Escargots au Lentment
Slow-cooked snails served slumbering under a puff-pastry dome. With creamy cognac sauce.

PLAT PRINCIPAL

Boeuf en Croûte

Corn-fed beef encased in a rich mollet crust. Stuffed with
mushroom duxelles and served with a red-wine reduction and
caramelized shallots.

with

Mashed "Couch" Potatoes

In the style of Joël Robuchon.

(Recipe on page 138)

DESSERT

Nipples of the Virgin

Breast-shaped pastry oozing with a rich cream/chocolate
filling. Served warm.

(Recipe on page 133)

DIGESTIF

John Barleycorn Brandy

American vintage (1920).

AN EVENT CATERED BY VATEL!

The Job of Eating Well

Only the most perverse of worlds would rank the pleasure of an afternoon nap among the greatest of sins. Can it really compare to murder? Does the indolent bum really rank down with the out-of-control capitalist? Sloth is a victimless crime if ever there was one, and yet, of the deadly seven, it is the vice most devoutly abhorred in modern America, at least judging by the rewards doled out to the professional practitioners of lust and pride. The gentle sloths among us, alas, receive no comparable compensation.

The practice of criminalizing foods that engender laziness first appeared in the legal code of the seventh-century B.C. Spartan civilization. The Spartans did everything they could to make dinner pure hell. Meals were served in communal mess halls and in portions designed to leave citizens hungry. Their national dish was a deliberately revolting "black broth," made of pork stock, blood, vinegar, and salt. Citizens whose generous paunches suggested covert snacking were thrown out of the country. Foreign ambassadors who dined with undue elegance were also expelled. The idea behind this madness, according to Plutarch, was to stop citizens from "spending their lives . . . laid on costly couches at splendid tables, delivering themselves up to the hands of their tradesmen and cooks, who fatten them in corners like greedy brutes." The code's creator, Lycurgus, took his creed so seriously he actually starved himself to death.

It's a notion that recurs regularly throughout Western history. The nineteenth-century English almost banned the potato for fear it would turn its working class into fornicating hobos, just as the French aristocrats outlawed soft white bread to ensure a hardy peasantry. Modern America has raised this technique to technological perfection; consider, for example, "convenience foods" like Oscar Meyer's infamous Sack of Sauce in a Can of Meat and premade chocolate sundaes designed so that the microwave melts the sauce but leaves the ice cream intact. TV dinners. McDonald's. Despite the technological differences between modern America and Sparta, the principle of using diet to create an ideal working class is identical. Where the Spartans banished citizens who enjoyed eating, modern America just pays them less—about 7 percent among female workers. Both today's fast-food outlets and Spartan mess halls are/were designed to discourage lingering over dinner and eliminate the need for people to "waste" their time cooking for the family. And, like the Spartans' legendarily bad food, many of these convenience foods are so unpleasant they make even work look good. They're also immensely profitable for the corporations who produce them. Perfect: American workers now pay more money for worse food so they can hurry back to jobs they hate.

The Spartans wanted to create a society of superwarriors because they believed waging war was the only worthwhile labor. They succeeded, and their fifth-century B.C. invasion of Athens helped end Greece's Golden Age of democracy, philosophy, and art. But before they fell, at least one Greek sybarite did a gastronomic tour of Sparta. "As he lay on the wooden benches and ate with them he remarked that he had always before been astounded to hear of the Spartan's courage," noted historian Athenaeus. "But now he did not think they were in any respect superior to other peoples . . . for surely the most cowardly man in the world would prefer to die rather than endure living that sort of life."

The Wonderful World of English Cookery

Food lovers have long regarded the English cook with awe. His boiled cabbage and overcooked beef. Those cannonball puddings. There is no foodstuff on Earth he has not reduced to an overcooked, flavorless monstrosity. But why? The French believe it's genetic. "The Englishman is naturally a glutton stuffed with beefsteaks and plum pudding, a boa quasi-asphyxiated by a gazelle he just swallowed," opined scholar Jean Saint-Arroman in 1852, "whereas the Frenchman is naturally sober . . . so it is to us [the French] the sun, fine weather and the most precious gifts of nature. To the English, fogs, coal, plum pudding, the spleen and consumptive diseases." It's a point of view that has some resonance for anyone who's experienced the splendors of English cookery (green eel pie, anyone?). There are, however, other theories. Historian Stephen Mennell, for instance, believes France's obvious culinary superiority to the English developed from Louis XIV's requirement that France's nobility live with him in Versailles. Louis had merely wanted to keep an eye on rebellious nobles. But by putting all the aristos under one roof, he inadvertently created a gastronomic hothouse where armies of chefs, pâtissiers, sommeliers, *boulangers,* and maîtres d'hôtel competed for the approval of the world's fussiest eaters.

One maître d', François Vatel, went so far as to throw himself on his sword when the fish arrived a half hour late. Voilà, the birth of French haute cuisine. British nobility, on the other hand, were not obliged to dwell at court, and, living on their own estates enjoyed less-elevated fare. If the fish arrived late, good—it meant two helpings of boiled beef.

Although this theory does explain the absence of a truly British high cuisine, my personal favorite relates to the so-called invention of childhood during the Victorian era of the 1800s. The Victorians were the first to completely embrace the notion that children are fundamentally different from adults. Juveniles were strictly segregated, dressed in funny clothes, and told specific bedtime stories. They also had special dietary needs, i.e., old potatoes. "New potatoes are *acceptable*," wrote Pye Henry Chavasse in his 1844 bestseller *Advice to Mothers on the Management of Their Offspring*, "but old potatoes, well cooked and *mealy*, are the best a child can have." Chavasse preached that children under ten should breakfast exclusively on lukewarm milk poured over stale bread that was "preferably seven days old." Sweets were "slow poison," as were green vegetables. Once children had reached their second decade, they could be served old mutton—never beef or pork—and weak beer. Onion and garlic were absolutely forbidden. "Meat, potatoes and bread, with hunger for their sauce is the best, and indeed should be the only dinner, they should have," he wrote. Chavasse was the Dr. Spock of his day, and middle-class Victorians followed his advice religiously. Children were shoved full of a gruel made of milk, crushed biscuits, and flour that had been boiled for seven hours. The students of Eton ate nothing but old mutton and potatoes 365 days of the year for both lunch and dinner until a compassionate graduate left a bequest to provide them with a plum pudding every Sunday. Their peers in France may have had to choke down an unreasonable number of baguettes, but almost a quarter of what they ate consisted of vegetables, eggs, and fish, not to mention half a bottle of wine every day. Even the boarding school in Provence that served nothing but cabbage soup 125 days of the year ranked above the English programs.

This sadistic approach to child nutrition was a perfect match for the theories of John Wesley, the founder of Methodism, who believed children were "natural atheists" because they enjoyed nature instead of God. He recommended bringing this under control by reminding them that "they are more ignorant and wicked than they could possibly believe," and breaking their spirit at every turn. Withholding pleasant food was considered a particularly plum way to do this because it trained them out of the expectation of "natural" pleasure at the table. Add this food guilt to the insanely bland food expectations created by Chavasse, and you have the pleasure-free cuisine that some claim helped create the stoic Victorian personality that led to Great Britain's domination of the world. It also explains why Victorian brats were so fond of American children's literature. It was the scenes of kids gorging on buckwheat pancakes with maple syrup, eggs, and sausage that they really liked.

Toast

Fresh-baked bread is as soft and warm as a newborn baby. It's like eating a living creature. No wonder Christians use bread to symbolize the flesh of Christ or that the Jews call it the Staff of Life or that the Mayans' thirteen-layer loaf macerated in honey mead, called *noh-wah*, was said to symbolize Heaven. Most people believe toast's divine status derives from its role as a dietary staple. It's more complicated than that, and a better explanation is the way it is made. Like beer, bread is created by allowing grain to ferment and then either baking or boiling the result. Today we know fermentation is just a yeast infection of sorts, but anybody who has seen a barrel of fermenting beer seething like a volcano, or a loaf rising, can understand how the humans who first witnessed it considered the process supernatural and akin to the swelling belly of a pregnant female. Italian women used to stand in front of their ovens gnashing their teeth and contorting their faces in a mock birth delivery to ensure a risen loaf. As late as the 1800s, it was traditional to force an older, unwed daughter to sit atop an oven baking bread to make her more attractive to suitors. The world's first bakers, in Egypt, actually doubled as gynecologists by selling wheat to women who suspected they "had a bun in the oven." The ladies would urinate on the wheat and, if pregnant, it would germinate in sympathy. If she was barren, the grain, too, would remain fallow (yes, this is largely effective).

But the people who took this equation most to heart were the French. The French believed the baker's oven to be the national womb and the baguette to be the penis, and great care was taken to ensure that only France's finest were involved in the act of consummation. The baking profession was restricted to devout Catholics. Village priests set aside an entire day each week to hear the confessions of the local *boulanger*, lest his sins be passed on to the bread-eating public, and journalists like George Sand claimed the bakers' role in shaping public morality was second only to that of the Church. The good people of Paris took the issue so seriously that they almost went to war over a bun called *pain mollet*. A loaf both light and rich, often enhanced with milk, soft as a baby's bottom, *mollet* had traditionally been reserved for the aristocratic table. (Everyone else made do with stuff that had to be cut with an ax.) By the late 1600s, however, Parisian bakers were baking *mollet*, also known as the "Queen's Bread," for the hoi polloi, and alarm bells began going off. "It is thirty years since an element of voluptuousness was introduced into the bread of the French," wrote one concerned police commissioner in 1710, "and since then, the bakeries have begun to resemble a brothel."

In his definitive *The Bakers of Paris*, historian Stanley Kaplan points out that the authorities' concern over *mollet* existed on a number of levels. "Bread became the innocent vector through which 'sensual pleasure' conquered (and cankered) the lower reaches of the body social," he wrote, ". . . blurring distinctions that structured the social order and undermining the sturdy values that had protected the 'little people' from the ravages of refinement." The police considered *mollet*'s luxurious texture its most obvious danger, because it introduced unrealistic expectations into the workers' daily lives. But they also objected to the way it was produced. Traditional French sourdough, called *au levain*, is made by "mounting" a huge mass of raw dough and kneading, beating, and massaging it into shape. The intense labor this required was thought to impart a moral character to the loaf, which, when eaten, helped create a race of equally hardworking peasants. *Pain mollet* (which is comparable to a good brioche) was called "fantasy bread" because it almost kneaded itself, a laziness that, of course, imparted equally slothful characteristics to the diner. This was fine for aristocrats, who were lounge lizards by right of birth, but definitely a faux pas for the lower classes.

The other concern related to the yeast used to make *mollet* rise. The historic method of starting the growth of yeast in *au levain* loaves was to set aside a small piece of uncooked dough from the previous night and add it to new batches. This not only produced a delicious and chewy bread with a wonderfully winey flavor, but the continuous transference of dough from one generation of bread to another gave loaves a pedigree that went back decades, if not centuries, to the baguettes gnawed by French yeoman of yore. In a culture obsessed with ancestry—and one that believed baking was sexual and yeast a kind of semen—this was no small potatoes. *Mollet* circumvented this process by using yeast obtained from Belgium beer to impregnate the loaf—dirty, unnatural, "foreign scum" that the French believed would produce similar unpatriotic characteristics in anyone who ate it. *Mollet*'s seminal fluid was doubly damned because it came from beer, a drink that France's wine-loving aristocrats traditionally held in contempt.

The controversy eventually split the capital in half. On one side were the Molletists, who indulged in the decadent habit known as "dunking," and claimed their lighter loaf was more intelligent than the "coarse and ponderous" sourdough. On the other side were the Anti-Molletists, who countered that excessive indulgence in the queen's bread was creating "a creeping feebleness in the State." In 1660 the Paris Faculty of Medicine banned *mollet*. The Parisians were outraged—as decadent, lazy scum they demanded the right to start their morning with something appropriately reprobate. A year later the government overturned the ban but proved their patriotism by forbidding the use of "foreign yeast." The arguments continued on and off for the next one hundred years and were celebrated in this lovely little ditty by Monsieur de la Condamine in the 1700s.

> *Then Perrault, the antagonist*
> *Said to all, "I am a Pain Molletist!*
> *And Gentlemen, I do insist*

This bread is pleasant to digest!"
Patin responded, "but the yeast,
(To say the least)
Is made from a beer of Belgium!
A modern, devilish, bad invention!"

That this should have been published a century after the controversy first erupted gives a pretty good idea with what gravity the French viewed their morning slice. It was, however, just the tip of the iceberg.

The Incredibly Sad Tale of Philippe the Shoemaker

(OR, THE POLITICS OF THE BAGUETTE)

It was a pleasant Parisian spring afternoon circa 1775 when Philippe Cordelois was awakened from his siesta by a knocking on the door. Kicking, actually. His visitors first reduced the building's main entrance to splinters. Then they charged up to his third-floor garret, shouting, "In the name of the King!" Philippe, a twenty-eight-year-old apprentice shoemaker, was puzzled; was his master in trouble with the police? The cops burst into his room and threw him against the wall. They knocked over the table, ripped open his mattress. Finally, the officer rummaging through his cupboard gave a shout and grabbed the shoemaker by the collar. He had found a piece of stale bread wedged into the back of one of the shelves. "Nothing to hide, eh?" shouted the officer. He shook the week-old crust in Philippe's face. "Then what, may I ask monsieur, is this?"

"The history of bread," wrote historian Piero Camporesi in

The Bread of Dreams, "is the dietary expression of a long battle between the classes." The earlier Parisian scandal over *mollet* had centered on the questions of yeast, nationalism, and ancestry. But the classic battle was all about color and class. Italians, for instance, have historically had only two real classes, according to Camporesi. There were the "fodder mouths," peasants who lived on dark brown bread, and "bread mouths," who dined only on white. The Roman elite would attack anyone who dared offer them a slice of brown bread, and Caesar made the inappropriate serving of dark bread a crime punishable with prison time.

By the time Philippe the shoemaker was arrested in 1775, the issue of who got to eat white, and who brown—and at what price—had become one of the touchiest political issues in France. Like the Italian peasants, most French citizens choked down coarse rye and barley breads. The authorities thought this fine and natural. Peasants, after all, were believed to be only marginally more evolved than pigs. The aristocrats suffered a supernaturally refined digestive system which, alas! could process nothing but the most meltingly delicious of baked goods, well buttered. There were a few concessions to the real world. The army had been on a white-only ration since an attempt to foist rye on the boys had led to an open revolt. Parisians also received special treatment, and even the lowliest gamin dined on the snowiest of breads. This discrepancy was one of the first things Napoleon Bonaparte noticed with horror when he arrived in the capital.

Like Napoleon, the French peasantry was passionately discontented with the situation. It finally blew up when a baker in the village of Beaumont-sur-Oise tried charging white prices for rye. Housewives hog-tied the villain and threw him into the pond, which would have been the end of it if the village's police chief (a notoriously shy man) had kept the situation under control. He didn't, and before you knew it, the ladies had embarked upon a daring but popular program of economic reform. After they'd given away all the baguettes in Beaumont, they headed over to the neighboring village of Meru, where their fiscal policies were again warmly received. Within ten days, over three hundred bread riots broke out. Markets were raided, bakers were forced to sell their loaves at one-tenth the market price, and whole barges were relieved of their flour. The uprising kept creeping closer and closer to Paris, but the police did nothing. They claimed so many people were participating that they'd have to arrest most of France.

The rioters finally reached Paris and gathered outside the office of the minister of finance, Anne-Robert Turgot, chanting, "Give us bread!" At least that's the popular version of the event. A more accurate translation of their plaint would probably be, "Give us a light yet savory bread with a crisp, caramel-colored crust and a pleasantly chewy, but not tough, interior at a reasonable price." They emphasized their point by threatening to clobber the riot police with stale baguettes. Stale *green* baguettes, to be precise. They claimed the bizarrely colored monstrosities, which ranged from very dark brown to gray to green to black, were now being sold by Parisian bakers as a result of Turgot's free-trade policies. This was too much for Turgot. He called the green baguettes "Turkish bread" and claimed they had been made from ashes and rye to serve as propaganda tools in a campaign to topple his government. Turgot's supporters then implied that the bread riots had been started not by peasant housewives but by sexual transvestites, "perverted men who were strangers to the villages which they had come to destroy." It was *they* who had made the green bread weeks earlier, Turgot claimed, so it would be nice and moldy in time for the riots, at which point they'd handed it out to real peasants whom they paid to say it had been purchased at the marketplace. It was obviously all a lie, the story went, because no one had seen a slice of dark brown bread in Paris—much less green—in centuries.

Enter Philippe the Shoemaker. Turgot had assigned the entire Parisian police force to find anyone possessing bread that was *bien brune* (quite brown) and bring the conspirators to justice. Hundreds were arrested and interrogated. The transcripts of their "confessions" can still be found today on a dusty shelf in the French National Archives, a foot-high stack of handwritten, crumbling papers liberally decorated with doodles. A number of them finger the shoemaker. One informant told the police he'd seen Philippe with a group of suspicious-looking country "ladies." Another put him drinking with bakers believed to be part of the conspiracy. The most damning report claims he was seen with a subversive baguette in his hands the day of the riots. Inspector Jean Baptiste Charles LeMaire was in charge of the investigation, and when he finally located Philippe's digs— only a block from Paris's central marketplace, Les Halles!— LeMaire struck. Philippe was charged with "possession of a *crouton* of bread that was absolutely brown" and taken to the sadistic interrogation chambers below place du Chatelet (now an equally annoying Metro station of the same name).

POLICE INSPECTOR LEMAIRE: Is it not true that you told the shopkeeper that this bread, this dark bread, was being sold in the central market of Paris?

PHILIPPE THE SHOEMAKER: *Mais, oui!* Yes, it is true I said that. But monsieur, I was only repeating what a man from the country had told me. He said that they were selling this bread in the market. It is he who gave me the dark bread!

[LeMaire must have been pleased since his job had been to find
   proof that the peasant rabble-rousers from Beaumont were
   also behind the disturbance in Paris.]

LEMAIRE: This is the one you met with the country "ladies"?

PHILIPPE: I saw three or four women who were showing everyone some round loaves, yes.

LEMAIRE: Did they speak to you?

PHILIPPE: I think they were selling bread. But in truth, monsieur,
   it was the man with them who approached me with the
   aforementioned bread that you found in my chamber.

LEMAIRE: And it is true, is it not, that those three or four women
   also gave you some bread that was quite dark?

PHILIPPE: No.

LEMAIRE: I think you are not telling the truth, monsieur. It is not
   a reasonable story. For instance, why were you in the market
   when there was all the tumult going on if you were not
   involved?

PHILIPPE: Oh, I was only curious.

LEMAIRE: Just curious! A likely story. Do you know where you
   are? Do you know what happens to people in these places?
   People who are "just curious" about rebellions against the
   King of France?

PHILIPPE: God save the King! Oh, mercy, monsieur . . .

LEMAIRE: Are you sure these so-called women did not give the
   bread to you?

PHILIPPE: Yes, no, no. I tell you it is the truth! It was the man who
   gave me the aforementioned bread. It was completely black!
   I remember he said to me, "This bread, eh? It is not so good,
   non? Not even a dog should eat such stuff!"

LEMAIRE: The rogue! Describe this man.

PHILIPPE: He was maybe five feet three inches, about thirty-six to forty years. Brown hair. I swear that I have no idea of his name. I had never seen him before.

LEMAIRE: And his clothes? What was he wearing?

PHILIPPE: I couldn't say. I remember thinking he had very poor fashion sense. *Très paysan.*

Philippe's story seems to have checked out, because LeMaire released him after a half dozen interrogations. There are, however, no records of his ever having married. Perhaps he died in the upcoming revolution, or returned to his village of Cambray, where people ate brown bread and were glad of it. The treasonous *crouton* found in his room was sent to the royal crime lab, where forensic experts determined that, contrary to Minister Turgot's theory, it had been baked the day of the riots and "turned green and black because of its ingredients." Turgot's theory that a deviant Svengali had masterminded the riots, however, was probably correct; Louis XVI was so horrified by the information in the final police report that he burned it himself (apparently it indicated that Louis's relative the Prince of Conti had been behind the whole thing). Turgot was forced from power soon after banning the powerful bakery guild. The question of who got what bread continued to smolder until Marie Antoinette finally introduced an element of sanity into the debate by suggesting that if the peasants were unhappy with their bread, why didn't they just eat cake? This simple observation was somehow taken the wrong way, and, soon thereafter, on the day the price of bread reached an all-time high, the people of Paris went shopping for her head.

Bread is the perfect bellwether of French neurosis. Once the revolution got into full swing, people began choosing their toast based on its political flavor. White was out. Proletariat brown became the toast of the town, and nary a marquis could be seen dunking his *mollet* in his *au lait*. Scholars quoted Pliny's praise of rye. Generals reminisced about how Roman gladiators scarfed down barley biscuits before battle. Even London's elite took note of the volatile situation and swore to eat "no wheaten bread of any finer quality than that produced from meal." But the bureaucrats of the French Revolution took the cake (not that they wanted any). Political committees railed against the class separation caused by *la mollesse* (luxury white breads) and urged that it be banned to "create a just uniformity." Court records from the era are full of bakers arrested for subversion or cheating or simply politically incorrect baking. The mayor of Paris urged the people to hunt down royalist pâtissiers, and some bakers were even lynched. The bread debate became so fierce that one of France's leading journalists furiously questioned the National Assembly as to whether the revolution had been simply over who was to have "more or less white bread."

The answer to his query, of course, was yes. In November 1793, only a month after Marie "let 'em eat cake" Antoinette had lost her head, the National Assembly voted to create a National Bread of Equality. It was to be made of three parts wheat, one part rye. "Wealth and poverty have no place in a regime of equality," opined the committee, "[so] there shall no longer be produced a bread of the finest flour for the rich . . . but this single and good type of bread, the Bread of Equality." It was the old *scandale mollet* reborn, a law that enshrined the belief that the people's daily bread defined their political and moral character, only now Paris's social engineers were using it to create a truly democratic nation. This utopian loaf law was passed on November 15 and sent on for final ratification. But it never came. Apparently even the French couldn't swallow this one. Instead, six weeks later the Parlement came up with what they thought was a better solution to the endless bickering over white and brown and luxe and *mollet* and your-bread-is-better-than-mine. They ordered every able-bodied Frenchman to start growing potatoes.

The Virgin's Nipples

The French may be the most vocal about sex and baking, but the Italians have the most colorful renditions. The bread called

Traditional image of St. Agatha offering her breasts on a serving platter; sketch by the author of a fresco in an unnamed Sicilian church.

copiette is made to resemble a couple having sex, a reference to the ancient tradition of schtupping in a wheat field to help ensure its fertility. Roman wives have a vagina-shaped pastry called *prucitanu* that they traditionally give their husbands at Christmas. If dissatisfied, they give him the *viscotta di San Martinu*, a phallic-looking biscuit named after the patron saint of cuckolded husbands. Well-hung grooms wear seven donut-shaped pastries called *xuccarati* on their member during the honeymoon to calm their fearful brides. One cookie is removed and eaten each day until she's ready for the full monty.

The most common of these erotic mouthfuls is the *minni di virgini*, or Nipples of the Virgin, a custard-filled pastry shaped like a woman's breast and topped with an aroused candied cherry nipple. Also sold—sans nipple—as *genovesi*. The story behind this delicious pastry, however, is enough to take away your appetite. It seems the pastry commemorates the martyrdom of St. Agatha, who had her breasts cut off by Roman pagans for refusing to renounce Christ. She's now the patron saint of breast cancer victims and is traditionally portrayed offering her breasts on a serving plate.

3 cups basic pastry dough
½ cup basic pastry cream
Candied *succatta* or chocolate pieces
Candied cherries cut in half
Confectioners' sugar

Preheat oven to 425°F (220°C). Divide the dough into seven pieces and roll into rectangles about 6″ × 4″ × ¼″. Place 2 tablespoons of pastry cream on one half of the rectangle and sprinkle with chopped candied pumpkin or chocolate (about ¼ tablespoon, or as you like). Fold the other half of the dough over it to make a square. Seal it well and then, with a glass or a pastry cutter, cut out a circle-shaped mound from the center about three inches in diameter. Put the halved candied cherry in the middle, and bake for six to eight minutes, or until lightly browned. Sprinkle with confectioners' sugar and serve.

Makes 8. Best enjoyed warm.

The Root of Laziness

The potato crept into Europe like a leper, a hideously deformed root that some Spanish conquistador, after raping an Indian village, had stuffed into his pocket and forgotten. When the European elite finally saw it in the 1500s, they immediately decided that it was unsuitable for themselves—so different than its deliciously tanned cousin, the sweet potato!—but *perfect* for those porcine peasants. "The potato is rightly held responsible for flatulence," remarked French scholar Denis Diderot in his influential eighteenth-century *Encyclopedie*. "But what is flatulence to the vigorous organs of peasants and workers?" The Russian aristocrats ordered their peasants to eat them. Italy's Catholics

urged the faithful to "try and try again . . . this delicious food."
The French published all-potato cookbooks. Only the English
hesitated. "I would see all these labourers hanged," wrote one
of the nation's most influential political thinkers in 1830, "and
be hanged with them myself, rather than see them live upon
potatoes."

The author in question was William T. Cobbett, an illiterate
peasant who became England's most influential journalist by a
unique combination of street savvy, demagoguery, and humor.
When a member of Parliament referred to his paper, *The Political
Register,* as "two-penny trash," Cobbett obligingly renamed it
Cobbett's Two-Penny Trash and watched the circulation increase.
When one of his editorials got him imprisoned for treason, he
simply ran the paper from his cell. His many loves, recorded in
excruciating detail, included universal suffrage, turnips, and
farming. His much more numerous hatreds included Shake-
speare, paper money, tea, and, above all, that damned Irish
potato. The Irish and the potato were inextricably woven together in the English thinking of the time, because while the
rest of Europe still considered it pig food, the Irish had em-
braced the root like a brother. It usurped bread as the local staple. Men grew extra long thumbnails to facilitate the peeling.
By the late 1700s the average Irish person was eating ten
pounds of taters every day.

English Protestants like Cobbett thought this was disgusting.
They believed wheat bread was the natural food of man and
that its replacement with a dirty root was transforming the Irish
into doglike creatures content to do nothing but sleep and forni-
cate. They dubbed it the "Lazy Root," a slur that lives on in
phrases like couch potato and potato head. Even drinking its
cooking water could cause irreversible moral damage, according
to Cobbett, and when his suggestion that it be banned from En-

gland was ignored, he urged workers to overthrow their government to stop the spread of this "depraved food." At one point, protesting mobs of Londoners paraded before Parliament with potatoes stuck on sticks like political placards. This bizarre combination of anti-Irish racism and half-baked dietary philosophy may seem like lunacy, but as Larry Zuckerman points out in *The Potato*, the underlying situation was quite serious. A single acre of potatoes—the so-called "lazy bed"—provided an Irish family of six with enough to eat all year long. This gave the Irish peasant sufficient freedom from his gouging British landlords not only to enjoy life and make lots of little 'uns, but to wonder how he'd ended up a virtual slave in his own country. That combination boded ill for the British land barons who controlled Ireland. "So long as Ireland was only occupied by a million, or a million and a half, of starving wretches, it was a comparatively easy task to hold them in servitude," wrote the prestigious *Edinburgh Review* in June 1822. "But, thanks to the Potatoe and the Cottage System, Ireland contains at this moment nearly *seven* millions of inhabitants . . . ," making physical repression no longer practical.

Despite Cobbett's occasional racist rants, he actually sympathized with the Irish because, like his own father, they were mainly small farmers. This love of the independent farming life is a constant theme in his writing, particularly a series of travelogues called *Cobbett's Rural Rides*, that he penned while riding about England during the 1820s. The author jeers at ornamental bridges and the "unnatural" act of pruning trees. The "damnable system of paper money" is often criticized. But most of all, Cobbett wrote, beware of "the blasphemous cant of *sleek-headed* Methodist thieves that would persuade you to live upon **Potatoes**." Near Crickdale, he reports seeing laborers living in hovels "the size of pig beds . . . digging up their little plots of *potatoes*. In my whole life I never saw Human Wretchedness equal to this." Soon afterward, he rides his horse through Kensington where "cherry trees are in full bloom" and the children are the fattest, cleanest, best-dressed brats he's ever seen. Why? "I have the very great pleasure to add, that I do not think I saw three acres of POTATOES in this whole tract of fine country." Lest we doubt the vegetables' deleterious affect on humanity, he reminds us it was the "devil himself . . . Sir Walter Raleigh, who (they say) first brought this root into England. He was beheaded at last! What a pity, since he was to be beheaded, the execution did not take place before he became such a mischievous devil. . . ."*

The story of Raleigh introducing the potato to England is probably rubbish—nobody knows how it got there—but Cobbett's nay-saying proved prophetic. By the early 1800s, over one-third of the Irish population had been reduced to surviving on nothing but potatoes, and in some places potatoes had replaced hard currency. Then in 1845 the peasants dug up their "lazy roots" to find only a putrid-smelling black mass of gooey flesh where their crops ought to have been. Within two years 90 percent of the nation's food supply lay rotting in the fields from potato blight, a previously unknown disease. The ensuing famine killed well over a million people. Another million fled the country. By the end of the century Ireland's population had been cut in half.

Cobbett did not live to see his prophecies fulfilled. After being elected twice to the same Parliament that had once imprisoned him for treason, he passed away on his beloved farm in 1835. His obituary in the *London Times* called him "in some respects, a more extraordinary man than any other of his time."

---

*All typographical emphasis is Cobbett's.

Potato Wars

It's hardly surprising that at the same time the English wanted to ban the potato, their cousins in France were making its consumption a patriotic duty. The French government published all-potato cookbooks. They made planting it mandatory. Marie Antoinette even tried to give it some chic by wearing potato flowers in her hair. The most successful ploy, however, came from Auguste Parmentier. The eighteenth-century scientist, who dedicated his life to the potato, realized that while the peasants would never accept a tuber as a gift, they'd be more than happy to steal them. So he put a field of potatoes under twenty-four-hour guard. When the plants were ripe for transplanting, Parmentier ordered the guards to leave the field unattended overnight. The peasants swarmed in, stealing every plant and replanting them in their own gardens. The birth of the french fry. Parmentier's efforts are memorialized in dishes like potatoes Parmentier, but it wasn't until the tail end of the twentieth century that his beloved became truly fashionable via the *purée de pommes de terre* (mashed potatoes) of Chef Joël Robuchon. Thanks to Robuchon, mashed potatoes became a "thing" among the French. Chefs like Jacques Barbery, of Paris's Le Café Marly, came forward to proclaim their version superior because it was 49 percent butter and cream, compared to Robuchon's miserly 25 percent, and had olive oil besides. The three-star chef of Burgundy's La Côte D'Or, Bernard Loiseau, pointed out that he had been serving all-potato menus years before Robuchon. One French company started selling *pommes de terre* nurtured on seaweed for 3,000 francs a kilo (about $250 a pound). Robuchon's Paris atelier closed in 1996, but his mashed potatoes live on at Japan's Taillevent-Robuchon, where local gourmands enjoy the dish in a Loire chateau transported stone by stone all the way from France.

While some have suggested that the secret to the following version of Robuchon's dish is its copious amounts of butter, the key is really the *la ratte* potato. Traditionally grown only in northern France, this breed became available in North America under the name *la princesse* in 1996. (Check the Endnotes for suppliers.)

Two pounds of potatoes, preferably *la princesse* (la ratte),
   all approximately the same size
Sea salt
One cup unsalted butter, chilled and cut into pieces
One cup whole milk

Wash the potatoes with their skins on and put them, whole, into a large pot. Cover with cold water, making sure to cover by at least an inch. Add salt, approximately one tablespoon per quart of water.

Simmer, uncovered, until done (about thirty minutes, or until a knife inserted into potato comes out easily).

Drain immediately and peel while still warm. Pass through a food mill set at the finest grind into a large saucepan set over low heat (alternatively, mash well and pass though a fine sieve, although this is not as good).

Stir vigorously to dry with a wooden spatula for five minutes and then start adding the butter piece by piece, stirring until each piece is incorporated, rather like making a *beurre blanc* sauce. The butter should be very cold.

Bring the milk to a boil and take off heat immediately.

Incorporate into the purée slowly, stirring vigorously all the while until it is completely absorbed.

If you want the purée even finer, pass though a fine-mesh drum sieve. If stiff, add more hot milk and butter. Season to taste. Can be made an hour or so in advance. Keep warm in a double boiler.

The Last Drop

On the day of his funeral, men stood weeping on street corners. Some stockpiled supplies against the coming Holocaust. Others gave away their most cherished possessions, and ten thousand people lined the streets to watch the pallbearers carrying the coffin to where America's most famous preacher waited to deliver the eulogy. But the most distraught of the mourners was a single man dressed as Lucifer, who stood by the great man's coffin weeping and throwing himself to the ground in despair. "Good-bye John," began the Reverend Billy Sunday at midnight. "You were the Devil's best friend. I hate you with a perfect hatred. . . . The reign of tears is over! The slum will soon be a memory. We can soon turn the prisons into factories and our jails into storehouses and corn cribs. Men may walk upright, women will smile, and the children will laugh."

The "man" in the coffin was John Barleycorn, the nickname for hard liquor, who "died" on January 17, 1920, the day the United States banned all forms of alcohol (that being the treasure men had been hoarding or giving away). Love or hate Prohibition, the fact that it happened verged on the miraculous. Westerners worship wine and adore beer, literally, because like all people we once believed that inebriating foods derived their power from resident spirits who would possess the imbiber.

Hence our nickname "spirits" for hard liquor. This liquid divinity has been considered largely benign, if not divine, since the wine-drinking Dionysian cults of ancient Greece. Most cultures agreed on some level—ancient Babylonian law required the poor be supplied with "food to eat, and beer to drink"—but Europeans took it the furthest. Not only did they incorporate alcohol into all religious rites, but they made it a dietary staple comparable to milk. Beer thickened with eggs and poured over bread was the original continental breakfast and remained common in Germany until the mid-1700s. Beer for breakfast, ale for lunch, stout with dinner, and a few mugs in between. "People," wrote Placutomus in 1551, "subsist more on this drink than they do on food." The average northern European, including women and children, drank three liters of beer a day. That's roughly two six-packs. People in positions of power, like the police, drank much more. Finnish soldiers enjoyed a ration of five liters of strong ale a day (the alcoholic equivalent of about six to eight six-packs, or about forty cans); monks in Sussex made do with twelve cans' worth. Orgiastic drinking contests were part of most religious festivals and occurred almost twice a week. "They must swallow half, then all of a drink in one gulp without stopping to take a single breath," wrote one German in 1599, "until they sink into a complete stupor . . . [then] the two heroes emerge and guzzle in competition with one another." Drinking and toasting became so excessive that the British created a semi-official ban in the late 1700s that inspired the lyrics "drink to me only with thine eyes . . . and I'll not ask for wine. . . ."

The fact that the most abusive drinking was in northern Europe led to a short-lived temperance movement there in the 1500s—a group of Germans who limited themselves to a mere seven glasses of wine per meal—but most of Europe staggered along as it always had. Doctors advised patients to drink themselves unconscious at least "once a month . . . as it stimulates general well-being," and booze was so respectable that churches would ring their bells at ten and two to let workers know it was time for a drink. It wasn't until the obviously horrible effects of alcohol on Native Americans that the first "dry state" was created by an Algonquin Indian leader in Canada; Chief Little Turtle of the Cherokee later convinced Thomas Jefferson to outlaw selling whiskey to his tribe. Although both these bans eventually failed, Christian leaders used these models, along with the image of the "murderous drunk" Indian, to promote the idea of an alcohol-free nation. This racial twist on Prohibition was amplified by sociologists like Arthur MacDonald, who claimed that white Americans, largely of northern European stock, "stand about midway between the maximum susceptibility of the American Indian [to liquor] and the minimum susceptibility of the Latin races" and thus required stringent laws to control their drinking.

The point argued most vigorously by American Prohibitionists was that banning alcohol would lead to a new era of prosperity. Worker production would increase, absenteeism would plummet, and, as Sunday said in his eulogy, "the slums would become a memory." It seemed to work at first. Drinking decreased by as much as 80 percent in the early 1920s. After this initial drop, however, it started climbing again and, by the end of the ban a decade later, was approaching pre-Prohibition levels. Only now, people drank less beer because its bulk made it more difficult to hide. Illegal gin became the drink of choice, but it was of such poor quality that there was a 400 percent increase in deaths due to alcohol poisoning. "The government used to murder by the bullet," commented comedian Will Rogers on the situation. "Now it's by the quart."

The prophesied death of sloth and crime proved equally elusive. While Prohibitionists crowed that they had stamped out "Blue Monday," the day hungover workers would supposedly report sick en masse, it turned out that for some inexplicable reason, worker productivity actually *increased* with heavier drinking. The anticipated growth in savings accounts overflowing with money not spent on tipple also failed to materialize. Instead of creating more jobs and greater prosperity, Prohibition destroyed legitimate work situations and decimated the government's tax revenues, according to sociologist Mark Thornton. Not that those people didn't find work elsewhere: Prohibition was the midwife to serious organized crime in this country. In the first year of Prohibition, overall crime jumped 25 percent; by the end, violent crime rates had increased over 50 percent, largely because of crimes related to illegal drinking. As soon as the law was repealed in 1933, the crime level dropped back to pre-Prohibition levels. Instead of turning "the jails into corn cribs," as Reverend Sunday had promised, the head of the Bureau of Prohibition, Henry Anderson, acknowledged that Prohibition had created "public disregard not only for this law, but for all laws." The only industry that benefited was the prison system. Inmate populations jumped by 30 percent in the first two years, and, by 1930, half of all prisoners were doing time for drinking violations. Not surprisingly, the cost of the federal prison system budget rose 1,000 percent. It all sounds so strangely familiar.

In one sense, however, Reverend Sunday was dead right about Prohibition's positive effect on national productivity. The first successful temperance societies in the 1800s were female church groups like the Women's Christian Temperance Union. Although it was considered "unladylike" to be involved with politics, anti-alcohol campaigning was considered appropriate because it came from a "motherly" urge to protect children against drunken husbands. This union was eventually taken over by Frances Willard who, in 1875, connected temperance with a woman's right to vote by arguing that "since women are the greatest sufferers of the rum curse, she ought to have the right [political power] to close the dram shop over her home." Female Christian groups like these had long opposed giving themselves the vote, but when the wily Willard put the question to them in the so-called Home Protection Ballot, they bit. She then doubled the group's membership, making it the largest in the world, and used its clout to make females fully enfranchised members of society.

In the Green Hour

Jeff and I stared doubtfully at the liquid dripping slowly into the glass.

"Does that look like it's turning green to you?" I asked.

"Well, no," Jeffrey drawled, "but maybe if we drank some more, it would."

"Sounds like a plan." I looked around. It was New Year's Eve, 1999, and we had ended up at a party thrown by a painter friend in the East Village of Manhattan. A small affair, good fun, but the libations weren't flowing with quite the fecundity one associates with the festivity in question, and we'd both become parched, particularly Jeff, who, as leader/singer of the renowned Lefty Jones Band, often suffers from inexplicable bouts of thirst. So we'd taken it upon ourselves to rummage through our host's personal belongings, and there, toward the back of the top shelf in a remote cupboard, we'd stumbled upon a bottle with its cork half-eaten away. *"Absinthe,"* read the moldy label. *"New Orleans, 1898."* I almost shrieked with delight. I'd been trying to get ahold of a bottle of the brew for over a year. The fact that it had been illegal worldwide for almost a century had made it a hard find. And there it was, perhaps one of only a few thousand bottles left in the world.

Absinthe was the cocaine of the fin de siècle and had as many nicknames as the White Lady herself. Opaline. *Le Fée Vert.* The Green Fairy. The Emerald Hell. Oscar Wilde eulogized it, Vincent van Gogh painted it, Toulouse Lautrec dedicated his liver to it. Absinthe is a 120-proof liqueur steeped with hallucinogenic herbs. Psychedelic vodka. But beautiful. One takes absinthe by suspending a sugar cube over a goblet on a special slotted spoon and then trickling water drop by drop onto the cube. As the sugar water hits the liqueur in the glass, it turns a dreamy opalescent green.

> *Green changed to white, emerald to opal:*
> *Nothing has changed.*
> *The man let the water trickle gently into his glass,*
> *and as the green clouded, a mist fell from his mind.*
> *Then he drank Opaline . . .*
> *He saw blue vistas of undiscovered countries, high prospects and a*
>   *quiet caressing sea.*
> *Green changed to white, emerald to opal; nothing had changed.*

Written by Oscar Wilde groupie Ernest Dowson, the poem "Absinthia Taetra" gives a good picture as to why the Impressionists so loved the stuff. But everyone drank it. France went through about 36 million liters a year, and, by the late 1800s, what we now call happy hour was known as *l'heure vert,* "the green hour," for the top hat–toting *absintheurs* who spent hours in the cafés of Paris lingering over a glass. Then habitués began to develop odd quirks. The poet Paul Verlaine, who once drank a hundred glasses in two days, set his wife's hair ablaze. The less artistic settled for dementia and spasms. Scientists reported that a few cups transformed a puppy into a monster with "convulsed face and twisted lips covered with foam, its eyes wide open, haggard, convulsive, mad, in which one reads an impulse to kill!" Politicians labeled it madness in a bottle. "Absinthe," wrote the newspaper *Gazette de Laussane* in a typical editorial from the time, "is the premier cause of bloodthirsty crimes in this country." Then in 1905 a Swiss peasant named Jean Lanfray brutally murdered his wife and two children. He was dead drunk at the time—like many peasants, Lanfray drank up to five liters of wine a day—but the police blamed his behavior on the two glasses of absinthe he'd taken earlier that day. Three years later the Swiss outlawed the brew. Holland followed suit in 1910 and the United States in 1912. France, the world's greatest consumer, held out until the beginning of World War I. It's been illegal worldwide ever since.

Absinthe's repression helped set the stage for the American Prohibition, but its psychoactive herbs make it something of a separate case. The main villain in the drink appears to be the herb *Artemisia absinthium*, popularly known as wormwood because it supposedly sprouted along the trail left by the serpent as it fled Eden. The Greeks used wormwood to aid in delivering babies (not to mention curing flatulent dogs) but its main fame is as a mild hallucinogen whose active chemical, *thujone,* is said to resemble the THC that gives marijuana its kick. Absinthe's power, however, is thought to have come from a little-understood interaction between wormwood and herbaceous flavorings like anise, hyssop, mint, coriander, parsley, and chamomile. Sadly, that was not the case with the bottle Jeff and I discovered that night. Once we'd convinced our gracious host, Bill Hudders, to crack open his bottle, we devoted ourselves to a night of intense research. We added sugar. We drank it straight. We injected it. We even added other psychoactive substances to the mix. All in vain. Although its 120 proof did not go unappreciated, there were definitely no hallucinations. It had no more effect than Pernod, the gutless imitation created when absinthe was banned. The only fireworks that night came when Times Square blew itself up at the stroke of the millennial midnight.

GREED

The difference between a rich man and a poor man is this—the former eats when he pleases, and the latter when he can get it.

Sir Walter Raleigh

GREED MENU

APÉRITIF

Leche de Mamasita
Vodka, cream, and green ink

FIRST COURSE

Crostini de Jesus
Crisp baked wafer spread with a messianic pâté.
Sprinkling of Rindfleisch.

SECOND HELPINGS

Smoked Green Makaku
Herb-flecked loin of baboon, slow smoked over endangered
tropical hardwoods.

MAIN COURSE

Fried Capitalist Pig
Deep-fried Haitian pork rind served in a bitter sauce.
Garnished with eye-of-the-needle pickles.

DESSERT

Rock Candy Mountain
Served in a pool of whiskey sauce.

WE SPECIALIZE IN CATERING
CORPORATE EVENTS.

The Greedy Diner

You might think that a romp through the historic relationship between greed and food would dwell (lovingly) on obscene feasts. Illicit delicacies. Evil gourmands snatching lollies from the hands of wailing babes. All good fun, which you will find richly represented in the chapter on gluttony, but not here, because the classical sin of greed consists of an insatiable desire to increase one's worldly wealth. Eating well is, of course, the ultimate expression of power, and some historians have argued that the ability to do so is the most important litmus test of one's power, and that, therefore, all political/financial struggles are fundamentally about who gets to eat what. In some Ecuadoran cultures this is literally true; the elder female who serves dinner has the power to designate the tribe's leader because she decides who gets the biggest portion at mealtimes. Conversely, in many places the female's exclusion from the power structure is indicated by the rule that she eat only after the men have dined. But more interesting to me is the ingenious ways power-hungry leaders from the Pope to lumber barons have manipulated food taboos in order to enrich themselves. The unintended results, ranging from the most horrific plagues of the twentieth century to medieval genocide, are poignant reminders of how strongly we feel not only about what dishes the waiter is allowed to bring to the table, but also who gets served the fattest slice.

Lazy Luscious Land

To get to the country the Dutch call *Luilekkerland,* "Lazy Luscious Land," you must eat your way through a ten-thousand-foot-tall mountain of rice pudding. The people of *Luilekkerland* live in houses constructed of chocolate cake surrounded by fences made of sausage. The flowers are made of scones—already buttered—and clouds of dreamy fried chicken float in a gravy-colored sky. It rains Chardonnay. Peasants doze under ravioli trees by streams that flow with melted goose fat. Even the shit, they say, is delightful: horses poop poached eggs; donkeys drop figs. But beware! Everywhere are "birds winging south/just gape—they'll fly into your mouth!"

> *The Hogs you meet on every street*
> *Are sleek and fat and crisply fried;*
> *They carry knives—it's very nice!*
> *And stand by while you carve your slice!*

Luilekkerland exists in almost every culture. The French call it *Cockaigne,* the Italians *Chucagna,* and the Germans *Schlaraffenlad,* but they're all folk utopias in which life is one long luxurious feast. Harmless enough, but when they first became popular in the medieval period, this lifestyle belonged exclusively to Europe's royalty, and any suggestion that others might deserve a sampling was considered dangerously unpatriotic. So when the

German version of *Luilekkerland* was finally put on paper in the 1600s, a surprise ending was added, which read, "To warn my readers this was writ/now go and do the opposite!" The writer was Hans Sachs, Germany's approved poet-for-the-poor, and his moralizing coda was a way of warning the lower classes to keep their hands out of the rich man's piggy bank. Peasants, went the subtext, should just forget about the rich and famous lifestyle and get back to work. Mapmakers emphasized the point by publishing maps that placed these utopias next to the Infernal Kingdom and populated them with cities named Dickhead, Incontinence, and *Wank en doff*.

Scholar Hal Rammell believes that Europe's nobility felt that these fairytale feasts contained "significant subversive implications" because they suggested "that hunger, and all the social constraints that perpetuate it," should be removed. As the ensuing centuries grew more politically restive, the subversive element of the tales grew. In a seventeenth-century English version, called *An Invitation to Lubberland*, we again read how ". . . hot roasted pigs will meet ye/they in the streets run up and down/all crying out, Come Eat Me!" But Lubberland is now also a place with no "law nor lawyer fees/all men are free . . . without a judge or jury." There are no landlords, and all men are created equal. The tale has morphed from one about everlasting dinner to one in which everyone has the right to sit at the aristocrats' dinner table, an idea soon realized when avant-garde London coffeehouses posted rules ending class-segregated seating. The Germans' get-back-to-work message was replaced with an outright suggestion that the reader should revolt; the last line tells all to hurry and join the ship for Lubberland, which "waits but for a gale" before setting out.

During America's Great Depression these quasi-socialistic utopias again became popular in songs by artists like Harry

"Haywire Mac" McClintock. His famous 1928 "Rock Candy Mountain" sings about a hobo-Heaven where bulldogs have rubber teeth and cops have wooden legs and "there's a lake of stew and of whisky too/you can paddle all around them in a big canoe." Even children's literature of the era was not safe from these subversive influences. In a chapter titled If the Ocean Was Whiskey, Dorothy—of *Wizard of Oz* fame—finds a tree that sprouts tin lunch boxes. In each box, attached to its side with a stem, Dorothy finds a sandwich, an apple, and two pickles. While some believe this kind of "free-lunch" populist imagery may have played a part in the banning of the Oz books from public libraries, America's moguls should have kept their shirts on. Author Frank Baum had put another shrub sprouting napkins next to the Lunch Box tree so everyone could clean up afterward. You can't get much more American than that.

The Magic Cannibal

The Fourth Lateran Council of 1215 was the most important political gathering of the Middle Ages, and representatives from secular and religious powers were packed so tight in the tiny church that one bishop was actually trampled to death. A number of interesting reforms were passed during the monthlong meeting—idiots and incompetents were banned from the priesthood, and Muslims and Jews were obliged to wear funny hats—but perhaps the most bizarre was the council's interpretation of the Eucharistic bread eaten during the Catholic High Mass. Until then, the eating of the communion wafer had been considered a symbolic breaking of bread between Christ and his followers. The Lateran Council ended that by declaring that in a "true" Christian ceremony, the wafer and wine of the communion were "*truly* changed by divine power into the body, the wine into the blood . . ." of Jesus Christ. Any other view was heresy punishable by death. From then on the Eucharist wafer was the literal and true flesh of Jesus Christ, raw human meat, and the taking of it cannibalism.

The man who convened the Fourth Lateran Council, Pope Innocent III, claimed to be merely taking at face value the passage in the New Testament where Christ says, "Take, eat; this is my body," while handing out bread to his followers. The reality is that the Pope was a sophisticated Roman who had devoted his life to making the church Europe's supreme power and not the kind of man to take the Bible literally. He was, however, keenly aware of the psychological power held by the sacred meal that crowned the Catholic High Mass.

Holy Communion is the most sensual of religious ceremonies: the priests in immaculate white robes glowing in the candlelight, the bloodred wine gurgling in massive golden goblets, the paper-thin wafer slipped reverently between the lips of the faithful. Religion as it should be. During Innocent's time, however, the Eucharist wafer's relevance was being undermined in every direction. Only 150 years earlier the Church's Eastern wing had left after a dispute over how to bake the wafer. Heretic cults, like the Albigenese Church, declared that the wafers had no meaning or made their ceremonies more dramatic by claiming to put human embryos into the dough. Considering these challenges to the holiness and authority of the Holy Communion, Innocent's "fundamentalist" interpretation looks less like a literal take on the Bible and more like an attempt to sensationalize his own Mass.

He was not, however, the first to note Christianity's man-eating propensities. The following description by the pagan Roman Minicus Felix of this new Jewish cult might even have given the Pope a few ideas.

As for the initiation of a new (Christian) member, the details are as disgusting as they are well known. The novice himself, deceived by the coating of dough (covering a sacrificial infant), thinks the stabs (into the bread) are harmless. Then it's horrible! They hungrily drink the blood and compete with one another as they divide (the child's) limbs . . .

That passage was written in the first century A.D., around a thousand years before Innocent came to power. But during the pope's own time there were huge outbreaks of cannibalism, including a scandal over baby eating among his church's knights on the First Crusade. Russian Tartars to the north were said to have an insatiable appetite for the succulent meat of young ladies' breasts, and firsthand accounts of the Egyptian famine of 1201 agreed, "It was not unusual to find people selling little children (their own or others), roasted or boiled." Early medieval Europe made cannibalism punishable with fines of not more than 200 shillings—the same fine levied if you killed another person's cow—indicating the act was too common for serious punishment to be practical. Holy Roman emperor Charlemagne soon upped the ante by making cannibalism punishable by death. His law, however, is something of a puzzle, because it bans not only man eating, but also the *belief* in it. Historians have hypothesized that this second clause indicated that Charlemagne wanted to curb superstitious rumors. An equally logical interpretation is that the Christian king was not outlawing belief *in* cannibalism but the beliefs *of* cannibalism, i.e., the rituals and religious ceremonies associated with the act.

Charlemagne might as well have banned prayer itself, at least judging from the writings of some scholars who imply that man eating, or at least sacrifice, was as common a religious practice as saying amen. One of the founders of the Celtic Church in the fifth century appears to have consecrated a church by burying a monk alive in the building's foundation and the Christian Mass itself is believed by many to have evolved from an ancient rite involving the sacrifice and eating of the firstborn child.

But the most sophisticated religious cannibals were in the New World, a group that inadvertently gave us the word itself when Christopher Columbus mispronounced the tribe *Carib* (Caribbean) as *Canib* (cannibal). The Aztecs of Mexico went through up to two hundred fifty thousand victims each year in their religious feasts. The most vivid descriptions come from the Spanish prisoners taken to what is now Mexico City in 1521, as in this one by soldier Bernal Diaz del Castillo:

Again there was sounded the dismal drum of Huichilobo and many other shells and horns and things like trumpets and the sound of them was terrifying. . . . We all looked towards the lofty *Cue* (temple-pyramid) where they were being sounded and saw that our comrades whom they had captured when they de-feated Cortes were being carried by force up the steps, and they were taking them to be sacrificed. When they got them up to a small square in front of the oratory, where their accursed idols are kept, we saw them place plumes on the heads of many of them and with things like fans in their hands they forced them to dance before Huichilobos, and after they had danced they im-mediately placed them on their backs on some rather narrow stones which had been prepared as places for sacrifice, and with stone knives they sawed open their chests and drew out their palpitating hearts and offered them to the idols that were there, and they kicked the bodies down the steps, and Indian butchers who were waiting below cut off the arms and feet and flayed the skin off the faces, and prepared it afterward like glove leather with the beards on, and kept those for the festivals when they celebrated drunken orgies, and the flesh they ate in *chilmole*.

The Aztecs fed the victims' hearts, called "precious eagle-cactus fruit," to the Sun. Mere mortals had to make do with the leftovers in a stew called *Tlacataolli* which, according to Aztec chronicler Fray Bernardino de Sahagun, was considered "something from Heaven, eaten with reverence and ritual."

Europe's most avid man eaters appear to have been the Celtic Druids of northern and western Europe. Roman historian Strabo reported in the first century B.C. that the Druids "count it an honorable thing, when their fathers die, to devour them," being, horror of horrors, "man eaters as well as *herb eaters*." Imperial Rome was constantly at war with the Celts, so these comments might have been mere war propaganda, but two-thirds of all of Europe's confirmed cannibal sites are in Celtic/Druid regions like Normandy, England, and Ireland. The Druids' recipes are, unfortunately, lost, but we do know that they kept the heads of their deceased leaders (or revered enemies) preserved in oil, an ancient method of conserving meat used today in the making of duck confit. This might have been the source of the "mystic meat" that Druid priests chewed while staring at breaking waves or smoke until they experienced a prophetic vision.

The exact extent to which these ancient practices continued during Innocent's era is impossible to measure. The Pope would, however, have been acutely aware of the Druid/Celtic belief in hallucinogenic meat thanks to King Arthur and the Holy Grail. This cycle of romantic tales, so popular it verged on a religious cult, essentially tells the story of how a Christlike King Arthur and his crew scoured the Celtic regions in search of a dish called the Grail. The popular belief is that the Grail held the blood of Christ. In fact, it also held his flesh. Arthur and company were essentially a group of Celtic priests actively seeking the body of Christ to consume it in a completely true and unsymbolic feast of cannibalism.

The notion that the Messiah's body was being gnawed by a group of warrior-priests in the Celtic regions posed a threat to Roman power because, if true, it meant that Christ's body was in England and therefore that the heretic Celtic churches had a stronger claim to being the center of Christianity than Rome. Catholic chroniclers agree that the Vatican was "very aware" of the threat posed by the Arthur cult but refrained from proclaiming it heresy for fear that doing so would have given it a theological legitimacy it then lacked. The Catholics held this fear with good cause—the tale of the Grail was one of the ecclesiastical arguments used by England's King Henry VIII when he created his anti-Roman Church of England.

Faced with so many threats centered on the dining rituals of the Holy Mass, Innocent's transubstantiation doctrine simply closed the circle and returned his church to its ancient roots of sacrifice and violence. It also made his Mass the wildest show in town. Declining church attendance soon revived, and the concept proved so popular that the Church established the Feast of Corpus Christi, literally the "Feast on the Body of Christ," which became one of the most popular of the medieval festivals. Some churches put up murals showing Christ being sliced into cookies and served up by the Pope. A more appropriate image would have shown Europe being consumed by the Pope; thanks to empire-building tactics like this, Innocent's successors soon controlled an estimated one-third of all the wealth in Europe.

By beatifying one of civilization's deepest taboos, however,

Innocent also flamed the passions of a society addicted to morbid fantasies. Peasants began reporting that consecrated hosts screamed in agony when bitten into. Some bled profusely, supposedly leaving permanent bloodstains on the faces of the faithful. Disbelieving prelates pulling a wafer out of a bag found their hands in a mass of raw, bleeding flesh, and according to the *X-Files* of the time, Caesarius's *Miraculorum*, a family who had put a wafer in their beehive to ensure sweeter honey returned to find thousands of bees gathered about the wafer on bended knee. The church made taking a host from a church a capital crime. Innocent himself barred Christian girls from working as nursemaids in Jewish homes, because "when such nurses accept the body and blood of Jesus [during High Mass], their employers force them for three days thereafter to spill their [now sanctified] milk into a latrine before again breast-feeding the [Jewish] children."

Then a Parisian Jew named Jonathan stole a consecrated host with the intent of proving how ridiculous the whole thing was by serving it to some Christian friends for breakfast. According to court documents, however, the bread refused to be cut by a knife. After a fruitless struggle, Jonathan attacked it with a small ax. The wafer then magically divided into three parts representing the Father, the Son, and the Holy Ghost. A piece tossed into boiling water turned to cooked flesh. The pot began overflowing with blood. The horrified Christians handed Jonathan over to the authorities, and his death at the stake became an annual Parisian festival for the next six hundred years. Similar accusations against a wealthy Belgium family—apparently part of a plot to gain their wealth—resulted in the burning of every Jew in Brussels, a massacre again celebrated with a holiday until the late 1800s. These slaughters continued sporadically until 1510, when thirty-eight people were burned alive in Berlin and Jews were banned from the city for two hundred years.

The most perverse of these pogroms was led by an obscure German nobleman with the unusual name of Rindfleisch ("Beef Man"), who, after another incident of Jews allegedly abusing the Christian wafer, gathered a small army of drunken peasants and in 1298 set out to eliminate "the accursed race" from Germany. For six months Rindfleisch and his henchmen ravaged the countryside. They stormed major cities and threw all Jews into the flames. Christians who tried to protect their Hebrew neighbors were overrun, and many Jews burned their own children alive rather than let them fall into the hands of the psychotic mob. In all, Rindfleisch destroyed 146 towns and killed an estimated one hundred thousand people, only ending his campaign when the weather grew inclement. Or perhaps it was only put on hiatus; almost a thousand years later, in nearby Lublin, Poland, a presumed descendant of Rindfleisch, camp doctor Untersturmführer SS Rindfleisch, oversaw the asphyxiation of Jewish children in the Nazi Majdanek extermination camp.

Scientists now believe these bleeding hosts were caused by the fungus *Prodigious microccous*, which grows on stale bread and secretes a red dye that could have been mistaken for drops of blood. Some were created by greedy priests who dipped wafers in blood to create miracles that gullible pilgrims would pay good money to see. But whatever the causes of these bizarre apparitions, the Pope had succeeded in manipulating the strong emotions tied to cannibalism to help make himself the world's wealthiest human being. His magic cannibalism had bound Christians together both as criminals and as God's Chosen, a brilliant merging of humanity's two most binding social contracts, while simultaneously driving a stake into the heart of the older religions by appropriating their most powerful rite into a ceremony that was exalted, refined, cruel, and forgiving. Men need no longer hide in darkened groves to eat mystic meats, for God had sacrificed His only Son and given us the body to feast upon in a ritual glittering with gold and white cloth, incense, music, and wine; the ultimate forbidden food was now divine, fulfilling the prophesy of the apostles who wrote that all shall be eaten and found delicious.

Smoked Green Makaku

It's been ten years since I took a rusty barge down the Congo River, but the memories remain vivid. Like the moment I realized my dorm cabin was doubling as the boat's brothel. Or the time our captain lost his temper and deliberately drove the boat aground for three days. Or the sweltering hot rooms below deck where stowaways were hung from their wrists and whipped. But it's the expressions of the smoked monkeys that I remember best. Faces contorted in an agonizing howl, lips blackened from smoke, eye sockets charred and empty. Smoked primate is the nouvelle cuisine of Central Africa and every day dugout canoes pulled up out of the endless jungle to unload stacks of them for delivery to the marketplace in Kisangani. By the end of the trip the decks were covered with what looked like piles of withered children curled up in fetal position. Occasionally someone would tear off an arm to make a bit of soup.

I didn't realize then that I was witnessing the birth of a culinary trend that many believe will finally lead to the extermination of mankind's closest relatives. Primates like chimps and apes have been on endangered species lists for many decades, but their numbers had stabilized until a recent breakdown in traditional food taboos put them back on the fast track for oblivion. "If the taste for bushmeat continues to spread at its current pace," says Anthony Rose of the Institute for Conservation Education, "all African apes and most other nonhuman primates may soon be threatened with extinction." Hundreds of wildlife organizations have recently made the issue a top priority, including famed ape specialist Jane Goodall, who has predicted the extinction of wild apes within fifty years if the culinary fad continues.

The problem began with logging companies sending foreign workers into the deepest parts of the African jungle. Keeping their workers fed in these areas is extraordinarily complicated. So to economize and maximize profits, many of these companies simply gave their workers guns to hunt "bushmeat" like gorillas, chimps, gazelles, anteaters, and whatever else they could find. Many of these animals have always been on the local menu, but most tribes considered primates taboo because of their obvious kinship to humans. Seeing foreigners munching on monkey chops for the last few decades, however, has normalized this as food. "You must come to my house," one of my fellow passengers used to urge. "My mother, she makes the best monkey!" (*"Ma mere, elle fait le mieux singe!"*) This local consumption has recently been exacerbated by a growing export market. The chimp jerky on my boat, for instance, was destined for the second-largest city in the Congo, Kisangani, so it could be shipped to places like Brussels, where African expatriates willingly pay up to $20 for a plate of Ma's smoked green *makaku* stew. The lure of this easy cash, combined with the local consumption and better guns, is causing slaughters in numbers unimaginable in the recent past. Some estimate the market is now worth a billion dollars a year and that 10 percent of the meat in some African towns comes from primates and that the international market—worth an estimated one billion dollars—consumes a quarter of a million metric tons of primate meat a year. With an estimated two hundred thousand chimps left in Africa, the math isn't hard to do. The recent extinction of Ghana's red colobus monkey has already been blamed on this phenomenon.

It's not just the monkeys that are threatened. Primates, whose genome code is 98 percent identical to that of humans, carry a version of the HIV/AIDS virus, and specialists have long suspected that this was the source of the human virus. Only nobody could figure out how it had been transmitted. Then in 1999 a team of researchers stumbled across a chimp that the U.S. Army had frozen twenty years earlier and, after an exhaustive genetic investigation, deduced that the first human victim of AIDS had been infected by a dish of chimp cooked about fifty years ago. An historic meal. The disease has already killed some 20 million people worldwide. In the area through which I was traveling, half the population is expected to die from AIDS before they reach the age of twenty.

The Laughing Man

The Congo is a hundred thousand square miles of jungle, mud roads, and diamond mines. Aside from the boat where I saw the smoked monkeys—which usually runs about three weeks late—the only way to get around is hitching rides. There's really nothing to see, but it requires so much effort to get anywhere, you've no energy left over to wonder what you're doing there once you arrive. One of the more popular tourist attractions is probably the cannibals. My first encounter came near the Uganda border. Our truck was passing through a typical Congo village of a dozen tipsy-looking huts scattered along a red mud road. Thatched grass roofs, bamboo doors. But there were no people. The line of waving children who had greeted us in every village was missing.

I asked the man sitting next to me on the truck's roof what had happened.

"Cannibals," Jacques explained calmly. Jacques was a Congolese man, perhaps eighteen, whom I'd met soon after getting off the Congo barge. "They have attacked this place. So the people, they have just left."

I laughed. Surely, I said, you don't believe cannibals still exist?

Jacques looked offended. "But it is only true! Sometimes you can even see the Laughing Man in my town of Kisangani."

The Laughing Man? I asked. Jacques explained: The Laughing Man is a sickness that comes to a cannibal when the spirits of the people he has eaten possess him. First he starts hearing their voices in his head. Then he begins to see things. He talks to invisible spirits. He can't stop smiling, and eventually he laughs himself to death.

At the time I wrote off Jacques's story as yet another African fairy tale, like the church whose followers scream themselves to sleep every night to scare away evil spirits, or the insect that lives exclusively on human corneas. I was wrong. The technical name for Laughing Man disease is *kuru*, although it has been documented only among the cannibals of Papua New Guinea. *Kuru* is closely related to today's infamous Mad Cow disease (the human version of which is Creutzfeldt-Jakob). Both are caused by institutionalized cannibalism: *Kuru* comes from humans eating the raw brains of their relatives, while Mad Cow first appeared when ranchers began feeding their steers the flesh/blood/brains/organs of other cattle. As in the case of the Laughing Man disease, the cattle's cannibalistic diet—created to maximize profit—appears to have allowed the spread of bizarre renegade proteins, called prions, that eat holes in the brain tissue and turn it into a spongelike glob. At present, some 3 million animals have died from these diseases, as well as an unknown number of people.

It's a gruesome tale of greed and how ignoring traditional taboos sometimes carries a price. What makes it particularly bizarre is what the symptoms shared by the cannibalistic diseases of Laughing Man and Mad Cow potentially indicate. The first signs of both include spasms of the limbs, and around the mouth. For human sufferers, this evolves into an uncontrollable urge to smile, followed by compulsive laughter. Then comes dementia, paralysis, and death. These symptoms are quite similar to a rare condition called St. Vitus's dance. Named after a saint who was made to dance on a bed of red-hot coals, St. Vitus causes sufferers to shiver in a mock spastic "dance" and is believed to have been the cause of the weird religious-dancing hysterias that swept Europe during the 1300s. The Papua New Guineans believed that spirits possessed victims of Laughing Man, just as Christians believed that demons possessed sufferers of St. Vitus's dance. Whereas eating a human brain transmits Laughing Man, St. Vitus results from eating rye bread infected by the fungus ergot, the active ingredient in the drug LSD. Not surprisingly, the first symptoms of an LSD trip are very similar to symptoms of both diseases: uncontrollable laughter and smiling, followed by hallucinations and temporary dementia.

People from Sigmund Freud to Montaigne have commented

on our irrational horror of eating one another. "It baffles all sense of logic," wrote Freud, "that we should kill one another, often to applause, but be horrified beyond words at even the thought of eating one another." The similarity in symptoms between diseases tied to cannibalism and hallucinogens opens an intriguing line of speculation, i.e., that our aversion might have roots in historic illnesses associated with eating human flesh, or a knowledge that it once had been some kind of sacred food, a category consistently dominated by mind-altering agents. This second possibility sheds a different kind of light on a number of historic oddities. The ancient Greeks, for instance, called their sacrificial victims *pharmakos*, which means atonement, but is related to the word *pharmakon*, which means drug (hence the word *pharmacy*). The Vatican's psychedelic description of how eating the flesh of Christ via the communion wafer creates a sensation of "immersion within a universal being" starts making a sort of sense. If eating raw brains causes psychic disturbances of some kind, the tradition of Druid priests chewing a "mystic meat" to see visions might be connected to their custom of preserving their leaders' heads in oil. Was the altered state the Druids achieved similar to the "spacy" feeling reported by humans infected by Creutzfeldt-Jakob disease? "It would be hazardous to dismiss this custom (of preserving heads) among the Celts as being merely a desire to collect trophies for the accumulation of marital prestige," wrote Celtic historian T. G. Powell. "It's more likely derived from an older cult relating to human fertility. . . ."

If eating one's fellow human was merely gross or unhealthy, like eating human feces, would cannibalism have developed so many mystical overtones? Probably not. "Cannibals care intensely *how* they ate people and also whom they ate, when and where," wrote Margaret Visser in her delightful book *The Rituals of Dinner*. She ascribes this fastidiousness to proper table manners. Another possible explanation lies in cannibalism's antecedents as a religious cult. In his book *Muelos: A Stone Age Superstition About Sexuality*, scholar Weston La Barre marshals an impressive array of evidence that there was once a religion centered on ingesting an intoxicating elixir produced in the human brain, a cult which grew into the world's head-hunting cultures. "There was a very ancient belief in human life power apparently resident in the skull," he writes, "to be obtained by eating brains of other men." While La Barre speculates that this substance, called *muelos*, was thought to provide a kind of sexual/psychic power related to semen, he points out that the rites are closely associated with the taking of psychotropic substances. The Bikim-Kuskusmin people of New Guinea say the two are one and the same because a spirit called Afek put his blood/semen/bone marrow into magical plants to give them their hallucinogenic powers.

European Druids and the tribes of Papua New Guinea are among the more famous cannibal sects. Both were unusually isolated societies and were more likely to retain traditions that disappeared elsewhere. The early Tibetan Buddhists *(Bonpo)* were equally isolated, and they, too, are thought to have ritually eaten their loved ones as a way of passing on their wisdom. I have a Tibetan skull bowl sitting on the desk in front of me. The interior is covered in mystic carvings in a manner identical to those seen in hundreds of Tibetan religious paintings. In the paintings it's usually held by a wild-eyed deity, who carries the skull bowl, called a *kapala*, in one hand and a knife, called *chugri*, in one of his other nine. The skulls in these paintings are heaped with a gelatinous gray substance called *amrita*, supposedly semen. The shape and whorl-like designs of the substance, however, make it look remarkably like a human brain. Today these images of brain eating are described as being purely metaphoric. The same metaphoric rationale is applied to the shapely demoness typically copulating with the gods in the same painting, primly ignoring the fact that Tibetan Buddhism is closely related to Tantric Yoga, a discipline well known for its religious sexual practices. If the sexual imagery is clearly more than a mere metaphor, why not the ones involving brains? Anthropologists have reported Tibetan rites that use skull bowls to serve a substance that looks like brains but is actually made of wheat, and Tibet's Mongolian cousins, the Kanjur, identify *amrita* specifically as a human brain.

These people were endo-cannibals and ate their friends to gain their wisdom. Endo-cannibals tend not to eat the actual meat, preferring to burn it to a powder or eat the brain exclusively. Exo-cannibals, a group who eats their enemy to gain their strength, generally prefer a good man chop. Common sense tells us that endo-cannibals eat their friends' brains because— obviously—that's the center of thought and knowledge.

Obviously. That was a trick sentence. We're all so sure that the brain is the organ of thought that eating it to gain wisdom seems almost rational. Yet, it is reasonable to question whether early Tibetans, or a Stone Age people from New Guinea, considered the brain in this light. The father of modern science, Aristotle, believed the brain's sole function was to cool the blood. Among the Fore tribes of highland Papua New Guinea— where the Laughing Man disease was discovered in the 1960s— the brain was reserved for the corpse's closest female relatives. Some scientists attribute this to the men demanding the tastiest bits and leaving the rest for the ladies. The brain, however, has long been among the most prized of dishes. Until the 1700s Europeans brought the head of whatever animal was being eaten to the guest of honor so he could smash the skull open and spoon out the contents to the table's applause (knives and forks were considered bad taste under the circumstance). Later, servants sawed an opening in the skull to make a removable "lid" that the guest could just pop open. Until quite recently, the eating of a cow's brain was a rite of manliness at many Texan barbecues.

While I would never imply that Texas is a den of neanderthal affectations, scholars believe ritual brain eating like this was particularly popular among Neanderthals for about two hundred fifty thousand years, and that the practice disappeared only during the Celtic Bronze Age. Others date it back to 400,000 B.C. Neanderthals no more thought the brain was the center of thought than chimpanzees do. Not that chimps don't think highly of the tidbit: According to Jane Goodall, the only food chimps refuse to share with one another is the head of their near relative, the baboon, which is *always* given to the group's alpha male. In cases where two baboons are simultaneously killed, the heads of both are still given to alpha chimp, who sucks them out with gusto. No one is suggesting that chimps value the snack because they think it is the repository of the soul. They just like the way it tastes. It excites them. It's delicious, so much so that it raises a number of questions about the amorphous line separating intoxicating from tasty. The most praised drink in the world is wine. Yet most think it's vile when they take their first sip. And with good reason—alcohol is a poison, and our body's immediate instinct is to reject it. It's only when we experience alcohol's ability to intoxicate that we realize how "delicious" it really is. We have rationalized the pleasures of intoxication in terms of taste.

So when the chimps exhibit such rabid enthusiasm for the raw brain of a sister species, it's reasonable to wonder precisely what has them so worked up. Is it a taste sensation, or something closer to the feline love of the intoxicating herb catnip? Likewise, when the cannibals of Papua New Guinea say they reserve the dead man's brain for the closest female relative because it is "special . . . precious," their meaning, before being interpreted by Western anthropologists, is unclear. A word like *precious*, in its original sense, was a reference to some kind of magical power and is the kind of language that shamans use in explaining how they receive their wisdom from peyote and other hallucinogens.

This is all in the never-never land of speculation, but it's reasonable to suggest that, given the connection so many cultures make between madness and inspiration and holiness, the dementia-like symptoms associated with brain-eating diseases could have led to cannibalism being associated with priest castes. A number of anthropologists have suggested that eating human brains or heads was the prerogative of the religious elite in a variety of cultures. The Aztecs, for instance, doled out their sacrificial victims according to social rank. The heart went to the Sun god, while the meat went to the nobles. But the heads went to the priests, according to documents from the time. No one knows for sure what the priests did with them, but archaeologists have recovered hundreds of skulls they believe came from sacrificial victims, and every single one of them had their brains removed. There were no organic remains found to indicate they had been discarded.

Thou Shalt Not Eat
Thy Mother

It was once the premiere dining spot on the planet. Friendly service. Convenient location. Great view. Fresh, hot food. And the price—talk about cheap! Mother's milk, straight from her breast, was the original blue plate special. Now veering toward extinction. Despite international campaigns to preserve humanity's first drinking straw, breast-feeding has been on a fifty-year decline. Americans were once assured two years a-suckle, but today a mere quarter of them have the pleasure, and then for only a few months. Similar declines are also occurring in many parts of Asia and Africa. This turning of the universal food into a near taboo has been blamed on everything from the spread of colonial Puritanism to the entry of mothers into the workforce, but most scholars agree that the predominant reason is the greed of a small group of businessmen who promote a reconstituted milklike product as a convenient replacement. "With millions of dollars' worth of baby formula sold each year," writes scholar Marilyn Yalom in her *History of the Breast*, "the growth of bottle feeding can be attributed sheerly to the profits involved . . . and their promotion by both the industry and the medical profession."

The cumulative result is comparable to the Holocaust. World health organizations estimate that 1.5 million babies die unnecessarily each year because they are nursed with baby formula instead of breast milk. These deaths are not the fault of the formula product itself, but stem from the unclean water used to reconstitute the stuff in some areas of the world. But countries with relatively clean water also suffer because bottle-fed children everywhere are more likely to be obese, score lower on IQ tests, and suffer serious allergies. Bottle-feeding is also some-times associated with learning disorders. The United States alone is thought to spend between $2 billion and $4 billion a year fighting diseases connected to bottle feeding.

Baby formulas were originally created to help mothers who could neither breast-feed nor afford a human milk nurse, and they were doubtless an improvement on the practice of nursing babies on donkey's milk. It quickly grew into a small industry with over twenty prefab brands on the market by the late 1800s, all emphasizing convenience and promoting the idea that a woman's breast was unhygienic. This notion, of course, is pure nonsense—a woman's nipple naturally exudes an anti-septic liquid—but it caught on in an era fraught with Puritan ethics and a love of modernity. The formulas' negative health effects were at first too subtle to measure, and so it wasn't until the companies began peddling their product in countries where the water was unsafe that obvious problems started popping up. The manufacturers could hardly have been unaware of the impending disaster they created. No matter—with money to be made, they flooded the areas with advertising. According to the book *Milk, Money, and Madness*, during August 1974 there were over 250 ads for baby formula in the tiny West African country of Sierra Leone alone. International agencies and corporations gave free samples of baby formula to hospitals in countries where they knew it should not be used, and pictures portraying healthy bottle-fed babies lined doctors' waiting rooms.

The most revolting marketing device was the hiring of women dressed as nurses who visited hospitals to urge new mothers to use a particular formula. According to one study, 87 percent of Nigerian mothers stopped breast-feeding because of visits from these so-called "milk nurses." Pranks like this led to the famous worldwide boycott of Nestlé products during the

1970s. When Nestlé sued a group for publishing a book titled *Nestlé Kills Babies*, it took the mega-corporation three trials to win, only to then be chastised by the judge for "dangerous and life-destroying [activities]."

The major baby formula manufacturers have since voluntarily signed an agreement to abide by restrictions akin to the ones imposed on cigarette and liquor manufacturers. This has moderated the most egregious abuses suffered, but many companies have just become more subtle in their marketing. Some now mail American mothers redeemable checks for up to $50 to purchase their products. Others send cases of formula free of charge. These "gifts" are timed to arrive as soon as possible after the mother has given birth. "It's a common practice," said Deborah Myers of the mother-baby program at Kaiser Hospital of Portland, Oregon, "and sends out an unfortunate message to new mothers when they are sleep deprived and most vulnerable to suggestion." Company officials say they send samples only to mothers who specifically ask for them; their customer service operators, however, told me "they use marketing lists all the time." The practice of encouraging mothers to take a break from breast nursing in the early stages is particularly deceptive because when she does her breasts stop producing milk, making it more difficult to resume, and her child loses the ability to latch on to the nipple. This essentially addicts her and her baby to formula.

Strangely enough, members of the $8-billion-a-year baby-formula business seem reluctant to concede that they have, at times, effectively tried to replace the maternal breast. Repeated requests for comments from various companies have been ignored, save a sole Nestlé representative who said that they vigorously abide by all voluntary labeling and marketing rules. Not that anyone's suggesting the industry wants to harm children or denies that formula sometimes saves lives. It's a question of marketing gone amok. Companies now put a label on their products stating that breast milk is superior to baby formula; some also suggest that the customer not prepare the formula with water out of the communal toilet. In 1999 breast-feeding in America increased ever so slightly for the first time in fifty years, and the country's president, Bill Clinton, finally made it legal to nurse children publicly on federal property. Mothers in the British government, however, have not fared as well. Members of Parliament were recently refused the right to nurse their babies in government chambers because Parliamentary rules forbid both refreshments and visitors. It appears breast-feeding "visiting" infants violated both regulations.

Got Milk?

Mother's milk may be the universal food, but that other stuff, the coagulated excretions of mammals, is most definitely not. An estimated 50 percent of the world have serious problems digesting cow's milk because of a complex sugar—called lactose—contained in all milk. Practically the only real true-blue milk drinkers appear to be the white boys from northern Europe who are thought to have learned the habit, in conjunction with their freaky skin color, some ten thousand years ago. Their ability to digest milk was developed to compensate for a lack of calcium when weather conditions eliminated many dark green plants in the north. According to scholar Marvin Harris, their fairer skin developed at the same time because it created a chemical reaction with sunlight, which facilitated the digestion of the dreck they sucked out of the pets' teats. All quite barbarous, according to Greek historian Herodotus, who condemned the northerners for "sow(ing) no crops . . . and moreover, they are drinkers of milk!" Even the cow-loving Hindus have trouble digesting milk, which is why, with the exception of lactose-tolerant Northern Indians, you will find so much more yogurt or butter than milk in their diet—the fermentation that produces yogurt and cheese breaks down lactose into simpler sugars that are easily digested. None of this is relevant to human breast milk, which is entirely different from cow's milk.

American Pigs

Haiti's last pig died on June 21, 1983. An American scientist killed it. There's no way of knowing what the Ph.D. thought as he put the bullet into the animal's brain. He or she probably thought of it as a favor to the Haitians. The island's pigs were supposed to be infected by a deadly disease. Besides, the good ol' U.S. of A. had promised that once all those dirty little black pigs were dead, they'd soon be replaced with nice white American ones. So what was all the fuss about?

The official reason for the extermination of Haiti's beloved *cochon-planche* was to stop African Swine Fever from spreading to the continental United States. The disease had first appeared in Haiti's neighbor, the Dominican Republic, in 1978, and soon a very small number of Haitian animals had tested positive. But although Swine Fever is normally 99 percent fatal to pigs (it doesn't affect humans), the Haitian subspecies appeared to have developed an immunity to the bug. Very few animals actually died, and by the time the American-sponsored eradication program began three years later, the disease had disappeared. Notwithstanding this—or the voracious objections of the Hai-

tian peasantry—Washington went ahead and spent $23 million
for an army of pig-hunting helicopters to ensure that the Haitian pig joined the pterodactyls among the annals of the extinct.

This is not the first time the Americans have tried to eliminate a species from the face of the Earth. During the 1800s they
tried to drive the American buffalo to extinction as part of a
campaign to destroy the Native American cultures that were
hindering white America's economic plans. The stated intent of
the Haitian policy was, as we read, different. But the results
were remarkably similar.

The vast majority of Haitians in the early 1980s were subsistence farmers with an annual income of about $130. The pigs
were the "master component of the Haitian peasant production
system," according to Haitian sociologist Jean-Jacques Honorat,
and helped make the farmers' poor but independent lifestyle
possible. The animals' scavenger diet cost the farmer nothing,
and the money earned by sale of their meat provided cash for
necessities like school uniforms and medicine. U.S. officials
understood the pig's importance. That's why they promised to
replace every scroungy little Haitian pig with a brand-new
superdeluxe American model. And what a pig it was! The
American *über-schweins* were three times the size of their Haitian relatives and bred to produce the best-tasting, leanest bacon
on the planet. But once all the Haitian pigs were dead, the
Yanks decided that only farmers with enough money to pay for
a special water system and concrete floors would be given replacement animals. Luxuries like these, however, were too expensive for most Haitian people to put in their homes, much
less in their pigsties. The Haitian pigs had survived off garbage
and insects and excrement, thus doubling as an outhouse on
legs and an insecticide that kept the farmer's lands free of pests.

The American beasts turned up their nose at anything less than a special vitamin-enriched feed that cost about $90 a year, more than half of the average peasant's annual income.

The result was predictable (in fact, the peasant farmers *had* predicted it). Relatively few pigs were actually handed out by the Americans. Those that were failed to survive because no one could afford the water-mist system the animals needed to survive in the heat. When school attendance dropped 25 percent because of the absent pig money, people tried to bring back the old black pigs. But the rabidly anti-Communist Haitian right-wing government had both pigs and their owners executed as Communists. The same officials, who were supposed to control prices for the American pig feed, then created shortages so they could enhance their profits. The peasants were soon locked out of the swine-breeding business, and ten years after the death of the last Haitian pig, almost all of them had been forced to sell their ancestral lands to make ends meet. Even one of the American officials involved with the program reportedly admitted it had been a tragic mistake.

Perhaps *mistake* is misleading. It turns out that a year before the Americans had started pushing to exterminate the black pigs, their friends at the World Bank had been pressuring the Haitian government to shift their island's economic focus from subsistence farming to growing crops for export. The idea was for corporations to take over the peasants' farms and grow coffee and flowers, while the farmers moved to the cities to become splendidly desperate factory workers creating cheap goods for North American consumers. The peasants, however, had held their noses at the idea—Haiti is home to the first successful slave rebellion in the Western Hemisphere and the area's first free black nation. So the idea of ending up on some white boy's corporate plantation went against their grain. The World Bank's plan, in fact, was going nowhere until the Yanks wiped out the pigs and "accidentally" destroyed the peasant economy. This forced farmers to sell off their family plots, which multinationals grabbed up at bargain prices. Within a decade Haiti had switched from subsistence to an export economy. Staple food production decreased by 30 percent, and the urban population doubled. Some Haitians are still saying the pigs were killed to force them to work in American factories for $1 a day. Then again, maybe it was the ghosts of the slave owners taking a long-delayed revenge: Haiti's 1804 slave revolution began with a voodoo ceremony that climaxed in the drinking of a pig's blood.

BLASPHEMY

"Know and understand; it is not what goes into the mouth that defiles a man, but that which comes out. . . ."

Book of Matthew, 15:10

BLASPHEMY MENU

APÉRITIF
Brandy "Masai" Alexander
Fresh cow blood mixed with ice, milk, and brandy.

FIRST COURSE
Fritatta with Marrano Sausage
With Lenten eggs and kosher pork sausage.

SECOND COURSE
Iguana Carpaccio
Hibiscus-fed iguana served with a Catholic sauce.

MAIN
Adafina with Matzoh Balls
A heretic stew of meats and chickpeas.
(Recipe on page 192)

DESSERT
Biscuit de Jesus
Unleavened wafers with naturally sweet manna jam.

The Sacred
Act of Eating

If you deconstruct most religious ceremonies, you wind up with a man dressed suspiciously like a chef serving some kind of snack. Eating is imbued with religious meaning, and some anthropologists believe the rituals and symbols of organized religion grew directly from dining etiquette. Most religions forbid a vast array of dishes as a way to both give their followers a coherent identity and discourage them from mingling with disbelievers who might plant the seed for blasphemous thinking. The Old Testament devotes most of the Book of Leviticus to listing blasphemous dishes; one rule, prohibiting the mixing of meat with milk, was considered so important that it was apparently among the original Ten Commandments. Christianity, however, is largely free of these taboos, an apparent attempt by Christ and his followers to depart from the mainstream of religious tradition (or maybe they figured it would just make conversion easier). Which isn't to say they weren't fussy eaters—devout Christians routinely swallowed five times when they drank, once each for the five wounds of Christ, and every morsel was sliced into four parts, three for the Holy Trinity and one for Mary. During the 1600s, the Spanish Inquisition even had "food police" roaming the streets, sniffing for heretic cooking. But Islam, Buddhism, Hinduism, and Judaism still retain their forbidden foods and the echoes of these beliefs have led to some of the more bizarre chapters in how we worship our Head Chef.

The Jewish Pig

Once upon a time, Jesus bumped into a rabbi sitting by the side of the road. The rabbi had just been arguing with his friends about the rumors that this guy Christ was the Messiah. So he decided to test His powers. "If you are truly the Messiah," the skeptical rabbi said to Jesus, "then you can surely see what lies beneath this barrel next to me." The rabbi believed some pigs were napping there. Unbeknownst to him, however, the pigs had been replaced by his own son. When Jesus told him that his son was sleeping under the barrel, the rabbi sneered—some Messiah! Christ tried to convince the rabbi of the truth, but the rabbi would not listen. So Christ simply turned the child into a pig and walked away. It's a relatively benign fable told by early European Christians to explain the Jewish aversion to pork as a fear Jews have of eating their own children. But the tale grew over the centuries into a series of beliefs that implied that Jews were actually a subhuman race that had sprung from swine. Christian Poles believed that Jewish women had horizontal vaginas, like sows, and that they carried their babies for only six months. Butchers renamed the most succulent part of the pig (a single vertebrae near the base of the spine) the Jewess, or Damsel in the Swine, and some parts of Germany created a "cloven foot" tax exclusively for Jewish visitors. Other cantons required them to swear to tell the truth in court while standing on the flayed skin of a sow, i.e., to literally swear "on their mother's body." If found guilty, Jews were hung upside down, as opposed to by the neck, in a parody of the way one slaughters and bleeds a hog. In a bizarre reversal, some pigs received court trials as humans: the famous French hog of Falaise was tried for murder while wearing a jacket, breeches, and gloves. When found guilty of murdering a child—an accusation frequently leveled at Jews—the animal was hung while wearing a human mask.

Then a curious figure called *der Judensau* (the Jewish pig) began to appear among the gargoyles guarding the churches of Central Europe. It showed Jewish people sucking on the teats of a pig and gave the Church's official seal of approval to the Jews-as-pigs myth. Peasants spread rumors that circumcision, then only performed by Jews, was actually a castration like the one performed on male pigs to help keep their flesh edible. The pig castrators of the French Pyrenees adopted a uniform parodying that worn by the Hebrew *mohel*, who performs the act of circumcision, including the *mohel*'s trademark red silk belt. Cutting off part of the ear was a traditional way of marking a pig whose flesh was inedible. So officials began mutilating "inferior humans," like Jews, in the same way, and the phrase "here's your father's ear" eventually became a popular anti-Semite jeer. The upside to this insanity was that it allowed the Romans to forgo the ritual murder that had kicked off their Easter rites. The tradition had been to put an elderly Jewish man into a barrel lined with spikes and roll him down the side of Mount Testaccio, according to Claudine Fabre-Vassas's mesmerizing *La Bête singulière* ("The Singular Beast"). By 1312 Jews and swine were considered so interchangeable that a pair of pigs were substituted for the gentleman, albeit only after being dressed in fine silk suits and driven in an elegant carriage to the mountaintop. Rome's Jewish community, of course, was forced to pay for the carriage.

The development of printing turned the *Judensau* into "a forceful image which kept imprinting itself on the mind, conditioning, indeed stereotyping, an attitude toward Jews," according to Isaiah Shachar's study of the subject, and soon graced the

The author's sketch of a judensau gargoyle on a fourteenth-century German church.

covers of popular travel guides. The printed version, however, had been "improved" by the addition of an elderly rabbi who was pictured eating excrement jetting out of the pig's rear. The father of Germany's Protestant revolution, Martin Luther, expounded upon this hateful bit of pornography in 1543. "The Rabbi," he wrote, "bows and stares with great attentiveness [into the pig's rectum] and into the Talmud [Judaic holy book] as if he wanted to read something intricate and extraordinary . . . and the letters that fall from this [they] gobble down." Luther's "analysis" was embellished over the next few centuries. One bestseller explained that in the past "pious Jews did not approve of the sow for eating [but] today the Jews ignore this and make her their mistress." Another used the *Judensau* image as proof that "the sow is the brother to the Jews." The concept was such a hit in Germany that Christian house painters hid the image on the walls of their Jewish customers by covering it with a layer of watery plaster that would eventually peel away and "miraculously" reveal the "true nature of Judaism."

The Jewish dietary taboo against consuming blood under-
went a similar metamorphosis and anti-Semites claimed that
Jews were actually obsessed with blood because they used it in
their religious ceremonies. The best blood was said to come
from Christian children, a belief that became so deep-rooted
that it was still causing riots among Polish Americans in the
1920s. This cocktail of bigotry, fear, and ignorance was unfortunately amplified by some Jewish dietary laws that limited communication between the two groups; followers were banned
from eating nonkosher foods, or anything touched by a nonbeliever. Sharing wine between the religions was also taboo in
some sects, as was eating together. "The Christians interpreted
these ancient laws—formulated long before Christianity—as
meaning that to a Jew everything Christian was unclean" wrote
historian Will Durant, and retaliated by banning "Jews and har-
lots" from touching food in the market. Kosher meat could only
be displayed in stalls selling diseased flesh.

These inversions of Hebraic food taboos would be laughable
were their ramifications not so ghastly. "If it was impossible for
men in the age of Enlightenment and later to conceive of Jews
as their fellow humans it was not just because of religious differences," wrote Shachar. "It seems clear that the *Judensau*—
honoring the Jew more or sometimes less humorously with
porcine ancestry—had been contributing to a transfer of the
Jews to a totally different, non-human category . . . or as the
German would put it, *unsereiner*." It was the *unsereiner* concept
that Nazi scientists modernized so effectively with the use of
scientific jargon. "Non Nordic man," wrote the authors of the
Nazi textbook *New Fundamental Problems of Racial Research*,
"occupies an intermediate zone between Nordic man and the
animal kingdom," and is worthy of extermination. Interviews
with Germans involved in Nazi massacres indicate that many

felt no revulsion at the murders themselves but only at the accompanying mess, which they compared to working in a butcher shop.

Human beings magically transformed into animals are the stuff of fairy tales. But racist propaganda is just that, bedtime stories told to frightened adults, and Hitler was merely a master storyteller who brought the medieval fable of the "Jewish pig" to life. First he used the quasi-science of eugenics to reclassify the Jews as a subhuman species. He then forced Christian women accused of fornicating with Jews to wear signs identifying them as sows. Then he moved the Jewish people into sty-like ghettoes and built a netherworld of slaughterhouses where millions of these "animals" were butchered. In the end, however, it was not the Jews that Hitler's fantasy transformed into animals, but his German followers. In the famous study of Nazi atrocities *Violence Without Moral Restraint*, Herbert Kelman points out that when people dehumanize their victims in order to rationalize violence, it is the aggressors who become "increasingly dehumanized . . . until they lose the capacity to act as moral beings." The Führer must have forgotten that fairy tales tend to have moral endings.

Dinner with the Spanish Inquisition

"The said Beatriz cooked and had cooked adafina and Jewish cuisine with meat, onions, chickpeas, spices all crushed. . . ." This excerpt from the trial of a housewife named Beatriz Lopez is a good indication of just how perilous a dinner party could be in sixteenth-century Spain. Catholic priests roamed the streets of Madrid sniffing for Jewish cookery; friends invited for dinner might be informers and show up with pork sausage to see if you would resist adding it to the stew you were cooking. To serve a Jewish dish, or even to use certain ingredients (like oil), was considered proof of heresy and invariably led to being burned at the stake. The Spanish Inquisition even published a kind of cookbook so Christian neighbors or servants could recognize suspicious cooking techniques. The Jews the Catholics were seeking—called *Marranos* (pork) because they'd feigned conversion to Christianity by publicly eating bacon—countered by developing fake food like their *chorizo di Marrano*, a sausage that omitted pork and substituted red-colored spices for blood. If an officer of the Spanish Inquisition dropped by a *Marrano*'s house, the inhabitant would pop one of these babies into a bun and have lunch to confuse the officer. People, both Catholic and Jewish, took to hanging hams outside their front door to ward off suspicion.

In a study of women accused of heresy by the Inquisition, scholar Renee Levine determined that almost all of their "crimes" consisted of cooking forbidden dishes and that they took the risk because, with all Jewish institutions destroyed, these household practices were the sole "remaining device for transmitting knowledge" of Jewish culture. The dish most often mentioned in the Inquisition's transcripts was a delicious stew of meat, chickpeas, and cabbage called *adafina*. It was a particularly incriminating meal because *adafina* was designed to cook overnight so as to avoid doing any work on the Sabbath in accordance with Jewish law. The fact that matzoh balls were one of the main ingredients couldn't have helped matters.

The following recipe for *cocido madrileño* comes from Juan Carlos Rodriguez, the chef and owner of a New York restaurant, 1492 Food, which specializes in modern versions of heretic Spanish cuisine (1492 was the year Jews and Muslims were expelled from Spain). Ironically, the Jewish *adafina* (of Moroccan background) became *cocido*, the national dish of Spain. Both are traditionally served in three courses, first the broth with the *relleno* meatballs or matzoh balls, then the vegetables, then the meat. The trial of Ms. Lopez seemed to hinge on this fact, as the prosecutor noted in his charges by writing, "after long cooking, the broth was extracted and the meat awaited . . . and thus she ate it with great devotion that [she] had for the laws of Moses." Beatriz Lopez was burned alive before the Spanish elite in the mid-1500s. A choir sang hymns to drown out her screams.

Make the *Relleno* first.

10 ounces (300 grams) chickpeas
1 pound (½ kilogram) veal shank
4 marrow bones (about ½ inch thick)
1 bone from a serrano ham
½ *morcilla de arroz* (blood sausage)
2 pounds (1 kilogram) cabbage in quarters or large chunks
1 pound (½ kilogram) carrots, thickly chopped
¼ Cornish game hen per person, cut into quarters
6 smallish potatoes, peeled
½ Spanish *chorizo* sausage
5 ounces (150 grams) *tocino* (whole bacon)
6 ounces (180 grams) *fideo* pasta
Salt
Freshly ground pepper

Soak chickpeas overnight, rinse, and pick over. Wrap in a cheesecloth bag and set aside.

Put the veal, marrow bones, ham bone, blood sausage, cabbage, and carrots into about three quarts (three liters) fresh, cold water. Bring to a boil and skim fat. Adjust heat to low and cook uncovered for approximately two and a half hours. Add chickpeas with hen or chicken (chickpeas should be on top), and cook another hour on low. Add peeled whole potatoes, *chorizo* sausage, and *tocino*. Simmer another thirty minutes or until potatoes are tender. Remove all ingredients and put the broth back on low heat and skim again. Season with salt and pepper to taste. You should have approximately two quarts (2 liters) of broth. Serve broth with *relleno* and noodles first. Then serve chickpeas and vegetables as a second course. Finish with the meats (some like to pile vegetables and chickpeas in the center of plate and surround with meat). Dampen with broth. Serves 6.

Relleno

¼ pound lean ground pork, lamb, or veal
1 egg, beaten
½ teaspoon thyme
½ teaspoon oregano
Salt
Fresh black pepper
1 cup bread crumbs or matzoh
Olive oil (for browning)

Combine all ingredients in a bowl and form into about 12 meatballs. Brown in hot olive oil, and set aside, then boil briefly with the *fideo* noodles for the soup course.

If you wish to make this dish kosher, simply replace all pork products with approximately two pounds of boneless lean lamb, cubed. Replace bacon and sausage with one veal foot or four lamb's feet. Add approximately a half dozen cloves of minced garlic and six raw eggs in the shell and approximately a tablespoon of ground cumin, and cook as before. The eggs are cooked like hardboiled eggs in the broth with the other ingredients, but served peeled and cut in half. If you wish, you can cook this for eighteen hours on very, very low heat (use a heat diffuser) or in an oven at 170°F. You should check from time to time to make sure that the liquid covers all ingredients.

The Kosher Question

There is so little agreement on the meaning of Jewish dietary laws that a New York court recently declared it unconstitutional for the government to certify a business as kosher. The rules, they said, were so incomprehensible it would force government employees to interpret religious doctrine thus violating the separation between church and state. In fact, the only thing that seems relatively clear is that the regime known as kosher, or *kashruth*, and its Islamic brother *halal*, both derive loosely from the biblical Book of Leviticus, which details the "beasts which ye shall eat among all the beasts that are on the earth." It lists about one hundred animals from rabbits to salamanders, but the underlying premise is relatively simple. God created the world in three sections, earth, water, and sky. The religious chefs of the day interpreted this to mean that an animal that lived within one of those realms was the Lord YHWH's pet and suitable for dinner. Beasts that straddled the line, however, came from the Devil's menagerie. So, mammals that are cloven-footed and chew the cud are kosher, but the pig, which has a cloven foot but apparently doesn't chew his food properly, is so blasphemous that some Jewish texts refer to it as "that which should not be named." Likewise, a fish with scales and fins belongs to the sea element and is kosher, whereas an amphibious salamander is not.

At any rate, that's the interpretation of some cultural theorists. Scientists persist in speculating that the antiporcine clause relates to pork's tendency to harbor trichinosis. Never mind that this disease is not necessarily fatal, or that cows and lambs were responsible for the much deadlier anthrax plagues. Historians fancy the notion that Jewish pig phobia stems from their stint as slaves in Egypt during the time when the cult of the god Seth held pigs to be exalted beasts. This may also explain the curious reports that certain Jewish cults used to have secret pork feasts once a year. According to scholar Frederick Simoons, when Seth was overthrown, his beloved spareribs became taboo for Egyptians, save for a yearly feast held at the full moon, a habit some Jews might have picked up. Why the full moon? Because the original sacred animal was not the pig, but the similar-looking hippo, which lives on the Moon. Hippos live on the Moon? Well, yes; the idea is that while some Pharaoh was meditating on the full moon reflected in the Nile, a hippo emerged from the reflection. . . .

For obvious reasons, most rabbis have given up on finding a coherent explanation. Even the great twelfth-century rabbinical scholar Maimonides, in his appropriately titled book *Guide for the Perplexed*, suggested that devout Jews should follow the food taboos but view them as an object of meditation and "whatever is possible for him to do in order to find a reason

for [following] it, he should." The result of this advice is the
delightfully Jewish chaos noted by the New York Supreme
Court: some sects ban certain types of fat or particular veins or
tomatoes. Some even express reservations about women suffering a yeast infection over the holiday because it goes against
the Passover ban on fermented substances. Only two questions, however, need concern the civilized creature. Why is traditional kosher wine so second-rate (it is often boiled); and, if
Muslims and Jews are the only people whose laws make them
(almost) each other's ideal dinner guests, why can't they get
along?

The Lawyer in Us

"One must be careful not to be taken in by appearances, even at
Lent feasts held by great ecclesiastics, where scandal should
have been easily avoided," wrote an Italian courtier in the eighteenth century. "I remember one where they appeared to be
serving white soups, red mullet, sole and trout." This note referred to a series of blasphemous feasts held by Roman priests
who'd disguised dishes to accord with Catholic Lenten laws restricting diners to fish and vegetables. The cream soups the letter described turned out to be made of finely minced capon.
That luscious trout on the table, head still on, was actually
pheasant covered in "scales" made of almonds.

This is a rather artistic example of what people will do to cir-
cumvent dietary taboos. There are plenty of simpler examples.
The clergy's classifying of newborn rabbits as "fish" suitable for
eating during Lent created such a demand that it led to the
modern method of rabbit domestication in pens because they
had to be killed as soon as they'd popped out of mama to qualify for the exemption. Missionaries in South America displayed

similar creativity by classifying iguanas as fish because the reptile's propensity for sunning itself in riverside trees revealed its "true nature." The iguana's refined diet of hibiscus flowers made it a welcome addition to fasting clerics, according to one happy abbot, who compared the flavor of saddle of iguana to sweet rabbit, "ugly but very tasty when you get over your disgust." Modern-day Japanese prove themselves no slackers at parsing a rule when they claim their slaughter of whales to provide whale bacon occurs in the course of legitimate scientific research. Hypocritical gibberish, of course, but no more so than that of Americans who bemoan the damage done to the environment by this whale slaughter, and then serenely allow the massive deforestation of Brazilian forests in order to ensure their supply of cheap hamburger meat.

The various vegetarian cults, however, are the most egregious hairsplitters. The Buddha himself put a "don't ask/don't tell" clause in his ban on meat, essentially stating that believers may enjoy *osso bucco* every day of the week if they had no direct and immediate knowledge—preferably typed and notarized— that the meat dish was prepared specifically for them. It's a loophole thousands of hungry Buddhists have driven through. The Tibetans used it to create a caste of Untouchable Muslim butchers, apparently reasoning that a Buddhist is simply incapable of truly understanding what goes on in the mind of a nonbeliever. Others used the precedent to semisanctify top sirloin, arguing that since a chicken and a cow have equal souls, it is better to slaughter a cow, and feed forty, than to slaughter a chicken and feed, at best, four. Pound per soul, the reasoning goes, it's a karmic bargain. The real legal eagles are the Buddhist monks of Thailand, some of whom have decided they can eat fish because they do not kill the creature so much as "remove it from the water."

Perhaps the earliest example of this comes to us in a bit of dialogue from Greece around 500 B.C.

FIRST MAN The Pythagoreans eat no living thing.
SECOND MAN But Epicharides the Pythagorean eats dog.
FIRST MAN Only after he's killed it.

Lent Egg

Lent is the only notable Christian dietary law, a forty-day regime leading up to Easter, during which one is supposed to forgo strong food like meat and eggs and even milk. Pretty mild stuff, despite which the counterfeiting of food for Lent became a minor art form in the Middle Ages. There was fake bacon in which salmon was made into a kind of pâté laced with pureed pike fish and almond milk to replicate the pork fat. The following curiosity comes from *A Noble Boke of Cookry: For a Prynch [Prince] Houssolde or Another Estately Houssolde*, a fifteenth-century cookbook largely devoted to this counterfeit cuisine. The translation, done by a Mrs. Alexander Napier in 1882, leaves much of the original medieval spelling intact, as have I (with some clarifications).

To roft egs in Lent take and blowe out the mete [meat, i.e., yolk and white] at the end of the egg and washe the shelles with warme water. Then take thick milk of almond and set it to the fyere till it be at the boiling. Then put it in a canvas and let the water run out and keep all that hangeth in the clothe and gadur it to gedure [gather it together] in a dyshe. Then put it to white sugar and colour one half with saffron and [add to flavor] pou-

dered ginger and cinnamon. Then put some of the white [unfla-
vored] in the eggshell and in the middle put in of the yellow to
be the yolk and fill it up with white. Then sit it in the fire to
roast. To fifteen eggs take a pound of almond milk and a quarter
of ginger and cinnamon.

𝒜 𝒲𝑒𝓁𝓁-𝑅𝒾𝓈𝑒𝓃 𝑀𝑒𝓈𝓈𝒾𝒶𝒽

Jewish cooks weren't the only ones persecuted for heretic cooking. Christian Europe actually tore itself in two because of a
squabble over a cookie recipe. A wafer, actually—or would that
be biscuit?—the one representing Jesus and served at the High
Mass. The Orthodox wing of the church, which dominates
Eastern Europe, Russia, and Greece, had always served a well-
risen, chewy Son of God at their Mass. The Romans preferred a
flat, crackerlike treat. In A.D. 1054 two leaders finally got together to create a unified recipe. There was plenty of room for
compromise, but judging from the two men's preconfab correspondence, the impending disaster was probably unavoidable.
"Unleavened bread is dead and lifeless," went one letter from
the Orthodox side, represented by Michael Cerularius, "because it lacks leaven, which is the soul, and salt, which is the
mind of the Messiah." Nonsense, had been the reply from the
Catholics' Cardinal Humbert. "If you do not with stubborn
mind stand in opposition to the plain truth," he wrote to Cerularius, "you will have to think as we do and confess that during
the meal (the Last Supper) it was unleavened bread Jesus Christ
distributed."

The exact reasons for these different recipes are rather
complex. The Orthodox Church believes that the leavening
that makes bread rise represents the life force of Christ. Greek

housewives still claim their breads rise by the will of Christ, in recollection of his ascension from the dead, and they lace special loaves with dried flowers from the altar. The Roman Catholic recipe comes from the matzoh bread Hebrews serve at Passover, a flat, crackerish fellow that was left unleavened because the Jews were in such a rush to get out of Egypt that there was no time to let the bread rise. Not that the Vatican was going to cop to "Jewish tendencies"—one of Humbert's main kvetches was that Orthodox leaders were "persecuting [Catholics] by calling them *Matzists*" because they used matzoh bread at Mass.

The two sides could easily have split the difference and opted for pita: delicious, easily stuffed, and only *partially* risen. But the negotiations didn't really get off on the right foot. In fact, it's not clear they ever got off at all. The Catholic Humbert, renowned for his unpleasant disposition, arrived in Istanbul after a long journey and was already furious over a letter he thought Cerularius had written condemning the Catholic wafer. Cerularius, however, had never even seen the letter, much less penned it—a Bulgarian archbishop was the author—and when some foreigner showed up at his house unannounced, shrieking about crackers and a mysterious letter, Cerularius failed to extend his fullest hospitality. It seems the Catholic Humbert had forgotten to write he was dropping by to discuss some theological disputes, and Cerularius came to the conclusion that Humbert was a spy *posing* as a papal ambassador. After a few days of cooling his heels in the Patriarch's reception room, Humbert packed his bags and headed back to Rome. On his way out he declared Cerularius, who was the head of the Orthodox Church, a blasphemer and emphasized his displeasure by nailing the order of excommunication to the Orthodox Church's holiest spot, the altar of St. Sophia in Istanbul. "Mad Michael [Cerularius], inappropriately named Patriarch," began the letter, and that was the nicest part. Cerularius returned the favor by declaring the Romans heretics for their *matzist* tendencies. He also banned shared meals between Orthodox and Catholic clergy.

This dispute split the world's most powerful organization in half and set in motion events that would divide Europe for centuries. It was this dispute that the Crusaders cited when they defiled the Orthodox Church by setting a prostitute on Cerularius's throne in 1204. The division between the two churches also sufficiently weakened the Christian empire to allow the Ottoman Turks to conquer Eastern Europe. This, in turn, laid the groundwork for Russian domination of Eastern Europe and set the boundaries of the Soviet Union's Iron Curtain. Even the recent Serbian conflict was affected—the Russians were reluctant to bomb Serbia because they both belonged to the Orthodox Church and shared a long history of being dressed down by self-righteous hypocrites from the West. The two churches finally made up nine-hundred-plus years later in 1965.

For What We Are About to Receive

We all know the routine of thanking Him before we break bread. "Oh, Lord, on this day/We Thank Ye for our daily bread. . . ." It's only good manners: God created the world that we feed upon and so as good guests we have to thank him. But not everyone views the situation that way. The Sherpa people of Nepal consider the gods as the guests, and moreover ones who had better behave Themselves. "They make the explicit analogy between the offering ritual and social hospitality," writes anthropologist Sherry Ortner. "The people are hosts, the gods their guests . . . who they make happy so they will want to help humanity." These Sherpa ceremonies start off a bit like a frat party. Incense is burned, loud music is played, and beer is poured out the window so "the guys" (normally local entities) will know there's a happening. When the supernatural guests arrive, they are invited to seat themselves in bread-and-butter sculptures that are up to seven feet high called *tormas*. To make sure there're no gate-crashers, similar bread-and-butter sculptures, *gyeks,* are baked for the demons and then tossed out the temple door as far as they can be thrown. Then an appetizer, usually seared fat from a goat's heart, is served to the guests, followed by a smorgasbord of *tso* (cooked) dishes. This party, however, is not about buttering up the deities and earning goodwill. The Sherpas are putting their guests under an obligation. "I am offering you the things which you eat," their prayer goes, "now You must do whatever I demand." Lest the gods think this thinly veiled coercion presumptuous, the Sherpas remind them it is the sacred duty of *all* guests not to offend their hosts, saying "that is not *my* order, but you have promised to work for me in the beginning of time. . . ."

O, Dog

"No one's eating dogs anymore," said Don Climent, head of San Francisco's International Rescue Committee. "My Laotian clients just needed information on what's acceptable to Americans in relationship to dogs. Besides, I think they were more interested in the squirrels."

Climent was explaining to me how it was that a group of dog lovers from Laos caused a national panic in the early 1980s.

It started one day in August when some cops found five head-less dogs lying in San Francisco's Golden Gate Park. As the offi-cers stood puzzling over the situation (now if I were a dog, where would I hide *my* head?), they noticed a number of Asians armed with bows and arrows wandering about. The dogs, it seemed, belonged to the Laotians in the gustatory sense. The incident appeared in the papers, and overnight Californians realized that a tribe of quasi-cannibals had invaded their state. Filipino sailors were accused of sneaking into suburbs for noc-turnal dog hunts. A lady in Sacramento discovered her chil-dren's favorite pooch hanging by its tail at a neighborhood barbecue, skinned, flayed, and waiting for the kiss of the smok-ing grill. A San Francisco man found his spaniel in a Chinese neighbor's garage under suspicious circumstances. A law pro-tecting pets was immediately proposed. Politicians fumed, im-migrant groups rationalized, and a brown-and-white springer spaniel named Ringo appeared before the California Assembly wearing a T-shirt emblazoned with "I'm for Loving NOT for EATING!" It all went to prove that there are two distinct species of dog in the world. There's the Western dog, hair flying in the wind as he rushes to the rescue, a pampered, petted deity Europeans revered so much they used dog blood in early trans-fusions. The other kind of dog is also loved, preferably roasted, sometimes sautéed. The Chinese call them "hornless goats" or "fragrant meat," and in some restaurants you can pick out which puppy you want cooked for dinner. Connoisseurs rec-ommend red-haired mutts with sprightly ears and black tongues for their veal-like flesh. Dog is an honorary dish, and the Vietnamese say, "It's going ill for the dogs," if a legal dispute is dragging on, because it was the custom to serve roast pup at all negotiations.

The Asian cultures are the only modern dog eaters, but the

most developed canine cuisine belongs to the people of the Pacific Isles and the New World. The Aztecs had huge puppy farms in which they bred a stocky chocolate-brown pooch related to the hairless Chihuahua. "There were four hundred large and small dogs tied up in crates, some already sold, some still for sale," wrote Spanish missionary Fray Diego Duran in the early 1500s. "And there were such piles of ordure that I was overwhelmed! When a Spaniard who was totally familiar with that region saw my amazement he asked 'But why are you astonished, my friend? I have never seen such a meager supply of dogs as today!' There was a tremendous shortage of them!" The Polynesians and Hawaiians had similar ranches where they raised poi dogs so toothsome that they were largely reserved for the king. The now-extinct poi was a curious creature: bug-eyed and unnaturally plump, it was a strict vegetarian that lived on nothing but sweet potatoes and soup. European visitors described them as semi-amphibious and so lacking in energy they eschewed barking in favor of listless little yelps. They were not, however, mere livestock. Dogs were often spiritually tied to a specific child, like a pet, and were breast-fed with the child at the mother's breast (a courtesy still offered to young piglets in some areas). If a child died, his or her puppy was killed and buried alongside to guard the infant during its journey in the afterlife. If it was the dog that passed away first, its teeth became a necklace the child wore to ward off sorcery. Dinner, however, was the more common fate. The puppy was usually suffocated by blocking its mouth and nostrils for fifteen minutes. Its delicious blood was made into a pudding by adding hot stones to the liquid, but the body was roasted luau-style in a pit covered with banana leaves and earth. "Few there were of the nicest of us," wrote Sir Joseph Banks of his time with Captain Cook's eighteenth-century expedition "but allowed a South Sea dog was next to an English lamb."

The when, where, how, and why of this split in humanity's feelings for the species is still hotly debated. Dogs are thought to have initially accepted humans as near-equals about 12,000 years ago, although some put the date as early as 125,000 years ago. The first alliance was over hunting, with humans relying on the wild dogs' keen sense of smell, while the dogs benefited from our weapons and flexible fingers. Canine historian Mary Thurston reports that as late as 1870 Native American hunters were followed by wolves for weeks, "at a distance of half a mile or so and at night, when he [the Indian] lies down to sleep, they will also crouch at a respectful distance." This business relationship turned personal when people adopted pups left orphaned by the packs that had begun to hang about the human tribes, a phenomenon which still occurs between Australia's Aborigines and the wild dingo dogs that loiter near their settlements.

The first dog worshipers were the followers of the Egyptian god Anubis who, 3,500 years ago, preached that their dog-headed deity walked humans to the afterlife. At one point they had a religious city populated by canine "priests" that humans petted to improve their karma, and archaeologists have found thousands of mummified puppies that were used in much the same way as Christians use crosses. The Romans later morphed this idea into "dog hospitals," where the ailing were given a healing lick. The thirteenth-century Italian St. Roch became famous for a "miracle dog" that kept him alive by feeding him with stolen bread. It is still the custom during the saint's mid-August festival to let all the village dogs into the church, where they are fed pastries.

The stronghold of the don't-eat-the-damn-dog contingent

seems to have been in Europe, perhaps because the colder climate killed off many edible plants and made hunting essential. My personal belief is that in this era humans and dogs actually ate and slept as equals, rubbing shoulders around the campfire, just as we do now. This hunting bond was so intense that until a few hundred years ago, European hunters still ritually gave their dogs the "soul" of any stag they'd hunted together by soaking bread in the prey's blood (thought to contain its soul), and then rewrapping it in the stag's skin. The dogs would then again tear the animal apart and devour its "soul" while the humans held the stag's head over the feasting pack. For some reason this relationship faded as humans headed east from Europe and into the Americas, at least as indicated by the practices of people from Asia to Mexico. But who really knows why such radically different attitudes developed? Islamic disgust for the canine species apparently formed when they conquered the Persian Zoroastrians around the eighth century. The Persians, it seems, had worshiped dogs and considered killing or eating them a crime, and as part of their cultural subjugation of the area, the Muslims took the opposite stance. The Californians, however, chose neither to demonize nor deify. Torn between the desire to be two kinds of politically correct—culturally sensitive and kind to animals—the politicians simply returned the legislation outlawing dog meat to committee for further consideration. That was in 1982. It has yet to reemerge.

Holy Cow

The weekly market in the coastal village of Anjuna, India, can be quite the scene. Rajasthani women peddle ten-pound silver bracelets; Nepalese merchants offer carved human skulls; English junkies pawn their tennis shoes; neo-Eastern-synthotechno-house-acid-rave-hip-hop-didgeridoo sound tracks fill the air. And there are celebrities everywhere—Julia Cow, Harrison Cow and, yes, even Keanu Reeves Cow—wandering about and mooing at anyone who fails to show respect. My beloved Nina J. and I had our own booth in Anjuna once upon a time. She peddled a soothing balm made of sandalwood. I sold delicious little gâteaus of honey and coconut. Business was rather slow until one day a cowlebrity swooped down on our humble little stall, and in one long, lascivious lick, inhaled every cake I possessed. It also blessed Nina's perfumes with a liberal douse of spittle. Nina and I were ecstatic, and, just to be sure everyone remembered our celebrity clientele, we built a papier-mâché cow's head, complete with a pair of glorious golden horns. The cakes looked splendid on its foot-long hot pink cardboard tongue the next market day. But not for long: our two-legged customers were soon lapping them up as quickly (if with less drool) as our Bollywood friend had the week before.

Indian cows live in a realm above and beyond the ordinary travails of mere mortals. Each and every one of them is said to house 330 million deities: Shiva has the nose and his sons the nostrils, while the tail belongs to Sri Hanar, the goddess of cleanliness. This extreme overcrowding means cows drip sanctity. All their products are sacred. Food cooked in butter is called *pacca*, and it's karmically delicious as a result of its submersion in a cow product. Lesser foods are called *kacca*. Some Hindus refuse to eat cauliflower because the Hindi word for it, *gobi*, is heretically close to that of cow, *gopa*. High-born Hindus returning from life abroad are often obliged to eat a pellet made of butter, yogurt, and urine, all bound up nicely with a bit of dung, to repurify themselves after life among the heathens.

Needless to say, no dutiful Hindu would think of eating the beast. It's a food taboo that has been widely criticized in the

West; how can a country where millions of people die every year from malnutrition, wails the Texas Cattle Rearing Association, afford "cow retirement" homes so a useless animal can end its days in peace? What's so special about a goddamn cow? The religious response is simple enough. In Hindu theosophy, it takes eighty-six reincarnations for a soul to climb up from a devil to a cow, but only one to leap the gap separating cattle from humankind. Hence, that steak on your dinner plate might have contained the soul of your newborn child. Historians prefer the idea that Hindu religious leaders became cow lovers two thousand years ago to prove that they were more compassionate than those upstart Buddhists. The ecological defense is that the cow's enormously complicated digestive system, comprising four stomachs, can turn the most wretched of weeds into milk, people food that is both delicious and nutritious. Its dung, dried and molded into patties, provides crucial fuel in the deforested continent. Its piss, chilled, has the same tart flavors associated with Chablis. To wantonly murder such a resource would be ludicrous. Rather, it is the West's steak fetish that is illogical, because the twenty-two pounds of grain needed to produce one pound of beef diverts human food resources to feed livestock.

Not that anyone is seriously suggesting that the Hindu fetish derives from a deeply logical impulse. Their passion runs too hot for that. When Indian Muslims want to start a ruckus, they need merely to drive a herd of implied ground round past a Hindu shrine. The Hindus elicit equally enthusiastic responses when they "accidentally" lead flocks of pigs to the nearest mosque. There are riots, murders, then everybody goes home with the glow of sanctity staining their cheeks.

It's the English, however, who proved themselves the masters of boor-dom by offending both Muslims and Hindus in one fell stroke. When the East India Company, then in control of India, armed their native troops with the Enfield rifle in the mid-1800s, the weapon was cutting-edge stuff: three times more accurate and ten times as fast on the reload. The secret was the grease that encased every Enfield bullet. Unfortunately, this supergrease was made from pig and cow fat, the two animals sacred or taboo to every native on the subcontinent. The fact that the soldiers had to bite off the bullet's tip to load the rifle was pure bad luck. The Indian officers explained their dilemma to the British. If we touch this bullet—much less put it in our mouths!—we will become Untouchables. How will we find wives? Our own mothers will disown us! The English officers wrote to London and urged that the bullets be coated in mutton fat. London bureaucrats told them not to be silly. Indian soldiers started to mutiny. Unrest spread throughout the region.

Then out of the jungle trotted a *sadhu* with four pieces of chapati bread stuck in his turban. To this day the Indians claim to be clueless as to the meaning of the Chapati Movement of 1857, but it appears to have been a culinary chain letter. The first *sadhu* gave his four chapati breads to a village elder with the message to share them with everyone in the village and then bake four more, which in turn were to be delivered to the next village with the same message, etc., etc. Historian Christopher Hibbert speculates that the chapati movement referred to rumors that the British were adding ground cow bones to local flour so as to destroy India's religious structure and facilitate converting the continent to Christianity. At the time, however, no one knew what it might mean, and everybody was on edge. The breaking point came when an Untouchable asked an Indian soldier for a drink from his canteen. When the soldier politely cited his caste as grounds for refusal, the Untouchable said,

"What does it matter? Soon you will be without any caste just like me. You chew the taboo bullets. Cow killer! Pig lover! You are all just Untouchables!"

The Hindu soldiers went wild and started massacring not just the English officials, but women and children. The British responded with a lamentable lack of restraint. They killed innocent children and shot rebelling soldiers out of cannons. Taking up the culinary motif, they sewed some Hindu soldiers into cow carcasses and left them to suffocate. Their behavior was so louche that the British government decided to take India away from the East India Company and make it a member of the British Empire. In fact, this early revolution probably failed only because the Indian soldiers, who outnumbered the English twenty-five to one, refused to use the hated Enfield rifles during the fight.

Revolutions over cow fat, riots over roast beef—it strikes Westerners as preposterous until you realize that we, too, have massacred and tortured thousands over the exact same issue. The first known portrait of God is a horned figure dancing on the walls of a Paleolithic cave in France. Horns, it seems, have always been a sign of supersexual or supernatural power. The ancient Babylonians used them like military stripes and gave their more powerful spirits an impossible number, like the seven-horned lamb in the Bible's Book of Revelation. At some point this horn fetish became focused on cattle. From the Greeks' bull-headed Minotaur to the mysterious horn temples of ancient Ur to the modern bullfights of Spain, the entire cradle of Western civilization was once a den of cattle worship. The most eccentric was the early Egyptian cult of Apis, in which a cow or bull was selected based on certain markings and worshiped as a god. The animal was particularly revered by baby-seeking ladies who flashed their genitals at the bemused beast to ensure conception. A pagan horned deity surrounded by naked women indulging in obscene rituals—any medieval Christian would have recognized HIM in a second. Witches kissing the Horned One's ass were little more than overwrought cow lovers. The Judeo-Christian Church had simply demonized earlier religions and turned the horned deity into Uncle Nick, first in the Golden Calf so disliked by Moses, and then in the horned Lucifer. People who persisted in this original faith were tortured, tenderized, and roasted at the stake. When Linda Blair was possessed by the Devil in Hollywood's *The Exorcist*, she shouldn't have spewed vomit and obscenities. She should have mooed.

You and Your Beautiful Hide

He was the most elongated man I'd ever met, seven feet tall, with ears that hung down to his shoulders. Would have made a terrier pup jealous. The Masai of northern Kenya are famous for elongating their earlobes to enhance their natural good looks, and his must have made him look pretty sweet. His outfit, however, left a little to be desired. He'd given up those traditional bloodred Masai robes and spears for a grimy guard's uniform and a shotgun, which he pointed at everyone who dared to enter the courtyard of our little hotel in the town of Isiolo. But he was definitely a Masai and loved nothing better than to talk about his family's cattle.

"We only have a few," he told me sadly while we shared a cigarette. "Ah, but they are just so beautiful. If you saw them . . ."

Everybody loves a good steak, but the beefy passions of

the Masai people of northeast Africa are so intense, so soul-consuming, that anthropologists have suggested they suffer from a collective neurosis called "the cattle complex." They pray to the beasts. They polish their horns. They drink their blood. They even name their children after cows. And every night, dressed in traditional crimson robes, spears in hand, the giant warrior-herders sing their beloved moo-moos to sleep.

> *God gave you to us long ago*
> *You are in our hearts*
> *Your smell is sweet to us.*

But is this true love? Anthropologists Keith Hart and Louise Sperling found crucial differences between the Masai and Hindu cattle fetishes. For one thing, the Masai eat their loved ones. Reluctantly, true, and they get the animals drunk before their throats are slit, but eat them they do, and apparently with gusto. The wills of high-ranking tribesman usually contain instructions on which members of his herd should be eaten at his wake and which skins he wishes to be buried in. In fact, it's actually a point of pride to live upon nothing but cow products, mainly milk and blood mixed together, or a kind of cheese made by curdling milk with cow urine. The only combination not allowed is milk and meat together, and the Masai will always take a special herb to make them vomit out any milk they have drunk before they eat beef. To eat anything "not cow," or even mix vegetables with cow products, is allowed, but it's terribly déclassé. The ultimate disgrace is to be banned to one of the tribes that actually grow and eat vegetables.

Equally odd is that although the Masai language has more than ten adjectives exclusively devoted to describing a cow's charms, they appear to be indifferent to the quality of any given animal. It's only the *size* of a man's herd that matters, and the chief's advisers are chosen not based on blood relation or geography, as is typical, but by the number of animals they own. I should say the number of animals they *stole*; the Masai are notorious cattle raiders (they don't view it as theft), and at one point owned 1 million head among forty thousand people. The anthropologists' conclusion was that a cow is no more sacred to the Masai than a lucrative NASDAQ share is to a Wall Street stockbroker. "Pastoral nomads (like the Masai) are some of the thickest-skinned capitalists on earth," they wrote in their paper *Cattle as Capital*, "and view the cattle as self-reproducing commodities ... representing future consumption." Their reluctance to sell or eat their animals is simply the capitalist's eternal hope for higher returns on the morrow.

The security guard I met that night would probably not have agreed. It was just one of those chance encounters that happens when one travels about mindlessly for months at a time. I was trying to meet a friend up toward the Ethiopian border and had gotten stuck in Isiolo because bandits had made trucks shy about heading north. I certainly had no interest in cows. But it's hard to avoid the topic when talking to Masai. My friend that starry desert night told me how the god Engapi used to send all the world's cattle to the Masai on a string between Heaven and Earth. When the Masai carelessly allowed the string to break, Engapi sentenced them to a life of "gathering" up all the cattle that were (of course) rightfully theirs. He told me that in his father's day his tribe had owned hundreds of cattle. He even reminisced about the great cattle wars when the men would form raiding bands with names like "Red Bull," because naming the group after a bull made them more attractive to the cattle.

One of their favorite tricks was to shoot arrows up in the air; when the dirt-loving farmers covered their heads with their shields, he said, they were shot in the stomach. Ha! Ha! Ha! He laughed, throwing his shotgun over his shoulder. Such foolish people!

ANGER

"Meat eaters are generally crueler and more ferocious than other men; the observation is from all places and all times. English barbarism is well known in this regard . . ."

Rousseau
Emile

A N G E R   M E N U

A P É R I T I F
Kir Royale
Champagne stained bloodred with crème de cassis

A M U S E - B O U C H E
Insanity Popcorn
Traditional popped kernels flecked with vicious chile.
(Recipe on page 241)

F I R S T   C O U R S E
Wagyu Beef Kabobs
Free-range beer-fed beef which was massaged to death.
Served saignant.

P L A T   P R I N C I P A L
The Sadean Goose
Served in two styles: seared liver with wild chanterelle
mushrooms (recipe page 237), and breast au jus,
roasted alive

VEGETARIAN OPTION

Buddha's Delight
(Lo Han Jai)

Winter-vegetable stew, cooked according to the precepts of the
Doctrine of Five Angry Vegetables (recipe page 246)

DESSERT

Twelve-Foot Trifles
Candied Jellies
Liquor-Soaked Muscadines
Mincemeat Pies
Plum Tarts
Raspberry Fools
Fruits Sauvage

Served in a traditional Tudor food fight.
Casual attire advised.

In the case that the host sets the house ablaze, guests are advised
to exit in an orderly manner.

The Civilized Sauce

Neurologists tell us that hunger and aggression are controlled by the same small part of the brain. Stick your finger in the hypothalamus region, they say, and people (or at least animals) will be overcome with an urge to attack or eat. Putting aside the question of some scientists' kinky habits, this finding highlights how deeply the two impulses are linked. It's classic Pavlov. Millenniums of sating our hunger by attacking other organisms has left us neuro-wired to feel the same impulse upon sighting a *saignant* steak as our Neanderthal ancestors did when they laid eyes on a juicy-looking mastodon: Kill it, grill it, sauce it, and eat it.

This instinctual connection between anger and eating is expressed in a number of curious ways. Some cultures wage war by throwing feasts in which victory is achieved when the enemy is unable to eat another bite. Others have banned foods with characteristics thought to induce violent behavior, a school of thought epitomized by the cult of vegetarianism. Fourteenth century Turkey actually created an army of cooks called the Janissary. Originally members of the Sultan's kitchen staff, these merciless killers were called the *ocak*, or hearth, and used a *qaza sarf*, or cooking pot, as their symbol. Officers were called *sorbadji*, soup men, and wore a special spoon in their headgear. Other ranks included *cörekci*, baker, and *gözlemici*, pancake maker. The highest officer was, of course, called Head Cook and when he decided to overthrow the Sultan—something he did with regularity—he called his followers into the kitchen and overturned a cauldron of soup, thus symbolically rejecting the Sultan's provender and all his policies.

The most refined reaction to the violence of eating came in Europe, which developed a style of cooking intent on removing all angry emotions from the dinner table. The secret was a good sauce, and the revolution reached its peak in the 1800s, according to writer Chatillon-Plessis, who divided the continent at the time into two groups: the "bleeding dish nations," like Germany and England, which served their meat in a savage and barbaric sauceless state, and the "sauce nations" like the French. "Compare these two," he wrote in his *La Vie à la table à la fin du 19th siècle*, "and see whether the character of the latter is not more civilized." Along with a growing propensity for concealing our meat under a blanket of *bernaise*, the tradition of carving whole carcasses before dinner guests disappeared, save for holidays, where custom demands we continue to attack defenseless animals like a pack of wolves. "Cruelty, violence and barbarism were the characteristics of men who fed upon the fiber of half-dressed meat," opined English social critic Lady Morgan, "[whereas] humanity, knowledge and refinement belong to the living generation, whose tastes and temperance are regulated by the science of such philosophers as Carême [a famous Parisian chef]." The hope was that by concealing the natural savagery of the rite known as dinner, one could wean man from his other, more barbaric, habits and world peace would ensue. Instead we ended up with the modern American supermarket, where nary a clue remains to remind consumers that they are walking in a mausoleum of death and suffering. All is sparkling white, celestial light, angelic muzak. Or, at least, so it seems on the surface.

The Sadistic Chef

Infants are ripped from the womb and thrown into boiling oil. There're dead bodies, flames, and the stench of burning flesh. Men in bloodstained smocks—their eyes bloodshot from wine and heat—scream abuse at the underlings. Grate, pound, whip, beat, sear, burn, blacken, chop, crack, mince; *Throw it on the grill,* the head chef growls, *and don't dare take it off until it's COM-PLETELY done, do you understand?*

"A true gourmand," wrote nineteenth-century gastronome Brillat-Savarin, "is as insensible to suffering as is a conqueror." My preceding description of a restaurant kitchen may be considered an exaggeration, but Savarin's comment was all too typical of his age. His contemporaries recommended that cooks tenderize their meat by whipping the animals to death. Pigs had red-hot irons thrust into their living bodies to make the meat "sweet and tender," and eels were thrown alive into the fire for extra flavor. True gourmets had pregnant sows kicked to death in order to mingle their milk with the embryos, which were then removed and served forth. One recipe recommended that geese be plucked, basted with butter, and then roasted alive. "But make not haste," instructs the seventeenth-century cook-book, which suggests placing dishes of water at the bird's side to ensure it does not die of thirst before properly cooked. The bird is done, the author writes, when "you see him run mad up and down, and to stumble . . . wherefore take him and set him on the table to our guests who will cry out as you pull off his parts; and you shall almost eat him up before he is dead!"

These practices, common up until the eighteenth century, were ostensibly done to produce a more succulent dish. The ancient Romans, however, were unapologetic about serving violence as an aperitif to revive the jaded palate. Some hosts executed criminals or staged gladiator duels on the dining table. But most merely let their guests watch the first course slowly die *à table*, according to Seneca.

> Mullets enclosed in glass jars are brought and their colour observed as they die. As they struggle for air death changes their colour into many hues. Others are killed by being pickled alive in garum (vinegar). . . . "There is nothing," you say, "more beautiful than a dying mullet. Let me hold in my hands the glass jar where the fish may leap and quiver in the struggle for life. See how the red becomes inflamed, more brilliant than any vermilion! Look at the veins which pulse along its sides! Look! You would think its belly were actual blood! What a bright kind of blue gleamed right under its brow! Now, between life and death, it is stretching out and going pale into a gradation of colour of infinitely subtle shades."

The old Romans found this appetizing, the theory goes, because they were more in touch with the essentially violent nature of the human species. Be that as it may, governments today have made these kinds of culinary highjinks illegal, and restauranteurs now go to enormous lengths to prove that their steaks died with a smile. Japan's famously effeminate Wagyu cattle, whose flesh sells for $150 a pound, enjoy free beer and massages before having their throats slit. Livestock raisers like California's Niman Ranch have made a fortune by claiming that their animals are not only killed in a painless manner, but spend their lives in a kind of free-range Club Med. And just as our ancestors' science believed that their sadistic cuisine was both healthy and delicious—some butchers who failed to torture their wares faced criminal prosecution—today's professors have conclusively proven that nice tastes nicer. Their secret elixir is glycogen, a carbohydrate found in animal tissue that provides energy for immediate action. If an animal dies after a horrific struggle, or even in extreme shock, its glycogen is depleted. This leads to tougher, more pungent meat, because when the animal dies its glycogen breaks down the flesh to make it more tender and flavorful. A cow that has died while stressed out, it seems, tastes like death. One that dies well rested is merely delicious.

Deep-Fried Murder

The notion that anger should be completely disassociated from eating has gone far beyond a question of sauce or butchering technique. The smallest clue that our food came from a living thing has become virtually taboo, as amply illustrated by a visit to any modern supermarket. Cattle are carefully ground up into a polite puree. Chickens come cubed and breaded. One rarely sees a head or hoof, and many children would no doubt be horrified to realize that their morning bacon once belonged to a cuddly little piggy-poo. Not everyone is pleased with this evisceration. Where, whine our intelligentsia, is the sweat of the farmer's brow, the anguish of the hunted beast? They should look in the snack-food aisle, where delights like potato chips have been specifically engineered to heighten the vicarious violence beloved by America's football warriors. Approximately half of the $19 billion worth of snack foods sold in the United

States every year falls into the category of "crunch" snacks. This sector increases about 50 percent every decade, but the fastest-growing subsector within the crunch family are the so-called "extreme foods," which put a premium on extreme auditory effects associated with anger: the splintering of skulls, the screams, the shattering bones, the sound track of mankind on the rampage.

Take a bag of Krunchers, which advertises it sells "no wimpy chips." First comes packaging designed to create a battle between bag and man, in which the latter drags his prey to ground and then, straining and swearing, disembowels it with his bare hands. The chips inside are almost useless as food. Just fat and salt. It's their shrieks of terror that we crave. In his book *The Secret House*, science writer David Bodanis does a marvelous job of explaining how every aspect of the product is designed by food engineers to manipulate our instinctual aggression. The chips themselves are made too large to close your mouth around, so their high-frequency roar will curve around your face and reach your ears without any loss of volume. They're also packed with miniscule, air-filled "cells" that cause "shrapnels of flying starch and fat" to ricochet within the mouth and produce more of that lovely roar. Bodanis notes the essential violence of the experience when he writes that further chaos is ensured by the "broken fragments boomeranging at high speed inside the now vacated cells, like the lethal metal slivers broken loose inside an enemy tank by the latest shoulder-fired optically tracked missiles. . . ."

Corporations refer to this as "exciting" and grow cagey when asked about the relationship. No doubt Frito-Lay's use of heavyweight boxing champion George Foreman as their spokesman was mere coincidence. It all really amounts to using a simulacrum of violence to whet our appetite, hence high-tech snacks like 3-D Doritos, which supposedly double the potential volume by creating an air pocket between two walls of high-tensile corn "glass." A tingling chili flavor is added to give us the teeniest adrenaline rush by simulating a mild burning sensation. Food futurists have speculated that chips like these will eventually contain chemical stimulants much like the increasingly controversial hypercaffeinated sodas and "herb" drinks flooding the markets.

It's a trend that causes people like *Salon*'s David Futrelle to question the long-term effect on our already jaded sensory threshold. "Taste in many cases is secondary; we're talking food as entertainment," he wrote, comparing some of the crunch snacks to violent video games. Both create not only similar thrills, but also similar action/response conditioning; just replace the tinny explosions and shrieks the video characters make as they are zapped with the chips' high-frequency roar as they are chewed. While most people accept that violent visual entertainment can inspire real anger, the impact of their culinary cousins is considerably murkier. A person eating a mouthful of potato chips is experiencing an approximately one-hundred-decibel sound level. According to a NASA study, 65 decibels of sporadic noise can cause a 40 percent rise in hypertension and mental illness, especially among children; other studies have found increased anxiety at levels as low as 51 decibels. Laboratory experiments involving college students found that the louder the noise the more aggressive people become. At 95 decibels of sporadic bursts of sound—roughly the volume of most crunchy snack foods—the students showed significant increased aggression. More important, their aggressive behavior continued after the noise ceased.

"One aspect of this [appeal of crunchy foods] is definitely a primitive sense of the act of destruction," said Alan Hirsch,

Neurological Director of the Smell and Taste Treatment and Research Foundation in Chicago. "When you destroy you get a certain sense of power, and that's why many people find the sensation of 'breaking' these foods so satisfying—they were expressing their subliminal anger."

If, as brain specialists say, eating and aggression emanate from the same part of the brain, which appetite does the crunch of the potato chip stimulate? We know junk-food junkies usually reach for their treats in moments of anxiety, but nobody knows if they're experiencing something that enhances their anger or something that soothes it. Hirsch believes high-crunch snacks probably act as a catharsis because the consumer has control over the sound, a belief that appears to be borne out by other sound/anger experiments. Violent visual entertainment, however, also has a cathartic element. Certainly, the connection between junk food and uncontrolled anger has been validated by the numerous juvenile detention facilities that have halved inmate violence by simply eliminating junk snacks from their inmates' diets. While experiments like these were focused on the effect of excessive sugar and salt typically contained in snack foods, the blood tests performed for hypoglycemia and lower blood sugar did not adequately explain the drop in violence, according to a paper by Stephen Schoenthaler in the *International Journal of Biosocial Research*. At any rate, there seems to be little doubt that crunch has a psychological impact. According to Hirsch, one study involving 3,193 people indicated that habitués develop a distinct "crunch craving" third in intensity only to cravings for chocolate and salt.

No one is implying that snack food manufacturers want to stimulate violent behavior. They just want to make their snacks fun to eat. The problem, if there is one, may lie in the average

American's growing inability to distinguish between the two concepts. Even our favorite beverages are a form of pleasant torture. Nobody drinks flat soda, because the drink's key, if not sole pleasure lies in the subclinical trigeminal pain caused by those bubbles of carbon dioxide exploding on the tongue. Without them they are as exciting as, well, a flat Coke. But then, every culture has its own way of invoking subliminal violence to stimulate appetite. The next time you go to a traditional French restaurant, take a moment to meditate on your *kir royale*; how the tongue shudders with titillating pinpricks as the bubbles explode; the way the champagne, stained bloodred with *cassis* liqueur, writhes sanguine in the candlelight. Time to eat.

Only if It Has a Face

A peach drifts down like an errant autumn leaf. You pick it up with a sleepy smile and take a bite. No need to peel, for you know it will be honey-sweet, soft, luscious, and divine. Perhaps you share it with a friend, and, sitting in the tree's fragrant shadow, the two of you make love before slipping into the perfect sleep. You wake up in the dead of night. Something wet is crawling across your feet. You look down and see a huge sabertooth tiger licking your toes. But no worries, mate. You are in the Muslims' *al-jannah*, the Greeks' Arcadia, the Druids' Avalon, the Judaic Eden, or one of a dozen primordial paradises that many religions remember as the place where we once lived free of death or fear or hunger or—most important of all—red meat.

The connection between the vegetarian diet and paradise is thought by some to date back to the Miocene period 8 million years ago, when it is conjectured that large parts of the Earth may have been free of significant predators, and hominoids, like everyone else, were strict vegetarians. The collective memory of this time, according to writers like Colin Spencer, supplied the imagery for this 2,500-year-old poem of paradise credited to Pythagoras.

> *There are the crops,*
> *Apples that bend the branches with their weight*
> *Grapes swelling on the vines: there are fresh herbs*
> *And those the tempered flame makes mellow*
> *Milk is ungrudged and honey from the thyme*
> *Earth lavishes her wealth, gives sustenance*
> *Benign, spreads, feasts unstained by blood and death*

This prehistoric love fest is thought to have evaporated when the weather went ratty and we were forced to become hunters. According to some dieticians, the increased protein provided by the switch to a carnivorous diet caused an unprecedented growth spurt of the part of the brain called the cerebrum responsible for higher reasoning. This quasi-scientific "fall from vegetarianism," however, reeks of the Bible. In both storylines, humanity breaks a food covenant—one with God (don't eat the apple), and the other with the animals (don't eat us)— precipitating a profound change in consciousness. Actually, the Bible repeatedly connects our fall from grace with a growing appetite for red meat. God kept us on a strict vegan diet until we got tossed out of Eden. In the second-class paradise where we found ourselves, meat was allowed but under the constraints outlined in the Book of Leviticus: no blood sausage, no fatty steaks, no pork chops, no cheeseburgers. Only after our behavior had grown so revolting that He drowned most of the human race in the flood were the survivors allowed full expression of their bloodthirsty ways. "Just as I gave you green plants,

I now give you everything," God tells Noah in despair. "Everything that lives and moves will be food to you." Some rabbis claim Jewish dietary laws are really just a ruse to limit Hebrew meat consumption and keep them closer to a vegetarianism suitable for the Chosen People.

All these theological trappings make perfect sense when you realize that vegetarianism is actually a religion. People "become" vegetarians, they have epiphanies. Vegetarians think they're better than the rest of us, and, surprisingly enough, we tend to agree. Surveys of students reveal that even devoted carnivores view vegetarians as more moral and spiritual. It is arguably the fastest-growing belief system on the face of the planet. The West's current interest, however, is, predictably, clothed in pseudo-science of diet and biochemistry. "It's meat, ma'am," says Mr. Bumble in the novel *Oliver Twist*. "If you had kept the boy on gruel, ma'am, this would never have happened." Mr. Bumble's explanation of Oliver's violent temper tantrum summarizes the belief of Dickens's time—when the term *vegetarianism* was first coined—that a meat diet led to unnatural bursts of violence, particularly in children. Other writers even credited English world dominance to the aggression created by their penchant for roast beef. At one point, Gandhi realized that his largely vegetarian Indian people could violently overthrow British rule only if they amplified their aggressive tendencies by becoming carnivores. "It began to grow on me that meat eating was good," he wrote, "and that if my whole country took to meat eating the English could finally be overcome!" He goes to a quiet spot and cooks up some goat, only to find it too tough to chew.

Goat, of course, is notorious for its propensity to toughen when overcooked. The meat-violence proposition underlying Gandhi's foray into barbecue, however, is interesting. One could no doubt make a statistical argument that cultures where vegetarianism is the norm, like India, have lower rates of violent crime than meat-gorging cultures like the United States, despite much higher levels of poverty and other crime. It's also fair to say that the act of eating meat plays on our species' memories of hunting and killing, which could potentially lead to a different kind of violence in certain individuals. Some vegetarians argue that butchering animals for meat engenders general violence by subliminally sanctioning killing, an argument quite similar to the one made by opponents of the death penalty, who claim that our government's endorsement of murder teaches our children that it is an acceptable way to solve problems. In 1847, lawyers for two London boys who'd killed their younger brother claimed that they had seen their own father slaughter a pig and were just repeating his behavior in play, the same defense offered in 2001 for an underage boy who'd pummeled a young girl to death, supposedly while imitating a wrestling match he had seen on TV.

The problem with all this is that there is no real evidence linking T-bone steaks to psycho killers. I believe vegetarianism's appeal lies not in this supposed ability to decrease aggression, but in its undeniable ability to amplify our capacity to love. Take the almost extinct Jivaro people of eastern Peru. The Jivaro eat meat but have a profound taboo against eating jungle deer. They point to the deer's nocturnal habits, its shyness, its quietness, the way it melts in and out of the jungle to appear, ghostlike, at the village edge. Then they point to the animal's fondness for grazing in gardens left abandoned when the people who tilled them died. The deer, the Jivaro conclude, are the ghosts of their dead neighbors returning to tend their gardens. We could never eat them, they say; they are our friends. This was the original reasoning of people like Pythagoras and Buddha, who introduced vegetarianism twenty-five hundred years ago. Like the Jivaro, they believed in a kind of reincarnation and that animals had "human" souls. It's this underlying concept that gives this religious diet its moral imperative, because by including all animals in "our tribe," it allows us psychologically to embrace and love more of God's world. Like throwing a stone into a pond and watching the ripples grow larger and larger and larger until the entire pond—from self to family to tribe to country to race, on to other species and all birds and beasts— falls within its magic circle.

Hitler's Last Meal

Adolf Hitler was the nicest man a pig could meet. Or a cow or a lamb, for that matter. The mass murderer was such a devout vegetarian that he would weep during movies that showed animals being harmed, covering his eyes and begging the others "to tell him when it was all over." Meat-eaters, he often said, were hypocritical "corpse eaters" and ultimately unsuitable as candidates for the master race. One early Nazi propaganda device was to sell boxes of cigarettes that contained a picture of the nature-loving Führer pensively peeling an apple. In fact, the German vegetarian community was so instrumental in his rise to power that he once considered making a meat-free diet part of the party platform, only stopping when he realized it would damage the food-supply system and hurt his war effort. When he finally came to power in 1933, leaders of the movement hailed him as their savior.

This bizarre character quirk has been explained in a number of ways. Hitler said it was the writings of opera composer Richard Wagner that made him a believer. "Did you know that Wagner has attributed much of the decay of our civilization to meat-eating?" he told Nazi chronicler Hermann Rauschning. "I don't touch meat, largely because of what Wagner says on the subject and says, I think, absolutely rightly." Traditional historians, however, suggest the diet was to alleviate Hitler's jumpy stomach. Psycho-historians point to his well-known oral fixations, like sucking his thumb during cabinet meetings, as well as to the guilt complex he developed after murdering his niece. It all certainly casts a shadow on the idea that vegetarians are innately peaceful, and to this day his fellow believers (dietary ones) still insist he was not a *real* vegetarian at all—didn't his vitamin capsules contain animal gelatin? they ask. His pastries lard?

Equally odd is the way Hitler treated his fellow carrot eaters once he got into power. According to historian Jane Barkas, Hitler first tried to turn the vegetarian/nature group Wandervogel into the super-Aryan Union of Teutonic Knights. Next he pressured the vegetarian colony Eden to teach Nazi race theories. When this failed, he banned the entire vegetarian movement. Their main magazine, *Vegetarian Warte,* was suppressed, and major meeting sites were turned into concentration camps. Known vegetarians were arrested, cookbooks were confiscated, and the owner of Cologne's popular Vega Restaurant, Walter Fleiss, appeared on the Gestapo's most-wanted list, apparently just for being a Jewish vegetarian. While the repression was part and parcel of Nazi paranoia about any "group," the traditional association between vegetarians and the peace movement, and the implication that the Führer was a closeted peacenik, were particularly galling to the war-hungry regime. And despite his backsliding during the war, Hitler remained as committed to vegetarian principles of morality as he was to cleaning the world of "subhuman" species. "He believes more than ever that meat-eating is harmful to humanity," wrote the author of *Hitler's Secret Conversations 1941–44* (supposedly propaganda minister Joseph Goebbels). "Of course, he knows that during the war we cannot completely upset our food system. After the war, however, he intends to tackle this problem also." The vegetarian Final Solution was never realized. The world's most-hated murderer and animal lover took his own life to the tune of Russian bombs tinkling down overhead. His beloved veggie cook, Fraulein Manzialy, was one of the few followers to commit suicide with him.

Little Nigoda

If Lewis Carroll were the head of a religious cult, I thought, he would have built a temple like this. The main building to my left was covered inside and out with thousands of bits of broken mirror, while a few *lungi*-clad priests sat meditating under a gaudy chandelier. The steeples looked as if they'd been squeezed out of a pastry tube. The building next to it was pure French baroque, albeit painted hot pink. Statues of the unlikeliest characters were scattered everywhere. Simpering English girls swirled parasols, boys in breeches cavorted with basset hounds. The largest was a six-foot-tall statue of an English soldier twirling his mustache with one hand and pointing furiously at the meditating priests with his other—*get up you bloody wogs*, his expression clearly said, *and get back to work!*

I looked at the man at my side, a priest actually, head of the entire complex, the Jain temple in Calcutta. He was a big-bellied fellow in a white *lungi* and skin-tight T-shirt. Jainism is the quintessential vegetarian religion, closely related to Buddhism, and I'd come to find out if it was true that followers wore gags to ensure they did not accidentally swallow a fly.

"So Jains eat no animals of any kind," I asked. "Not even fish?"

"No fish," said the priest. "Never."

"Only vegetables—like beans or potatoes." A confused look crept across the priest's face. I tried to remember the Hindi word for potato. *"Alu,"* I said. "Jain eat only *alu* and . . ."

"No!" he bellowed, raising his hands in horror. "No *alu!*" You'd have thought I'd suggested he liked to eat little girls. "Jain no eat *alu!*"

It turned out Jainism not only forbids the eating of animals but also considers most root vegetables taboo. Mere vegetarians, in their eyes, are little better than cannibals. The restrictions vary among the world's 4 million Jainists, but it boils down to eating almost nothing but leafy greens. Potatoes are particularly naughty because they are a kind of root and therefore are akin to seeds. Figs are also a no-no because they contain so many seeds, as no doubt are kiwi, corn, and almost every other food that makes the vegetarians' life occasionally bearable. The guiding principle behind these regulations is a belief in *nigodas,* or simple souls, which are beginning their long journey through endless reincarnations. They are thought to inhabit almost every fruit or vegetable, as well as substances like honey, hence the saying "He who eats honey commits a sin equal to murdering seven villages!"

Despite what seems like a fanatical veneration of life, the Jains' motivation is curiously anti-life, at least life on Earth. Every *nigoda* a Jain sucks down inhabits his or her body, and, because *nigodas* are young souls facing many earthly lives, their presence in the body increases the host's earthly attachments. This makes attaining *moksa,* or Nirvana, much more difficult, forcing the Jain to return to Earth for yet another life. This thought is apparently so unappealing that Jains condone suicide if followers starve themselves to death and so empty themselves of *nigodas*—the real sin of suicide would be if they took the life of some not-ready-for-*moksa*-soul(s) that happened to be in their lower intestine. True believers follow these principles to insane degrees. The ground on which they walk is preswept to ensure nobody gets squashed underfoot. Sudden movement in the dark and on grass is forbidden for the same reason. Even defecation is limited to stony places so one can see what's underneath, lest a *nigoda* inadvertently meet a truly unsavory end. The three-thousand-year-old cult is slowly disappearing, but you can still see their dust collectors in the streets of India. Look for an old man pulling a cart decorated with the Jain symbol of purity, the swastika. His job is to collect dust swept up by Jain housewives and store it in a sealed room for twenty years so the life forms in the dirt can die a natural death.

The French Connection

The main holdout in today's free-range love fest between the diner and his dinner is the revered, the delicious, the divine, *le foie gras.* "The goose is nothing," rhapsodizes *Larousse Gastronomique,* "but man has made of it a kind of living hothouse in which there grows the supreme fruit of gastronomy." The gem in question is created by shoving enormous amounts of feed down a goose or duck's arguably willing throat until its liver has doubled or tripled in size. Needless to say, animal-rights activists routinely protest the treatment as inhumane. Some countries have recently banned foie gras, and the European Union is currently considering passing a continent-wide ban on the practice of force-feeding. While farmers generally claim that the animals don't mind—the French government even measured the endorphin levels of force-fed ducks to prove they love the process—many have seen the writing on the wall and are experimenting with herbal appetite stimulants and electrode probes to stimulate the brain center responsible for eating, thereby making the geese gorge themselves voluntarily.

None of this, however, deters world-class *cuisinier* Jean-Louis Palladin, who happily became an international criminal for *le Foie* in the 1970s. The American government at the time had banned the importation of raw foie gras for fear that it would bring foreign diseases into the country. But Palladin, now chef at the acclaimed Napa Restaurant in Las Vegas, conspired with culinary legends like Jean Banchet of Chicago's Le Francais and Andre Soltner of New York's Lutece in a liver-smuggling cartel intent on addicting America. At some point one of the chefs even traveled the country cooking the contraband for gourmands, but the tour came to an abrupt halt when he accidentally burned down the mansion of a Texas wine collector.

"It was the work of a very small handful of dedicated chefs," says Michael Ginor, author of *Foie Gras: A Passion*. "They were among the first to bring true world class French cuisine to this country."

The most popular method of hiding the livers was to stick them down the gullets of monstrously large monkfish flown in from France; the last place most customs officials care to stick their arm. Palladin claims he used to slip about twenty of the jewels past federal customs inspectors each week. Although the clientele at his Jean-Louis Restaurant in D.C.'s Watergate Hotel included dozens of high-profile politicians, no one seemed to notice the federal offenses featured nightly. "We never put it on the printed menu, so there would be no evidence, you see?" explained Palladin. "It was only recited by the waiters, and besides, I am thinking the restaurant it was too expensive for the customs people to eat there."

Seared Foie Gras with Polenta and Mushroom Ragout, Port Reduction

This concoction comes from Michael Ginor, owner of Hudson Valley Foie Gras. Be aware that foie gras's high fat content, about 90 percent, means that overcooking can lead to disastrous results.

FOR THE
WILD MUSHROOM RAGOUT:

1 tablespoon olive oil
1 pound assorted mushrooms like shitake, chanterelle, portabello, trimmed and wiped clean
1 shallot, diced
2 tablespoons unsalted butter
¾ cup ruby port
¼ cup balsamic vinegar
1 cup dark duck stock
1 teaspoon fresh thyme
½ teaspoon kosher salt
¼ teaspoon ground black pepper

Heat a large skillet over medium heat. Add olive oil and heat. Add the mushrooms and shallot and toss. Add butter and cook until the mushrooms are golden and tender, about ten minutes. Remove from pan. Add port and balsamic vinegar and swirl around the pan. Continue cooking while scraping the bottom of the pan. Add duck stock, thyme, and salt and pepper, and simmer until reduced to a saucelike consistency, about ten minutes. Return the mushrooms to the pan and toss thoroughly. Set aside and keep warm.

FOR THE CREAMY POLENTA:

8 cups water

2 teaspoons kosher salt

2 cups stone-ground yellow cornmeal

4 tablespoons unsalted butter, at room temperature

1 cup heavy cream

½ cup grated Pecorino Romano cheese

½ teaspoon black pepper, or to taste

Bring water and salt to boil over high heat in a medium-size pot. Gradually pour in the cornmeal, whisking constantly. When the mixture begins to bubble, reduce the heat to medium-low and cook, stirring, until the cornmeal begins to thicken, about ten to fifteen minutes. Slowly whisk in the remaining ingredients. Continue cooking until the polenta just begins to pull away from the sides of the pan, about three to five minutes. Serve soft, as soon as it is ready.

FOR THE FOIE GRAS:

1 fresh foie gras, grade A (about 1½ pounds)

Kosher salt to taste

Freshly ground black pepper to taste

Devein the foie gras. Slice in ½-inch-thick slabs. Score one side of each slice in a crosshatch pattern with a sharp paring knife. Season both sides liberally with salt and pepper. Heat a dry skillet on medium-high heat. Add foie gras a few slices at a time and sear about forty-five seconds. Turn over and cook another forty-five seconds, until medium rare. Remove and drain on paper towel. Discard any rendered fat and repeat until all slices are cooked. Serve immediately, scored-side up.

TO ASSEMBLE:

Have mushroom ragout and polenta ready to serve. Sear foie gras according to instructions. Place approximately ¾ cup of polenta in the center of a heated plate. Top with two slices of foie gras and ladle mushroom ragout around polenta. Sprinkle a few grains of sea salt on top of the foie gras and sprinkle some chopped chives hither and thither. Serve.

Vicious Little Red Man

When a gang of California cops tortured some environmentalists in 1997 by pouring pepper spray directly onto their eyeballs, a chili-savvy jurist should have had but one question: Was the officers' spray *pasilla*-based or *habanero*-based? If it was the ultrahot *habanero*, the cops should have faced felony charges. But if it was just smoky-mild *pasilla*, well, a misdemeanor would do.

Chili peppers have been associated with violence since Christopher Columbus met them in the New World five hundred years ago. He'd been hoping to make a fortune buying India's precious black pepper. When he realized he'd failed to reach Asia, the wily Portuguese simply dubbed the brown-skinned Americans *Indians*, and their piquant spice *chili pepper,* to convince his backers they'd almost gotten to India and so ensure funding for the next expedition. The so-called Indians proved exceptionally generous with their spices. They literally threw them at the Europeans in the form of "chili bombs"— calabashes full of smoldering *habaneros*—that they tossed over Columbus's fortress walls in an attempt to drive the foreigners out of their country. While not as theatrical as the medieval habit of tossing plague-infected cadavers into besieged cities, it was probably quite effective; burning chilies emit gases that make it almost impossible to breathe.

The Native Americans (Mayans, Aztecs, etc.) have used chilies like this for ages. Mayans disciplined children by holding them over smoldering jalapeños, a child-rearing trick still popular among their descendants in the Mexican highlands. Ancient Panamanians strung them on their canoe prows to discourage marauding sharks. When the Incas of South America met Europeans in battle, they threw the invaders off balance by burning huge piles of *rocoto* chilies (so named because they're potent enough to raise the dead) as the two armies collided. The more peaceful Hopi Indians simply placed rows of them on their doorsteps to keep out the white spirits. It didn't work, but people today still hang chili crosses over cribs to ward off evil.

The chili pepper's violent nature derives from a tasteless chemical called capsaicin that's so potent 1 part in 11 million causes a sizzling sensation. It's akin to putting a lit match in your mouth, and biting into a well-endowed chili causes the body to produce a host of compounds designed to help us deal with danger or pain. The first high comes from adrenaline, a natural chemical that sometimes enables people to perform incredible acts of strength and violence. This rush is probably why fighting cocks in Mexico are force-fed chilies before they go into battle, and why the government of Peru banned hot-pepper sauce in their prisons. This initial buzz is followed by the release of endorphins produced by the body to dull pain. Chilies, however, produce only the illusion of heat by depleting nerve endings of something called Substance P. Since there's no "real" pain to dull, the endorphins produce a quasi-narcotic bliss instead. This, in turn, leads to what Dr. Andrew Weil has called "mouth surfing," where groups of gastro-masochistic degenerates spend their evenings going from *pasilla* to *serrano* to *chipotle* in search of ever-greater "rushes that enforces concentration and brings about a high state of consciousness" until, ears steaming, eyes popping out of their sockets and howling at the moon, they seek refuge in a cool, crisp Corona. It's the equivalent of bungee jumping–chili scholars call it "constrained risk seeking"— and has been fetishized in hot-pepper sauces with names like Psycho Bitch, Mad Dog Inferno, Sudden Death (with ginseng!) and the classic Dave's Insanity Sauce.

A South American plant that produces short, intense rushes followed by a false sense of well-being. Sounds a bit like cocaine. You could even still blame the (Christopher) Colombian cartel. Perhaps it says something about our culture that although we have often outlawed foods that engender love or sloth, the one most closely associated with anger has only been banned once. Homicide Salsa, which featured a murder victim's body outline on the label, was temporarily withdrawn from Chicago markets last year when a preacher objected that it glamorized violence.

Insanity Popcorn

The nastiest, the most viciously nerve-shredding torture is generally agreed to be Dave's Insanity Sauce. It was Dave's concoction that inspired the Guatemalan Insanity Sauce that gave Homer Simpson a psychedelic experience in the classic 1997 *Simpsons* episode. Dave's also has the honor of having been banned from the National Fiery Food Show in Albuquerque, New Mexico (an elderly customer tried it and suffered a slight heart attack). So beware. Creator David Hirshkop, who wears a straitjacket to chili-sauce shows, suggests that you never use more than one drop at a time. For those with more reasonable appetites, there's Temporary Insanity Sauce.

To indulge in this masochist-machismo, first pop ¾ cup of popcorn. While it's exploding in the background, melt 2 tablespoons of butter with 1 tablespoon of brown sugar and 1 teaspoon of Lowry's seasoning salt (or something similar) and exactly one drop of Dave's Insanity Sauce. Melt slowly, don't brown the butter. Pour on finished popcorn and toss to coat. Make sure you do not get any of this stuff in your eyes.

Stinking Infidels

The Queen of Sheba's hometown is not much to look at nowadays. There're lots of empty bottles of Bijan perfume. Goats munch blue plastic trash bags. Dust. It's a dump, but three thousand years ago the town we now call Mar'ib (in Yemen) was the center of the world. Its temple to the Moon goddess was the most holy spot in Arabia. It also possessed the world's first serious dam. But the true measure of Mar'ib's sophistication was its stand against halitosis. You can read about it on some ancient bronze tablets in the Moon Temple, how the Moon goddess struck down two men with a terrible disease for the sin of having "prayed in Her temple after eating a meal of stinking plants and onions."

Their sin had been bad breath, in other words. Garlic breath to be precise, since the stinking plant mentioned is the Stinking Rose, which, along with its henchmen the onion and the leek, continues to divide the world into admirers and sworn enemies. Many office-bound *Homo sapiens* today still forgo the herb, lest they, like the two Arabs in the inscription, offend the powers that be—just replace the word *gods* with its workplace equivalent. "The gods, being imagined anthropomorphically, were held to be influenced by odor," wrote Semitic scholar K. van der Toorn in his analysis of the Maribean tablets. "Thus one could please the god by burning fragrant materials as a 'soothing odor' . . . and caution not to offend the deity by foul breath could be the corollary." The outrageousness of the duo's breath can be measured by the fact that they had to perform the same penance as some men who'd been caught sodomizing each other on the temple's grounds.

The idea that bad breath and sodomy (in church) are comparable offenses might strike some as odd, but one shouldn't underestimate how strongly people used to feel about stench. With reason. Tests indicate that people who lose their sense of smell or taste also tend to lose all sexual impulses, and over 90 percent suffer serious depression. The reason for this is hard to pin down, but these senses are the only ones that interact directly with the part of the brain that controls our most primitive emotions. They have a particularly strong relationship to anger and fear because of their original role as a means of alerting us to dangerous predators or poisonous food. Some human behaviorists even believe the way we express anger evolved largely from our reaction to dangerous tastes, hence the peculiar facial grimaces associated with these emotions. That's pretty damn hard to prove, but a good indication of the extreme early importance of these senses is that our body has only four genes to govern the sense of sight, but over a thousand devoted to smell/taste.

Smelling good has always been particularly important when dealing with the gods. The world's earliest international trade routes developed to transport perfumes. Egyptians were so concerned about afterlife B.O. that they drowned their mummies in myrrh and frankincense. The first Christmas presents were perfumes, and any number of Catholic saints owe their beatitude to their corpses' propensity to smell like roses. These are all what Toorn would call "soothing odors," pleasing to the gods. More pungent odors enjoyed a less-savory reputation, particularly the Allium family of onion and garlic, which is said to have sprouted from the Devil's footsteps as he fled the Garden of Eden (garlic from his left footprint, onion from his right). Egyptian priests had to abstain from the duo, and until the nineteenth century, no devout Muslim would go near his mosque smelling of the stuff. Likewise, although the Bible records how Jews pined for garlic while starving in the desert, their rules once forbade eating these delights before noon. Priests who ignored the regulation were removed from the synagogue.

Instead, garlic's powerful ectoplasmic emissions were used to inflict a supernatural violence. One Sanskrit manuscript calls it "The Slayer of Monsters," and though King Tut's mummy may have reeked of myrrh, his cronies made sure to leave a few heads of garlic in case their Pharaoh needed to fight off enemies. Thousands of years before its current California incarnation, the Persians held an annual Garlic Festival at which they served demons a dish made of garlic, rue, and vinegar. The soup was supposed to taste so bad that the spirits would leave in a huff. Babylonians held aloft a clove when exorcising possessing spirits, and Romania's cathartic dancers, the *calusari*, used copious amounts of the raw stuff in their rituals. I will pass lightly over the obvious connection to the long-suffering vampires of central Europe.

Garlic was also employed against earthly enemies. The Hindu warrior caste was encouraged to indulge, and both Julius

Caesar and Alexander the Great pledged the plant to their war gods because they believed it made their soldiers fiercer in battle. "Now bolt down these cloves of garlic," wrote the Greek playwright Aristophanes around the fourth century B.C. "Well primed with garlic you will have greater mettle to fight!" The principle is no different than howling to unnerve your foe, and no doubt the stench emanating from the mouths of Roman Legionnaires was pretty damn shocking since their wartime staple was a brew made of raw garlic, barley, and sour wine. The Welsh claim that a famous seventh-century victory resulted from the warriors wearing cut sprigs of wild garlic in their hats. Some say the plants merely helped the Welsh soldiers recognize one another, but folklore holds it was the notoriously pungent odor of the local wild garlic that unmanned the Saxons and led to victory. The leek (as in gar-leek) remains their national plant, and its colors still adorn the flag.

The two garlic lovers from Mar'ib who offended the Moon goddess so long ago would have found none of this surprising. They knew that nothing offends like unsavory breath, and that nothing is more pleasing than an appetizing aroma. And like all men, they knew the best smell in the entire universe is of someone cooking you dinner. So when the Moon priests told them to make amends by roasting the head of a cow in the desert night, they understood its justice. Having taken away the Moon's appetite with their breath, they were now obliged to restore it by sending the succulent scent of roast beef floating up to her pale face peering over the desert horizon.

Five Angry Vegetables

A novice Buddhist monk once asked Lama Kalu Rimpoche whether eating garlic would prevent his attaining enlightenment. The Rimpoche replied with a parable. Many eons ago, he told the young monk, a demon drank a magic elixir to increase his powers. He flew high among the clouds and changed the color of the sea. But the gods eventually shot him down. The demon's blood fell upon the Earth, and from it sprouted garlic. This, he said, was the birth of the Five Angry Vegetables doctrine, which prohibits Buddhist monks from eating not only garlic, but also onions, chives, spring onions, and any member of the Allium family. The following deliciously crunchy-smooth dish called *Lo Han Jai*, or Buddhist Vegetarian Delight, is the traditional culinary embodiment of the law's principles because the absence of garlic or onion is thought to help monks control the angry passions. Lay Chinese like to start the New Year with a dish.

There are many variations on this soothing dish, so you may adjust the following recipe according to your personal level of enlightenment. Serve with hot rice.

1 cup dried black shitake mushrooms
½ cup dried snow fungus or cloud ear fungus
3 ounces dried bean curd stick (about 2 cups)
½ cup canned bamboo shoots, drained and sliced
2 ounces dried mung bean thread (about 1 cup)
1 cup firm fried tofu cut into 1-inch cubes
4 cups shredded Chinese or Napa cabbage
½ cup sliced carrots
3 tablespoons soy sauce

2 tablespoons sugar
3 cups water, plus water for soaking
½ cup raw peanuts
1 cup drained sliced water chestnuts
½ cup straw mushrooms
1 teaspoon oriental sesame oil
Sea salt, to taste

Soak the following ingredients individually in warm water for fifteen minutes: dried black shitake mushrooms, dried snow fungus, dried bean curd stick, and dried mung bean thread. Drain, rinse, and set aside.

If you cannot find prefried tofu, deep-fry firm tofu in a cup of oil for about five minutes, or until golden. Remove and drain on paper towels. Pour off all but ¼ cup of the oil and return heat to medium. Add cabbage, canned bamboo shoots, and carrots. Stir-fry for one minute. Add black shitake mushrooms, snow fungus, bean curd sticks, mung bean thread, bamboo shoots, fried tofu, soy sauce, and sugar. Mix well and add the 3 cups of water, peanuts, and all other ingredients except sesame oil. Simmer covered about fifteen or twenty minutes or until vegetables are tender. Season with salt and sesame oil. Serves 6.

Feasting to the Death

When a member of the Kalauna tribe on Goodenough Island catches his wife fornicating with another fellow, his revenge is swift. He picks his best sweet potatoes. He slaughters his fattest pig. Then he throws a dinner party for the man who cuckolded him, chuckling with delight as the guest grows infuriated at such generosity. The next morning there's bound to be a knock on the husband's door, and there, as expected, stands the home-wrecker with a single, shriveled sweet potato in his left hand. He hands this to the husband. "What," sneers the husband, "is this all your garden grows?" The other guy gestures, and his friends come out of the jungle carrying baskets brimming with taro root and roast pig and yam and pineapples and dried fish. "You think we cannot pay back your yams?" he snickers, tossing the food at the husband's feet. "Yes, now you see that *we* at least do not spend all our time bonking our wives as you do!"

The battle is on, and it continues until the one who throws the largest feast is declared victorious. This behavior, detailed in anthropologist Michael Young's *Fighting with Food*, is actually relatively restrained. Similar orgies in nearby Indonesia involved building sixty-foot-high walls made of pigs, fish, and fruit. The Kwakiutl people of northwest Canada replaced traditional warfare with enormous potlatches, or feasts, where guests/foes were stuffed with smoked salmon and berries, deluged with blankets and buttons. When the guests were too full to continue eating, the merciless host simply threw food into the fire until the flames leaped ten to fifteen feet high. When the guests remained by the roaring flames—shivering with cold and sneering about their host's miserly heating arrangements—even more food and seal fat were tossed on the fire. If the house burned down, as it often did, the owner earned extra glory, and his guests rowed back to their island in a huff; the only way for them to avoid defeat now was to burn down an even bigger house.

These are particularly extreme examples of how people have used food to express aggression, but they are hardly unique. When the last Duke of Burgundy, Charles the Bold, wanted to underline for visiting dignitaries that his tiny kingdom remained strong, he made the banquet look like a military en-

campment by serving thirty pies individually enclosed in minia-
ture tents. Each pie was gilded in gold with the initial of a town
controlled by Charles's army. When another noble decided he
had to resolve a conflict over who controlled the town of
Breisach, he invited the feuding parties to a dinner the main
dish of which consisted of two marzipan soldiers standing
guard over a smoked ham. Needless to say, Breisach was noted
for its outstanding smoked meats. State dinners like these were
"not merely entertainments and celebrations, they were a
means of asserting rank and power," according to historian
Stephen Mennell, and they grew increasingly popular with nobility as actually going to war proved more and more inconvenient.

You would think nobles must have rather looked forward to
some of these skirmishes, but that all depended on the chef.
When the Italian Medici family married off their son to the
French princess Marguerite-Louise in 1661, the nuptial feasts
clearly reflected the fact that this wedding was all about war
and power, not love (the couple loathed each other so much
they were officially married by proxy). One prenuptial to-do
began with a huge roast guinea fowl split down the middle and
opened to create a two-headed fowl to represent the Medicis'
double-headed heraldic eagle. Pine nuts arranged in a flower
garnished its breasts, and the whole thing was covered with a
rainbow of colored jelly. The fowl's heads, of course, were
crowned with sugar coronets picked in gold leaf. Next to this
strutting symbol of Medici aggression was an elongated pie
shaped into the letter *S*, after the princess's nickname, and filled
with layers of candied citron, pistachios, eggs, marzipan, lean
ham, roast capon, sweetbreads, sugar, and cinnamon. A dish
doubtless as rich and sweet as the bride herself. The pièce de
résistance, according to historian Elizabeth David, again celebrated the Medici power in a sumptuous dish of "pigeons *en*

daube in the Catalan manner, the breasts larded, first half-roasted then stewed in muscatel wine with lemon juice, powdered *mostaccioli* [spiced and musk-scented biscuits] and pounded candied citron, this sauce to be reduced to a jelly-like consistency and poured over the cold pigeons, the dish garnished with ten rose-shaped tartlets filled with five different sweet jellies—red quince, bitter cherry, white quince, *agresta* and plum—the jellies stuck with little candied cinnamon sticks and pistachios, the tartlets then covered in marzipan paste in the shape of the Grand Duchess's oak tree arms, with a sugar icing flecked with gold." There were, of course, other *amuse-gueules* on which to nibble, like musky confits, Tuscan spring cheeses, peach sweetmeats, and a dish of larded capons set on slices of roasted sweetbreads and *ortolans* and deep-fried pig cheeks with a thick sweet-and-sour sauce of verjuice. The only dish that apparently bothered to celebrate the joining of the two families was a parsimonious plate of blancmange shaped into the lady's heraldic lion and surrounded by the Medicis' lilies. The marriage was a disaster.

All this pomp and aggression sometimes spilled off the table. English Tudor mansions had a separate room where, after the main meal, guests would adjourn to nibble on sweets like twelve-foot-tall trifles, jellies, tarts, and liquor-soaked muscadines before a crowd of commoners. The feast was officially over when the host allowed the spectators to rush into the room and have a massive food fight that would leave everybody covered head to foot.

Using dinner to sate the aggressive instinct makes the most delicious of sense. First, put the weaponry of knives and forks into your enemies' hands and let them loose on a battlefield groaning with corpses and bloody-colored liqueurs. When they lay near death in a gluttonous coma you, the host, pick up a sprig of parsley and nibble it with a patronizing air—you have proved yourself the wealthiest, the most powerful, the most capable of digesting death. You have won. Normally one goes to war and the victors feast. Here, one feasts and he who feasts best is declared the king. It's life lived in reverse, which is as it should be; Lord knows, the world only makes sense when you stand it on its head. At least that's how the Kwakiutl tribe seemed to think. "Of olden times others ill-treated our forefathers and we fought them so that the blood ran over the ground," rhapsodized one of their chiefs a hundred years ago. "But now we fight with butter and blankets, smiling at each other. Ah, yes, how good is the new time!"

THE

E IGHT H

S IN

"A Cucumber should be well sliced, and dressed with pepper and vinegar, and then thrown out, as good for nothing."

Samuel Johnson

When Everything Is Allowed and Nothing Has Flavor

*A*fter writing a book like this one, even casual meals can take on alarming overtones. A recent lunch with some publishers from Scotland is a case in point. It started well enough. Booze was flowing, everybody was smoking; then one of the Scots ordered a plate of steak tartare. Raw meat. I was appalled, in part because of the biblical taboo against eating blood, but also because I knew that tartare was traditionally ordered by British businessmen desirous of gaining an advantage by intimidation. I had been under the impression that this was to be a casual, get-acquainted kind of chow down. Just what the devil was going on? What was the *real* agenda? Then the other publisher ordered. Sweetbreads with puff pastry. A mixed message. Puff pastry is related to the *mollet* bread restricted to European aristocrats; it spoke of a heartless refinement and indicated he was the brain behind whatever mischief was afoot. The ordering of a peculiar organ meat seemed another attempt to disorient me, and no doubt most Americans would have been terrified of these raw meat and organ–eating barbarians from Scotland. *Why, Henrietta, I done hear they wear skirts and eat deep-fried pizza over there!* But I knew better (well, actually, they *do* eat deep-fried pizza in Scotland) and so when the waiter asked my pleasure, I, too, ordered sweetbreads, thus letting my lunch companions know that this Yank, at least, remained unmoved by their Neanderthal propensities and was as bloodthirsty as even the most literate of Scotsmen.

It's not just paranoid writers who are prone to such overreaction. My stereotyping of the raw beef–eating editor as a dangerous opponent, for example, is typical. Many people say they avoid rare or raw meat because they are uncomfortable with the violent emotions it arouses; one can almost hear the nineteenth-century condemnation of the barbaric behavior of "bleeding dish nations" in the sentiment. In fact, the food taboos and their attendant attitudes that are the subject of this book continue to permeate almost every aspect of our lives. People seem to still think you are, literally, what you eat. In one 1989 study, college students who believed a certain person ate pork invariably attributed piglike characteristics to that person. When told the same person ate only chicken, those "piglike" traits were immediately replaced with chickenish ones. This has interesting implications, because we are constantly picking up information about one another's eating habits via body odors that are perceived on a subconscious level. So the characteristics we attribute to certain foods—attitudes formed from beliefs that go back centuries—flavor all our social interactions, from work, to romance, to whom we move away from on the bus. For instance, when we sit next to someone eating or smelling of potato chips, studies indicate we immediately classify that person as lazy and immoral, the same belief about the potato that led the English to denounce the root in the eighteenth century. People say they eschew garlic because of its strong odor, but it was only a century ago when American newspapers featured editorials condemning garlic eaters as "moral degenerates," a pretty clear indication that this attitude has its roots in something deeper than odor.

How deep our feelings on sin and food run is most clearly illustrated today by attitudes toward certain intoxicants. It's a complicated issue, but what binds these two situations together is the subliminal belief that what you take into your body has the ability to radically transform; you are what you eat, the reasoning goes, so you are what you smoke/snort/shoot. This is arguably more rational when discussing psychoactive substances, as opposed to food, but a look at the history of chocolate and cocaine shows how porous that border can be. The American government is currently using a dangerous kind of chemical weaponry to eliminate the coca plant—the source of cocaine—because we consider it to be a dangerous drug; the people of the Andes, however, consider coca to be a food and its leaves, chewed, provide essential nutrients in their traditional diet. Likewise, although we now consider chocolate to be a food, when it first came to Europe it was thought to be a powerful intoxicant. Eighteenth-century Europeans believed chocolate transformed women into sex-hungry whores; the popular image of cocaine/crack as a substance that transforms female users into animal-like prostitutes is remarkably similar. In fact, the 1990s hysteria over deformed "crack babies" (now largely discredited) had a parallel hysteria among the eighteenth-century French who banned chocolate over "cocoa babies," which they believed were being born pitch black as a result of their mothers' hot chocolate habit (this theory, too, has been discredited). The fact that both ages allowed the devastation wreaked by alcohol to continue suggests that social and health concerns were not the real reasons for these taboos, but rather that they are/were both motivated by a desire to keep un-Christian/foreign substances out of the social body. Otherwise, wouldn't we today be spraying poison on the brandy-producing vineyards of Europe, and not just on the coca fields of Colombia? It's perhaps telling that the first Western war against the coca plant was waged by Spanish missionaries who attempted to eradicate it (along with guinea pigs) in the 1600s because they considered both sacred to Satan.

So perhaps Westerners shouldn't be patting themselves on the back just yet for their rational attitudes about what people put in their bodies. Yet, it is true that almost all of the foods once forbidden are now allowed, and that absolute dietary taboos are now a thing of the past in mainstream society. The question is whether this new freedom has left us better off. There's certainly no doubt that Westerners enjoy a richer and more varied diet now than at any point in history. Yet, many people report that they find eating less satisfying than ever. Cultural historian Piero Camporesi attributes this dissatisfaction to a "profound disruption with the past," and compares the abandonment of food taboos to our discarding of sexual mores in the late-1900s. He believes that these changes have eviscerated the meaning of both sex and eating, and have produced a tendency to indulge in shallow and meaningless pleasure that leads to a kind of moral decay. It's an interesting comparison; sex and food are our two most basic drives and there's a long tradition tying the family unit to both sex and communal meals. There's certainly no denying that, as meals lose social and spiritual meaning, we spend less time eating together, or that as the communal family meal withers, so do our table manners and the general level of civility, leading to the creation of the current fast-food hamburger culture, in which everything is immediate, rude, meaningless, and disposable.

The point is that these archaic food taboos and rules, however preposterous and evil they may have at times been, also deepened our lives by imbuing our most common social gathering with meaning. Dinner gave us not just physical nutrition but spiritual nutrition as well. The laws governing what we ate also gave a sensory dimension to our sense of culture and time; one could tell the day by the smells of the special foods being cooked, which, in turn, led to unconscious meditations on the religious holiday being celebrated and its corresponding moral message. These aromatic links to liturgical time, in turn, bound us to the eternal cycles of spring and fall, winter and summer, life and death; it's no coincidence that the month of dietary restrictions that marks the Christian fast of Lent occurs in the last barren months of winter, or that its ending with the feast of Easter—celebrating Christ's resurrection from death—coincides with the first days of spring, when life returns to Earth's fields. The food laws of holidays like Easter or Ramadan were a crucial part of a multisensory celebration of nature, religion, and morality that marked the cycle of rebirth; they also reminded us that there is a naturally fallow season innate to life, a lesson often forgotten in our new artificial Eden, where all pleasures are always available, if perhaps too often plastic-wrapped and lacking true savor.

It almost makes the notion of returning to the traditional canon of food laws attractive. A ridiculous idea, of course, for every age will develop its own taboos and rituals to give meaning to the fulfillment of our most basic need. But we might want to hesitate before so blithely discarding the ones we've taken millenniums to produce. And we should perhaps pause for a moment before creating new rules, because what we outlaw reveals not only our society's priorities, it also shapes them by giving the avant-garde from Eve onward a wall over which to jump. The urge to break the rules is, after all, the most human of pleasures.

Acknowledgments

I first want to thank my editor at Ballantine, Dan Smetanka, for all his insight and patience, and Jennifer Hengen and Neeti Madan at Sterling Lord Literistic. Grovels to Jeff "Left Jones" Harris for his devoted research into the nature of absinthe. Special gratitude to everyone who contributed recipes to the book—their names are mentioned in the relevant sections—and those scholars who have become specialists in a variety of fields, in particular Stanley Kaplan, Frederic Simoons, the writers at *Petit Propos Culinaire*, Piero Camporesi, and many others, without whose work researching a book like this would have been pure hell. I'm sure at times I've misunderstood their thoughts, and I apologize in advance. All mistakes are mine. A variety of people were helpful in many ways, including David Lindsey, Zarela Martinez, Jerry Feldman, Jean-Louis Palladin, Michael Ginor, Robert Darnton, Zata Vickers, David Kileast, George Faison, Christene Gabriele, John Surinde, Bill Hudders, John the rickshaw driver, Annabel Bentley, Andy Tomassi, Troy and Paula Allen (not to mention Jackson), Pio, the staff at New York's Veselka Restaurant and at Williamsburg's Girdle Factory. Particular thanks to Allison Dickens for her forbearance. My especial gratitude to the staffs of the following institutions:

the British National Library in London, the Indian National Library in Calcutta, the private Buddhist library in Dharamsala, London's Guild Library, Columbia University, New York University, the French National Archives, the archives of the *Mairie* of Paris, and various Peruvian witchdoctors. I owe a special debt to the staff at the Humanities Library in Manhattan, one of the most efficient gulags I've had the pleasure to encounter. Bittersweet thanks (and condolences) to the staff at the new French National Library—may the architect responsible for that edifice from hell be consigned to a special purgatory reserved for those who put ego before function. I suppose the "will call" section of his library would do in a pinch.

But above all, my deepest thanks and buckets of love to Nina J., toast-eater and literary *wunderkind*, who made this book so much better than I ever could have.

ENDNOTES

$\mathcal{L}ust$

FIRST BITE (PAGES 7–11)

The debate over the precise identity of the Bible's Forbidden Fruit will never end. It seems fair to say, however, that the Latin of northern Europe, where Celtic civilizations were largely centered, used the word *pomum* to mean apple, while the Latin of Southern Europe used it to mean fruit. Avitus (full name Alcimus Ecdicius Avitus) was a prominent member of the Burgundy Church in Gaul located roughly five hundred miles from the former Celtic capitol at Aix-en-Provence. He uses two words in his poem: *fructus* (fruit), seemingly for the general abundance of the Garden, and *pomum*, for the specific fruit Eve eats. Most translators have determined the latter to mean the fruit we know as the apple. The version I referred to was in Avitus' *The Fall of Man*, edited and translated by Daniel J. Nodes, who used a ninth-century edition thought to be one of the earliest extant copies. The poem's text is given in both English and Latin. The conflict between the Romans and Celts, however, predates Christianity. In the first century A.D. Emperor Claudius outlawed all aspects of Celtic religion as "anti-Roman," and as recently as a few centuries ago Northern Protestants, a group that grew out of the Celtic Church, were still calling the Catholic grape "corrupt" as compared to their "temperate" apple (the controversy appears to have had something to do with the different fruits' methods of reproduction). The classifying of the apple as an aphrodisiac was universal but it appeared to be particularly popular in the Latin countries, where seventeenth-century priests like Juan Ludovico de la Cerda wrote "the apple to be under the jurisdiction of Venus," while Daldanius said to dream of them "foretold of venereal fruits." There's a host of folktales characterizing them as love charms.

The details on the Spanish alterations of the Aztec flower myths come from *"L'Arbre interdit du Paradis Azteque"* and "Myths of Paradise Lost," by Michael Graulich, in *Revue de l'histoire des religions* and *Current Anthropology*, respectively. He attributes the information on the Catholic appropriation to *Codex Telleriano-Remensis* and *Vaticanus*, which is identified by a commenting scholar as "intended to be tools in the hands of missionaries." The anecdote of the Mayans blaming the loss of their flowered drinks for their societal despair is mentioned in Sophie Coe's *First American Cuisine*. Whether or not the drinks contained an actual flower is not quite clear; scholars like Gordon Wasson have suggested it was peyote or a similar psychoactive plant. Other accounts identify the drink as being honey mead, called *balche*, that was infused with leaves or bark from a tree that was supposedly exterminated by the Spanish.

The tale of the Celtic apple "crucified" on a Christian tree comes from "The Apple Mystery in Arthurian Romance" by Jessie L. Weston, in which she describes a curious allegory in the Arthurian mythos called *Le Pèlerinage de l'ame*. It consists of a dialog about a wild (Celtic) apple that will produce only bitter fruit until it is grafted onto a desiccated tree that she identifies as representing Christianity. The illustration shows Christ nailed to a tree and covered in foliage. "Why should the redeemer of the world be represented under the form of an apple?" she writes. "Unless I am very much mistaken we are here dealing with an attempt on the part of the church to Christianize an already existing pagan ritual." The manuscript dates from the eleventh century, but the tale appears to be much older and probably accounts for a curious series of religious paintings showing the baby Christ with an apple in his hand, which he appears to be offering to the viewer.

Some of the Celt's sacred apple groves were located near Carlisle, which the Romans called *Aballaba* for its revered apple orchards. Many of these sacred Druid groves inspired Christian saints with names like Our Lady of the Pines.

LOVE APPLE (PAGES 17–22)

The etymology of the tomato's name is rather confusing. Tomato derives from the Aztec *xitomatl*, but the Italian name of *pommo d'oro* (golden apple) has been attributed to a misunderstanding of *pommo di moor* (the Moor's apple), *pommo di morti* (apple of death) and *pommo di amour* (love apple). The reference to the mandrake root and broomsticks relates to an unguent made of mandrake, belladonna, and baby fat which was rubbed on brooms that were inserted into the vagina, thus allowing the substance to be absorbed into the bloodstream. Other mandrake relatives were also notorious as glorifiers of fleshly pleasures, particularly the belladonna that Italian *contessas* used as an eyedrop in order to dilate their pupils and give them an unnatural beauty. In addition to the stream of tales connecting the tomato to Eden, there is lots of interesting art that underscores that belief. The popular plant guide *Paradisi in sole*, from 1625, shows Adam and Eve romping about under pineapple trees. Eve is shown picking a vegetable off a low-lying bush that appears to be a member of the nightshade family, although it's impossible to say if it's a tomato. The seventeenth century painter Isakk Van Oosten was famous for putting guinea pigs from South America in his painting of the Garden of Eden. The popular fifth-century bestiary *Physiologus naturalis*, details how two elephants representing Adam and Eve were ejected from Paradise after eating fruits identified as "love apples," meaning mandrakes. Although there are reports of Italians in the 1600s eating fried tomatoes, this was probably a reference to green tomatoes and was not the norm, according to Camporesi's *The Magic Harvest*, which mentions that the 1890 edition of *Rei de cuoci* calls tomato coulis only a garnish. It also contains the full quote of the Italian prelate Giovani Battista Occhiolini urging the Vatican's Prefect of Public Order in 1784 to promote potato eating. The list of disapproved foods by Abbot Chiari is in his book *Lettere scelte di varie materie pieacvolie, 1752*; he calls them "drugs," i.e., spices, and it seems to have been a reference to the growing use of tomato sauce at that time. The sad tale of the fork-loving *princessa* can be found in Norbert's *The Civilizing Process*.

VENOMOUS GREEN (PAGES 25–27)

Frederic Simmons reports that one twentieth-century census indicated that thousands of people in northern India still consider the plant *tulsi* their primary religion. There's a curious coda to Vrinda's tale. On the twelfth day of the bright moon of Kartk, Hindus celebrate how Vrinda, reincarnated as Rukmini, married Krishna, who was an avatar of Vishnu, the god who helped murder Vrinda's husband by seducing her. It's all very confusing and appropriately celebrated by smearing cow dung on the basil pot.

THE KING'S CHOCOLATE (PAGES 31–37)

The name *Theobroma* (food of the gods) is the genus classification assigned to cacao when it arrived in Europe during the 1500s; whether it was an appellation of approbation or a reference to Aztec beliefs is not clear. Most of the details on the early American use of chocolate come from Sophie Coe's *The True History of Chocolate* and Gordon Wasson's *Wondrous Mushrooms*. The chocolate/Lent controversy was finally settled by ruling that chocolate made with water, but not milk, was permissible while fasting. The story of the Queen of France being banned from drinking chocolate in public comes from the *Memoires de la Duchesse de Montpensier* as mentioned in LeGrand, who expresses doubt about the anecdote.

In his analysis of chocolate's relationship to the aristocracy, Wolfgang Schivelbush points out that with the fall of the ancien régime, chocolate as a morning beverage ceased except for its use among children, often the place where outmoded and discarded customs like fairy tales end up. French social philosopher Roland Barthes coined the phrase "Sadean chocolate," which he explains as a personification of the de Sade aesthetic involving "abundant, delicate soft food . . . to restore, to poison, to fatten, to evacuate; everything planned in relation to vice." Sophie Coe was the first to speculate that the Europeans stopped calling chocolate cacao (from the Mayan *ka-ka-w*) because of its similarity to the slang for excrement. The speculation that the references to chocolate and Madame du Barry imply some kind of anal sex originates in my perverted little mind alone. Robert Darnton, probably the leading authority on

French *libelles*, told me he is skeptical of the idea, but it's worth noting anal sex is still sometimes referred to as "fudge packing."

GAY GOURMAND (PAGES 38–41)

The taboos on hyenas, rabbits, etc., are in the *Epistle of Barnabas*, part of the apocrypha material deleted from the Bible. Various details on American taboos come from Laura Shapiro's *Perfection Salad*. The quotes in the discussion of fellatio among the Sambia come from Robert Stoller and Gilbert Herdt's "The Development of Masculinity," in the *Journal of the American Psychoanalytic Association*. Not everyone is so sexually insecure about dinner. The Hua men of New Guinea say women's food is soft, disgusting, wretched, revolting. But they gobble it up when no one is looking—it's the only way to get her secret powers.

BEIJING LIBIDO (PAGES 41–42)

This is, of course, only a partial list of aphrodisiacs. Apparently the rhino's penis, not its horn, was originally considered the aphrodisiac. To be fair, consumption of both rhino horns and tiger penes for medical purposes was declared illegal by the State Council of the People's Republic of China in May 1993. The law appears to have enjoyed limited enforcement.

THE RAINBOW EGG (PAGES 42–45)

The South Carolina study is cited in Simoons's *Eat Not This Flesh*. It's intriguing to speculate what role these African beliefs, transmitted via slavery, may have played in America's un-Euro aversion to wet omelets. Langercrantz, however, suggests that texture plays a significant role in these taboos and notes that many Central Africans with egg taboos will sometimes eat them if they are very, very well cooked; while wetter eggs remain be-

yond the pale. While the idea that the Rainbow Egg refers to
the arch of the rainbow is entirely mine, it seems borne out by
other references in Aboriginal myths to world-creating Double
Rainbow Eggs. The translation for the Orphic poem comes
from Newall.

Gluttony

PORCUS TROIANU (PAGES 52–56)

The adaptation of Ovis Apalis (Eggs in Pinenut Sauce) comes
from Ilaria Gozzini Giacosa's *A Taste of Ancient Rome*, with
permission.

COCKTAILS WITH THE DEVIL (PAGES 57–60)

The foodies in the Irish *Vision of Merlino* moan, "In recom-
pense for the food we refused not/and the evil of our not
keeping the fasts/great hunger and this/is ever on us to our consuming." The Islamic sunken garden referred to in the text still
exists in Seville. The numerological breakdown of the garden
comes from al-Haythami's *Majia al-zawa'id*, which also stipu-
lates that every man's sexual stamina shall be increased one
hundredfold. Although he does not mention how this was to be
achieved, one presumes that chickpeas were well represented
among Heaven's forty-nine hundred courses; the legumes were
considered so rousing that merely drinking their cooking water
was said to give the imbiber the power to "deflower 72 virgin
goats." The comments on bodily waste in Paradise have been
attributed to *Sahih Muslim Book 39*, #6798 by Jabir ibn Abdulla,
who states, "I heard Allah's Apostle as saying that the inmates
of Paradise would eat and drink but would neither spit, nor pass
water, nor void excrement, nor suffer catarrh. It was said: Then,
what would happen with food? Thereupon he said: They

would belch and sweat (and it would be over with their food), and their sweat would be that of musk and they would glorify and praise Allah as easily as you breathe." The details on heavenly sexual provender come from Koranic verses 76:19 and 37:40. Presumably female faithful suffer similar rewards, although the Koran states only that Allah will also provide "boys of perpetual freshness" to the blessed in Heaven. Whose pleasure they are intended to fulfill—male or female—is unclear. The poems cited appear in Jan van Gelder's excellent study of Arabic food imagery, *Of Dishes and Discourse*, and A. J. Arberry's *Islamic Culture*. For the record, the most temperate Paradise I've bumped into is the Buddhist *Tavatimsa*, which seems to consist only of silver-colored streams and psychedelic lotus blossoms.

THE SULTAN'S DATE (PAGES 60–61)

Waines's book (published by Riad El-Rayyes in Lebanon) recommends simply mixing equal parts sugar and powdered cinnamon, which is fine but not quite the same as the original, which called for flavoring the sugar with musk, camphor, and hyacinth. Admittedly, some of these ingredients are extinct, but there are interesting substitutes. The first step is to replace hyacinth with violets.

1) Violet-scented sugar: Carefully wash and dry ½ cup violets (do not use pink or white) and partially pulverize in mortar or processor. Mix with equal amount superfine (castor) sugar and spread on foil-lined tray and dry for one hour at 50° C. Cool.

2) Musk: This can be replaced with *ambrette* seeds (*Abelmoschus moschatus*), which are available from various herbal stores.

3) Camphor: The easiest replacement is cinnamon. Alternately, there's so-called edible camphor, still used in Bengali

sweets and called *kacha karpoor*. You should add approximately the amount that would cover the tip of a pin. Do not use camphor oil or inedible synthetic camphor. Most forms of camphor are inedible and should not be eaten under any circumstances.

One source of fresh dates is Western Date Ranches in Yuma, AZ (520-726-7006).

Angel Food Cake (pages 61–63)

Medieval speculation about angels' appetites grew so intense that the Vatican finally ruled that they neither ate nor fornicated and were genderless. There are actually a variety of foods called manna, such as a quasi honey that drips off the desert tamarisk trees and that is made into a kind of *halvah* around Turkey. Another manna is used in making the laxative mannitol. The lichen manna, however, is thought to be the likeliest source of the biblical chow because of the reference to it falling from the skies.

Saints and Supermodels (pages 63–67)

While there were a number of centuries separating Jerome (who was reputed to be something of a gourmet) and the super-slim saints of the late medieval period, many of their diaries seem highly influenced by his teaching. Angela of Foligno, for example, said she starved for years to cool her "hot little body," and when that failed literally burned herself to extinguish the internal "heat" of lust. Interestingly, the dieting diaries of some of the saints seem as image conscious as the ones given out by celebrities; the famous St. Catherine of Siena buttressed her fasting by "devoutly receiving Holy Communion very frequently indeed," according to her confessor. The statistics from America's *Psychology Today* are similar to numbers for Europe that indicate in countries like Britain about 15 percent of all teenage girls will eat only one meal a day in order to keep their weight down. Roughly a quarter of all models qualify as ano- rexic, according to federal health guidelines. Girls are twenty times more likely to suffer anorexia than boys, and approxi- mately 10 percent of those afflicted die from the condition. For information and on-line counseling visit www.edauk.com.

THE JOY OF FAT (PAGES 70–72)

It wasn't just fat that people loved in Trusler's time. Any- thing quivery and squirty seemed appealing, including an eye- ball, "which is to be cut from its socket by forcing the point of the carving knife down to the bottom," and the sweet tooth "being full of jelly." Fletcherism, which entails chewing every morsel approximately thirty times, was discovered in 1898 by Horace Fletcher, a.k.a. "the Great Masticator." It's said to be quite an effective way to lose weight. The Mayans' reservations on basting are mentioned in Coe, who sources it to *Cronicas de Michoacan*, edited by Gomez de Orozco.

MITTERRAND'S LAST SUPPER (PAGES 72–75)

The idea of covering one's head while feasting has a curious parallel among the Gurage people of Southwest Ethiopia. When a man there loses his appetite, he is thought to be possessed, the only cure for which is for him to cover his head and eat massive amounts of food, shoving it in as quickly as he can. Some of these snacks go for up to twelve hours, or until he fi- nally says, *"Tafwahum,"* "I am satisfied."

$\mathcal{P}ride$

THE EGOTIST AT DINNER *(PAGES 81–83)*

The patriotic ode to sauerkraut comes from the 1935 cookbook *Deutsch Heimatküche (German Homeland Cooking)* as translated by Bertram M. Bordon.

THE DIRT EATERS *(PAGES 83–85)*

Dirt eating, known as geophagy, is a commercial enterprise in parts of the southern United States, where small bags of kaolin can be found in supermarkets for about $1.50 a shot. Longstreet's imputation of a characteristic associated with Africans to the white Ransy Sniffle is merely one quirk in the curious social relationship between poor southern whites and blacks. In one school of thought, the so-called "white trash" (defined as a group of permanently unemployed Caucasian individuals specializing in incest and drunkenness) are a kind of "anti-aristocracy" created by the freeing of African slaves. The idea is that poor, unskilled whites in the color-obsessed American South could not engage in simple manual work because it was "colored folks' work" and for them to do so would entail losing social/racial rank. So they became versions of European aristocrats, who also often went penniless rather than lose caste by engaging in productive labor. Many of the "Euro trash" resolved their dilemma by marrying wealthy American heiresses interested in an Old World title. Mr. Sniffle and company merely created the Ku Klux Klan.

A DINNER PARTY IN KISHAN GARHI *(PAGES 85–88)*

The detailed analysis of the goings-on in Kishan Garhi is drawn from Mckin Marriott's "Caste Ranking and Food Transactions:

A Matrix Analysis," in *Structure and Change in Indian Society*. The suggestion of cow dung place mats is credited to tenth-century writer al-Biruni in Mahedra Singh's *Life in Ancient India*, which quotes al-Biruni as saying, "they prepared a separate table-cloth for each person by pouring water over a spot and plastering it with the dung of the cow . . ."

The Azande people of Sudan provide a much more congenial explanation for these taboos on communal dining. According to them, a feud between two gentlemen named Yapu-tapu and Nagilinugo over who got to have a hen with their porridge led to King Gbudue ruling that henceforth different groups should eat out of one another's sight in order to prevent unnecessary jealousy.

HUMBLE PIE (PAGES 91–99)

The connection between chicken liver pâté and Etruscan divination comes from Giuseppe Alessi, author of *Etruschi: Il Mito a Tavola (The Etruscans: The Myth at the Dinner Table)*. Alessi's book is available only in Italian, but you can try his re-creations of ancient Tuscan cuisine at his Florence restaurant, Pentola dell'Oro.

IMPURE INDIAN CORN AND THE BUTTERFLY PEOPLE (PAGES 101–6)

The first cookbook to include a corn recipe was *American Cookery* by Amelia Simmons, circa 1796, according to Tannahill. Prior to that date, American cuisine was considered undeserving of the printed page. The reference to corn being "the food of the servants" has been attributed to "Report of the Journey of Francis Louis Michel from Berne, 1701." Corn's despised status was so well known that Tom Sawyer even remarked on it in Mark Twain's classic. White America's intentions toward the buffalo were made relatively clear by General Philip Sheridan, who told the Texas Legislature in the mid-1800s, "let the hunters kill and skin and sell until the buffalo is exterminated, as it is the only way to bring about lasting peace." Buffalo Bill, hired by the railroads to help exterminate the animals that were blocking their lines, once bragged he killed four thousand in twelve months and left the bodies to rot.

There's actually no direct record of whether Native Americans were aware of the nutritional significance of nixtamalization but they seem to have had an inkling because they reserved non-nixtamalized bread for holidays when they did not eat other dietary essentials like salt and chili peppers. Corn's "murder trial" is mentioned in Daphne Roe, who credits it to Ebbie Watson, Commissioner of the Department of Agriculture in South Carolina. In the early 1900s, approximately nine thousand Americans a year were dying from pellagra. Although foreign foods and alcohol are one of the main health problems among native people in the Southwest, it's thought that the introduction of sweeter hybrid corns about forty years ago has really made the diabetes rate jump. In addition to the corn's higher sugar content, the sugar is also fast-releasing, rendering it doubly difficult to digest for some. Details about corn's cultural importance to the Hopi come from Fussell's work.

GHOST AT THE DINNER TABLE! (PAGES 107–10)

Whether or not our feelings about flatulence have ties to the Pythagorean theorem is difficult to say. The West's aversion to passing gas certainly diminished after the Classic civilizations fell apart—at least judging by accounts of medieval table manners—only to be fully resurrected when Renaissance scholars rediscovered the wonders of Greek antiquity in the fifteenth century or so. The most famous admonition comes from the scholar Erasmus's *De Civilitate morum puerilium* ("On the Civility of the Behavior of Boys"), which suggests not only that one

leave the dining room to vomit but also urges children not to
squirm about on their seat because "it gives the appearance of
repeatedly farting, or trying to do so." It remains a standard
parental nag even though most have no idea as to its original
meaning.

The overall idea that legumes make you lazy was so wide-
spread that the word *lentus*, meaning slow, became the root for
the word *lentils*. Roman general Marcus Crassus knew his army
would lose against the Parthians, because his men had been reduced to eating beans (Plutarch, *Vita Crassi*). Tannahill's suggestion that an aversion to beans played a significant role in Roman
and Greek agriculture is in her *Food in History*, in which she
points out that although the Classicists knew that planting
beans on alternate years replenished the soil, they refused to
do so.

KING'S CAKE (PAGES 110–12)

La galette des rois, dreikonigskuche, Twelfth Night cake, *bolo
rei*—there are as many names as there are versions for this cake.
Some are filled with almond paste or apples, or flavored with
port. There are cheesecake and fruitcake versions. All have at
some point included the ceremony of the crowning of the child
as the "bean king." According to *Les Fèves des rois* by Huguette
Botella and Monique Joannes, the rite was started by followers
of the two-headed Roman god Janus, who made the person
who picked the magic bean king until nightfall, at which point
his head was cut off. This custom eventually split into two
fêtes. The kids got the *fête des rois*. The adults ended up muddled into what we call Carnival (Rio de Janeiro's being the most
famous), originally called the Festival of the Crazy, a day when
lower classes were allowed to parody the elite by feasting and

drinking until morning. They point out that the revolutionary denouncement of *les gâteaux des rois* might have been reasonable because monarchists later made a point of buying the cakes decorated with the royal *fleur-de-lis* and a cross to show support for a return to a religious monarchy. Renaming the cake after beggars also led to the kindly tradition of requiring the child "king" to donate money to the poor. An interesting mystical story of this tradition is J. R. R. Tolkien's short story "Smith of Wooton Major."

Sloth

THE WONDERFUL WORLD OF ENGLISH COOKERY (PAGES 119–21)

The tale of François Vatel has been recounted numerous times and might even be true. It first appears in the correspondence of Mme. Marie de Sevigne, who describes him as a chef of the Prince of Condé who, while preparing a feast for the court of Louis XIV, killed himself over the missing fish. The fish arrived at the castle a half hour later. There is now a French school of hospitality named after him. English children's love of American literature is discussed in Sarah Freeman's *Mutton and Oysters: The Victorians and Their Food*, which quotes people like Lord Frederic Hamilton as saying that he liked books like *The Wide, Wide World* as a child because "there [was] plenty of drinking and eating." For more information on the concept of Victorian childhood, try "The Victorian Invention of Childhood," by LuAnn Walther. Despite the many barbs flung at English cooking, there's always been a tradition of good, honest fare there, as indicated by the following passage from the eighteenth-century *The Art of Cookery Made Plain and Easy*, in which author Hannah Glasse rails against the fashion for French cooks. "If gentlemen will have French Cooks they must pay for French tricks. I have heard of a Cook that used six Pounds of Butter to fry 12 Eggs, when every Body knows, that understands cooking, that Half a Pound is enough."

TOAST AND THE INCREDIBLY SAD TALE OF PHILIPPE THE SHOEMAKER (PAGES 121–32)

The historic relationship between beer and bread is too well documented to require specific references, although *Food: The Gift of Osiris* is a good starting point. The first "official" bread is thought to have been sun-baked loaves with a moist, chewy interior, but the first bread/beer/porridges were probably like the *chang* barley beer enjoyed in the Himalayas. It is served in a bamboo trunk with the "head" being a mass of fermented barley that resembles a diseased cauliflower; you get to the liquor by sipping through a wooden straw. Delicious when fresh. An interesting parallel to the European notion that ancestral characteristics can be passed through bread existed among the Zuni Indians who, according to turn-of-the-century anthropologist Frank Cushing, added a nut called *k'u'-shu-tsi* to their corn breads because it was the food of their ancestors and so eating it passed on ancestral wisdom (in *Zuni Breadstuffs*). The description of the Egyptian pregnancy tests comes from "On an Ancient Method of Diagnosing Pregnancy and Determining Sex" by P. Ghalioungui in *Medical History*. Much of the material relating to the controversy of *mollet* comes from Kaplan's massive *Bakers of Paris*, and manuscripts in the French National Archives. The police report quoted is *Traite de la Police* by Police Commissioner Delamare (available in various editions), but particularly the one from 1710. For the *panisvores* among you, yes, baguettes were not invented until much later, but I'm using the word generically for bread. Besides, the baguette, too, was criticized for epitomizing Parisian shallowness with its emphasis on excessive crust. Blame for the translation of the poem by Condamine belongs to me.

The transvestites supposedly leading the bread riots were not necessarily sexual transvestites, but merely men in drag because they thought the soldiers were less likely to shoot at women. Other accounts suggest that there were also females dressed as men. Many historians have debated whether or not Marie Antoinette actually made her famous cake remark. The classic version, re: starving peasants, was *"Qu'ils mangent de la brioche,"* a reference to a delicate type of bread similar to *mollet*. It is usually translated into English as "Let them eat cake." If the queen never made a remark about who should eat what kind of bread, well then, she must have been the only person in France who had failed to express an opinion.

The white bread vs. brown wasn't merely a question of social standing. The darker the bread, the easier it was for unprincipled bakers to hide adulterations in the loaf like acorns, bark, mud, sawdust, dog weeds, and God knows what else. Some even added poisons like bay leaves or the herb darnel to make so-called "dazed bread." Dark rye loafs also sometimes contained grain infected with the mold ergot, the base for the drug LSD, which people like Camporesi believe caused some of the bizarre religious "dancing" hysterias that swept through medieval Europe.

THE VIRGIN'S NIPPLES (PAGES 132–33)

If you're interested in seeing some older samples of erotic Italian pastry, there is a collection on display at Rome's Museo delle Tradizioni Popolari. The recipe is based on June di Schino's

"The Waning of Sexually Allusive Monastic Confectionary in Southern Italy."

THE ROOT OF LAZINESS (PAGES 133–39)

Modern nutritionists now say potatoes may indeed induce sloth because they help produce serotonin, which causes people to relax, a belief epitomized in the recent book of Kathleen DesMaisons, *Potatoes Not Prozac*. Cobbett was not the only Englishman to see the potato as the root from hell. Many considered the potato famine divine justice for Irish sloth, and believed the best possible outcome would be partial extinction of the Irish and total extermination of the potato. Others suggested outlawing small farms to prevent the growing of potatoes. La pricesse or la ratta potatoes can be found at PricessePotato.com Tel 631 537-9404; Fax 631 537-5436. Available October through late March.

THE LAST DROP (PAGES 139–43)

Reverend Billy Sunday's eulogy is to be found in *Ardent Spirits* by John Kobler, as are many of the other particulars on the history of Prohibition. Sunday was a former professional baseball player whom an estimated one million Americans trekked out to see preach by the time he peaked in 1917. Most of the statistics on the economics of Prohibition come from the Cato Institute's *Alcohol Prohibition Was a Failure* by Mark Thornton (also in his book *The Economics of Prohibition*), which details Richard Cowan's "Iron Law of Prohibition," i.e., that the more intense the law enforcement, the more potent the dope gets ("How the Narcs Created Crack," *National Review,* 12/5/86). Thornton notes that although the Eighteenth Amendment was repealed in 1933, its spirit lives on in the current "drug war," which has (predictably) had the same results of increasing criminal power and putting harmless people in prison. Interestingly, some believe that narcotics got a foothold during Prohibition because their smaller size made them an attractive smuggling alternative. The pro-Prohibition statistics come from *The Encyclopedia of Prohibition* and *Prohibition, the Way to National Prosperity* by Reverend T.M.C. The role of the women's movement is detailed in *Women and Temperance: The Quest for Power and Liberty, 1873–1900* by Ruth Bordin. For an alternate view, there's always Ralph Waldo Harley's *The Age of Unreason: Prohibition, and Women and What They're Doing*, which points out that "chain store flappers, private office concubines, dance hall shimmy-shakers, bobbed-headed movie rats, hip-wriggling bridge hounds, adultery billboards . . . and female men" are "hell bent" on imposing their morality on the world. His circular analysis on the futility of giving women the right to vote is remarkable. "If all wives vote *with* their husbands," he writes, "the ratio remains unchanged." If all women vote *against* their spouses, again nothing changes. So why give them the vote? Not every barkeep objected to the women's crusade—some found the hymn-singing ladies such a draw that they hired actors to imitate them and put on two shows a day.

IN THE GREEN HOUR (PAGES 143–46)

Wormwood's active compound *thujone* is also found in sage, probably accounting for the popularity of the "exhilarating" sage beer during the medieval period. Michael Albert-Puleo speculates in his essay on the mythology of the sage plant that the old saying "he who would live for aye, must eat Sage in May," might refer to how sage's *thujone* content peaks in spring. Absinthe has made a comeback in the last five years, via versions from Romania and Czechoslovakia. You can buy it in England, but by all accounts it lacks any serious wormwood punch. The stuff sold in the United States, called Absente, has even less psychoactive punch (the manufacturer claims that its *thujone* content increases when you add sugar, in the traditional manner of drinking). If you want to get the real thing, there are still moonshiners in Switzerland and France who follow the same recipes used a century ago. Just head up to the hills and ask around.

Greed

THE MAGIC CANNIBAL (PAGES 154–62)

Much of the information on various aspects of medieval law on cannibalism comes from Tannahill. There are, however, different interpretations of the sixth-century Salic and eighth-century Charlemagne laws in other works. The translation of Castillo's man-feast is by A. Maudslay in "The Discovery and Conquest of Mexico 1517–1521." Innocent's concern about the Arthurian cult is detailed in *The Catholic Encyclopedia*, which also quotes eighth-century chronicler Helinandus on the grail, "called Gradalis or Gradale, means a dish [scutella], wide and somewhat deep, in which *precious viands* [meat] are wont to be served to the rich in degrees [gradatim], one morsel after another." The word *precious* in its truest sense means magical. According to Helinandus, the *precious viands* referred to would have been lamb; Christ is commonly referred to as the Lamb of God. St. Philip Neri seemed to understand that the chalice was all about cannibalism—apparently he licked and sucked on the Eucharistic goblet so intensely he left tooth marks in its rim.

The Irish saint who apparently used a human sacrifice was Columba who, in founding his church at Iona, suggested to his followers, "it is permitted that one of you should go under the clay of this island to hallow it." One of Columba's disciples, Odran, replied, "If thou shouldst take me I am ready for that." Columba accepts and "then Odran went to heaven." That would have been in the sixth century, and various other public Druid rites apparently related to ritual cannibalism are well documented until the 1300s. As recently as the 1950s Catholic nuns were warning children to not bite the host with their teeth lest it bleed. Rindfleisch's Nazi relation is mentioned in the "Communique of the Polish-Soviet Extraordinary Commission for Investigating the Crimes Committed by the Germans in the Majdanek Extermination Camp in Lublin," translated by Philip Trauring. He appears to have specialized in vicious "medical" experimentation. The Bishop of Amalfi, trampled to death by his fellow prelates at the Fourth Lateran Council, was rewarded with a marble tomb in the Vatican for the inconvenience.

SMOKED GREEN MAKAKU (PAGES 162–64)

The horrified expression of the smoked monkeys on the boat was apparently caused by their facial muscles contracting during the smoking process. I refer to the country by its new name, Democratic Republic of Congo, but when I was there it was known as Zaire, although previously it had been known as the Belgian Congo, not to be confused with the much smaller Republic of Congo on Africa's Atlantic seaboard.

THE LAUGHING MAN (PAGES 164–71)

Kuru was first diagnosed by Nobel winner D. Carleton Gajdusek in the mid-1900s. Although there have been some recent reports of *kuru* in Papua New Guinea, both it and St. Vitus's dance (also known as ergotism and St. Anthony's Fire) are basically extinct diseases, and there is a lack of understanding as to precisely how they functioned. Mad Cow disease is now believed to be caused by renegade proteins called prions, which essentially eat the brain. How these prions work, however, is still controversial, as are the workings of drugs like LSD. Although LSD's symptoms are normally temporary, it's worth noting that long-term users of its sister, the hallucinogenic fly agaric mushroom, can develop these traits permanently. According to Waldemar Jochelson, a turn-of-the-century explorer who lived with a group of Siberian agaric enthusiasts, "long term users [of agaric] can be detected . . . even when they are in a normal condition, by an uncontrollable twitching of the face, and an uneven gait." Most of the information on the prehistoric brain-eating cults comes from Weston La Barre. The sites he and others refer to belong to Solo Man of Java (150,000 B.C.) and Peking man (400,000 B.C.). Anthropologists like David Snellgrove have reported on a number of Tibetan ceremonies involving skull bowls containing mock human brains made of flour. Jane Goodall's observations have been confirmed by other scientists and, although there have been contradictory reports, all agree that the head is the first thing eaten. The information about the missing brains of Aztec sacrificial victims comes from Sophie Coe's *First American Cuisine*, which credits anthropologist Eduardo Contreras of the Mexican Institute of Anthropology (citing research from the 1960s). The reference to Texan barbecues is in *Eating in America*, by Waverly Root. My personal encounter with cannibalism in Zaire was in the early 1990s, but I was also later told that when the military wiped out a village they sometimes spread rumors of cannibal attacks to deter any investigations.

For those interested in learning about the religious eating of human brains firsthand, I understand from reliable sources that certain extreme sects of Hindu Sadhus still partake as part of their disciplines. It is apparently popular in the industrial hell-hole Paradeep near Orissa in eastern India, where some bodies are buried rather than cremated.

THOU SHALT NOT EAT THY MOTHER (PAGES 172–75)

The statistics on the health effects of bottle feeding come from a variety of studies in publications like *American Journal of Nutrition* (Sept. 1999) and those of the World Health Organization. Many of the other facts come from Yalom's book and *Milk, Money, and Madness*, by Naomi Baumslag. As to whether or not these companies currently use mailing lists, a friend of mine received a box full of free baby formula a year or so ago when she was accidentally put on some sort of mailing list for brides-to-be. Nestlé failed to respond to numerous requests for comments on the content of this piece.

AMERICAN PIGS (PAGES 176–79)

The relationship between the World Bank and the USDA's apparently overlapping agendas is detailed in "AIDing and Abetting Mayhem," by Jim Ridgeway and Billy Treger in the November 1994 issue of *Multinational Monitor*.

Blasphemy

THE JEWISH PIG (PAGES 186–90)

Most of the information on European customs comes from Fabre-Vassas. Details about the Judensau is in Schacher's "The Judensau: A Medieval anti-Jewish Motif and its History." When you analyze how some of these misunderstandings developed, it's almost funny. For instance, Fabre-Vassas reports that some Jewish circumcisions entailed filling the mouth with wine and then sucking three times on the baby's penis to disinfect the wound. The wine was then apparently spat into a bowl and sipped by all the men in the room. One can image superstitious Christians spying on their stand-offish neighbors through a crack in the wall and seeing the screaming children, the men with the red-stained lips—hardly surprising they gave it all the worst possible interpretation. The most unusual explanation for the Jewish need for Christian blood comes from Thomas of Cantimpre's *Bonum Universale de Apibus*, which claims it was used to treat hemorrhoids. No instructions on application available. Exactly how kosher laws restricting social integration played into European anti-Semitism is a touchy subject, but Eduard Bernstein, a Jew who said he had become assimilated into German culture by giving up kosher laws in the 1920s, is quoted in Robertson's work as having written in the 1920s *Der Jude* that "Separationist meals . . . are a dividing wall that prevent the development and establishment of a true sense of social cohesion." The information on the attitude of Germans toward the Jews they slaughtered comes primarily from Glass's *Life Unworthy of Living*, in which he analyzes the motivations of a group of nonmilitary, middle-class, middle-aged men who murdered a thousand women and children in a Polish village in July 1942. He summarizes their feeling as akin "to witnessing for the first time the blood and gore of a sausage factory."

FOR WHAT WE ARE ABOUT TO RECEIVE (PAGES 201–2)

According to Sherry Ortner, what kind of *torma* a god is offered depends on his or her diet. Carnivorous deities get red ones, veggie godlets get white. The technique of binding a spirit with the rules of hospitality is also used in Tibetan funeral services, in which a special seat is constructed for the deceased's ghost, thus obliging it to stay until the priests have finished reading the Book of the Dead. For more information on the wafer controversy see Mahlon Smith's work.

O, DOG *(PAGES 202–6)*

Most descriptions of the Polynesian poi dog come from Margaret Titcomb's work. The species has been lost in the cross breeding with animals introduced by Europeans but there is a project to re-create the species in Hawaii, presumably for purely academic reasons. Poi dogs were not the only pooches force-fed for dinner—Moroccan dogs destined for dinner were fed dates. The account of the wolves following American Indian hunters comes from Thurston's excellent *The Lost History of the Canine Race*, in which she cites a nameless account written by Reverend J. G. Wood in 1870. For more information on the Egyptian dog city Hardai, check Thurston's work, or *Food: The Gift of Osiris* by William Darby and company. According to this, at one point there were respective sacred fish and dog cities that went to war because their citizens were eating each other's deities. "In my day the fish worshipers caught a dog and ate it up as if it had been sacrificial meat because the people of Hardai were eating the fish known as the oxyrhynchus," wrote Plutarch. "Both sides became involved in a war and inflicted great harm on each other."

HOLY COW *(PAGE 206–11)*

Most of the material relating to horns and devils, cows and demons, comes from *The God of the Witches*, by Margaret Murray. The cow's rep as stud divine is generally attributed to its agricultural role in pulling plows, but some anthropologists suggest that cattle were originally merely forced to walk over a field about to be planted so as to transmit some of their bovine mojo into the soil. The conduits for this energy were their horns, which is why farmers in some areas still attach special strings to the appendages and let them drag in the soil while plowing. Details on the Sepoy Rebellion come largely from *The Great Mutiny of India 1857*, by Christopher Hibbert. This was a four-course war, by the way, because in one anecdote the Hindu soldiers mistook a box full of canned lobster for munitions and actually fired them at the British troops (in 1867's *Shrimp and Lobster Lore*). If you want to try the honey cakes I sold at Anjuna, you'll find the baker at the edge of the dirt road leading into the teeny village of Arambol in Goa. I forget his name, but he lives in a small shack just opposite the village cricket field.

Anger

THE CIVILIZED SAUCE (PAGES 219–21)

The information on the Janissary army is mentioned in Clifford Wright's massive *A Mediterranean Feast*.

THE SADISTIC CHEF (PAGES 221–23)

Some of the details about sadistic cuisine are mentioned in Philippa Pullar's *Consuming Passions*, which attributes them to a lecture given by Keith Thomas to the London Guild of Food Writers in 1990. The goose recipe comes from a book titled *Natural Magick*, by John Baptista Porta and published in London in 1658. It appears to be a reprint of a similar recipe mentioned in many other publications. The birth of modern cruelty-free butchery was first made official in Switzerland in 1892. According to some, it was actually tied into the wave of anti-Semitism during that era. Certainly the German ban on cruelty to animals appears to have been a swipe at Judaic culinary/butchery traditions. At one point a bill was introduced into the New York Senate requiring that meat be labeled as "humane" or "kosher," according to Seymour Freedman's *The Book of Kashruth*. The bill failed.

DEEP-FRIED MURDER (PAGES 223–27)

The only measurement of the decibel noise experienced by an eater of crunchy foods that I was able to discover comes from food engineers Zata Vickers and Carol Christensen in the late 1970s. They got over the problem of measuring the sound experienced by the chewer by having him or her wear headphones playing noise, the decibel level of which would be adjusted according to the food the person was eating. If they could no longer hear the sound of themselves chewing, that was assumed to be the approximate sound volume experienced by the ear. Foods such as chips and carrots measured between 110 and 120, according to Vickers. Spokeswomen for Frito-Lay declined to comment on the relationship between food sound volume/crunch and aggression.

ONLY IF IT HAS A FACE (PAGES 227–31)

Much of the general information on the relationship between meat and violence comes from *The Heretic's Feast*, by Colin Spencer, as well as other publications. The Hmong people of Laos have a particularly charming version of the universal tale of how a broken dietary covenant landed humanity in purgatory. According to them, the crops of the field used to pick themselves out of the soil and line up outside the farmer's hut so he could choose which ones he wanted for dinner. One day the farmer was too hungover to get out of bed and asked them all to come back the next day. The same thing happened every day for a week, and finally the veggies said, Well, maybe from now on we should just stay in the ground, and when you're ready to choose you can come and pick us. And so work was invented. The Jivaro are a tribe of about twenty thousand who live in the tropical area near the Maranon River in eastern Peru and Ecuador.

HITLER'S LAST MEAL (PAGES 231–33)

Jane Barkas's *The Vegetable Passion* goes into more detail on this subject than any sane person could ever want to know, including Hitler's passion for Jewish pastries (apparently the only thing that could lure him into a Jewish establishment), and how his chef secretly added bone marrow to his food. Hitler's plan to turn Germany into a raw food cult is mentioned by Bertram M. Gordon in "Fascism, the Neo Right" in the 1987 Oxford symposium on Food & Cookery. Walter Fleiss, the veggie restauranteur who made the Gestapo's most-wanted list, reopened his Vega Restaurant in London's Leicester Square, where it became an institution. He even convinced the Salon Culinaire Food Competition to include a veggie category in their prestigious contests.

VICIOUS LITTLE RED MAN (PAGES 239–41)

It appears that pre-chili Asian cuisine used a fruit called *fagara*, or prickly ash, which is comparable to horseradish and wasabi. These, however, have only an initial burn that quickly fades, as compared to chili's long-lasting agony. One of the more unusual uses of chili powder is in birthing—the powder is flung into the mother's face, precipitating contractions. Most of the information on the 1997 California incident comes from newspaper clips, Amnesty International reports, and "Spring," one of the victims who is currently suing the officers involved. All officers involved were found not guilty of any criminal offense.

STINKING INFIDELS (PAGES 242–45)

The two Mar'ib men's sins are detailed in Jacques Ryckman's *Les Confessions publiques Sabeennes*. Ryckman refers to the men who apparently committed sodomy as being guilty of "special sex." The two men accused of bad breath actually hailed from outside Mar'ib, and only made pilgrimage when their local priests were unable to cure their disease. This entailed not only a dangerous journey but also arranging a "truce of God" between the eternally warring tribes of Yemen. It was only when they arrived in Mar'ib that they learned exactly why the Moon was so miffed with them. The question as to why garlic became so closely associated with demons might relate to the fact that its stench results from sulfide compounds, sulfur being the eau de cologne of Old Horny. The tribes in Yemen, by the way, are still squabbling away.

FEASTING TO THE DEATH (PAGES 247–51)

The information on the Tudor banquets comes from C. Anne Wilson's work *Banquetting Stuffe*. Details and quotes from various potlatch ceremonies can be found in Helen Codere's *Fighting with Property*. The Kwakiutl were so fond of the potlatch ceremonies that they refused loans from the Canadian government to replace houses incinerated during the festivities because they thought the white officials would try to limit the size of the house to prevent further parties. One amusing account of food as weaponry is told in an anonymous work from the 1700s called *Origen de los Mexicanos* which claims the Aztecs were so proud of their cuisine that they would cook dishes before besieged cities so that "the smoke will enter their city and the smell will make the women miscarry, the children waste away, and the old men weaken and die of longing and desire to eat that which is unobtainable." This passage, mentioned in Coe, probably refers to burning chili peppers. Elizabeth David's account of the Medici marriage feast can be found in her piece on ice molds, "Savour of Ice and of Roses," in *Petit Propos Culinaire*.

The potlatches were perhaps the most extreme version of the eating-as-aggression phenomenon, but it also played a part in the creation of the so-called California Cuisine of the late twentieth century. According to Jesse Drew's "Call Any Vegetable" essay in *San Francisco: History, Politics and Culture*, a group of politically motivated food activists inadvertently led to the California aesthetic. The key group was the San Francisco Food Conspiracy, which formed in the 1960s to overthrow the corporate American power structure. "There are conspiracies all over the city," wrote San Francisco's *Good Times* in 1972 of the group, "[intent on] breaking down the master-servant trip of grocery stores." The conspiracy was constructed using classic Marxist guidelines for guerrilla warfare in dozens of independent cells—Uprisings Bakery, Red Star Cheese, the People's Warehouse—that produced subversive foodstuffs for worker-owned co-ops that distributed them to the masses. The Conspiracy hoped these would replace America's soul-less supermarkets and their Wonder-Bread-and-mayonnaise sandwiches with "real food." This would inevitably put Americans more in tune with The People and inevitably lead to world peace, not to mention universal happiness.

The conspiracy was only one of a number of "food happenings" during the 1960s. The huge free meals thrown by the radical Diggers' group were staged so that nine-to-five working stiffs could see them, and were as much political theater as was the "pie encampment" of Charles the Bold. Another contemporaneous group, the New World Liberation Front, even bombed Safeway supermarkets apparently to force them to stock better produce. It was curiously effective, if in an unanticipated way. The Conspiracy's co-ops dispensed organic, fresh food, free of preservatives, with an emphasis on ethnic dishes. It was food few white people had tasted, not surprising in an era that believed that processed, packaged foods were superior to the stuff that came straight out of the dirt. Brown rice, tofu, ripe tomatoes, real cheese—every bite was a sensory rejection of everything for which 1950s America stood. These politically inspired mantras of fresh/simple/seasonal in turn became the culinary guidelines for people like Alice Waters, the great guru of California cuisine, who opened her world famous Chez Panisse restaurant during the conspiracy's heyday. The Panisse alumni list reads like the who's who of American cuisine—Wolfgang Puck, Joyce Goldstein, Mark Miller, Jeremiah Towers—all of whom are still chanting the culinary mantras of the original guerrillas. All they lack are the beards and red stars.

That it took this bizarre mélange of Chairman Mao and Jacques Pepin to get Americans to appreciate good food is not all that surprising since, like the Germans and the English, Americans generally feel politics to be more worthy of conversation than pleasure. Radicals appalled at this co-opting of the revolution by today's balsamic-swilling gourmands can console themselves with the fact that the original Conspiracy stayed true to its roots; in classic leftist rebellion style, the San Francisco Food Conspiracy movement ended with a gun battle between competing factions.

BIBLIOGRAPHY

"Communique of the Polish-Soviet Extraordinary Commission for Investigating the Crimes Committed by the Germans in the Majdanek Extermination Camp in Lublin," translated by Philip Trauring.

Ackerman, Diane. *A Natural History of the Senses.* New York: Random House, 1990.

Ackerman, Marie. *Das Schlaraffenland in German Literature and Folk Song.* Chicago: Chicago University Press, 1944.

Acton, Harold. *The Last Medici.* London: Faber & Faber, 1932.

Adair, Nancy (ed.) *Word Is Out: Stories of Some of Our Lives.* San Francisco: New Glide, 1978.

Albert-Puleo, Michael. "The Botany, Pharmacology and Chemistry of Thujone-containing Plants." *Economic Botany* 32 (Jan. 1978).

Aldana-Benitez, Cornelia (ed). *Unmasking a Giant.* Philippines: IBON, 1992. Includes *The Silent Slaughter* by Fides Lim of Philippine Center for Investigative Journalism.

Al-Gazalli. *The Revival of Religious Learnings or Gazzali's ihya Ulum-id-Din,* translated by Alhaj Maulana Fazlul Karim. Dacca: F. K. Islam Mission Trust, 1971.

Allen, Louis A. *Time Before Morning: Art and Myth of the Australian Aborigines.* New York: Crowell, 1975.

Allen. J. B. (ed). *First Images of America.* Berkeley: University of California Press, 1976.

Allison, Dorothy. *Trash.* Ithaca, New York: Firebrand Books, 1988.

Amnesty International. "USA: Police Use of Pepper Spray Tantamount to Torture." Nov. 4, 1997.

Andrews, Jean. *Red Hot Peppers.* New York: Macmillan, 1993.

Archetti, Duardo. *Guinea-Pigs: Food, Symbol and Conflict of Knowledge in Ecuador.* Oxford, England: Oxford Press, 1997.

Archives of Mairie Du Paris, 1970–95.

Aristophanes. *The Eccliszausae,* translated by Benjamin Bickley Rogers. Cambridge, Mass.: Harvard Press, 1924.

Ashton, John. *The History of Bread: From Pre-Historic to Modern Times.* London: Religious Tract Society, 1904.

Associated Press. "Last Pig in Haiti Is Dead" (June 21, 1983).

Astin, Alan. *Cato the Censor.* Oxford, England: Clarendon Press, 1978.

Avitus, Ecdicius Alcimus. *The Fall of Man (De spiritalis historiae gestis libri I–III).* Edited by Daniel J. Nodes. Toronto: Center for Medieval Studies, Pontifical Institute of Medieval Studies, 1985.

Baker, Linda. "Message in a Bottle." *In These Times* (Aug. 21, 1995).

Baker, Sophie. *Caste: At Home in Hindu India.* London: Jonathan Cape, 1990.

Baleesta, Henri. *Absinthe et absintheurs.* Paris: n.p., 1860.

Barkas, Jane. *The Vegetable Passion: A History of the Vegetarian State of Mind.* London: Routledge & Kegan Paul, 1975.

Barry, Madame du. *Drame en cinq actes: la Comtesse du Barry.* Paris: n.p., 1878.

Bataille, Christophe. *Absinthe.* Paris: Arlea, 1994.

Baudet, E. H. P. *Paradise on Earth.* New Haven, Conn.: Yale University Press, 1965.

Baum, Frank. *Ozma of Oz.* New York: Reilly & Lee, 1907.

Bauman, James. "Les Galettes des Rois: The Eating of Fine Art." In *Petit Propos Culinaire,* vol. 27.

Baumslag, Naomi, and Dia Michels. *Milk, Money and Madness: The*

Culture and Politics of Breastfeeding. Connecticut/London: Bergin & Garvey, 1995.

Beaumelle, L. A. *Memoire pour Madame Maintenon.* London: A. Millar, 1759.

Bell, Rudolph. *Holy Anorexia.* Chicago: Bell, 1985.

Beller, Scott. *Fat and Thin: A Natural History.* New York: Farrar, Straus, and Giraux, 1977.

Berry, Elizabeth. *The Great Bean Book.* Berkeley, Calif.: Ten Speed Press, 1999.

Beverly, Robert. *In the Historical and Present State of Virginia.* n.p., 1705.

Bharati, Agehananda. *The Tantric Tradition.* New York: Doubleday, 1970.

Bingen, Hildegard von. *Physica.* Rochester, Vt.: Hildegard Healing Arts Press, 1998.

Black, Matthew. *The Scrolls and Christian Origins: Studies in the Jewish Background of the New Testament.* Calif.: Scholars Press, 1961. From a Series of Lectures at the Union Theological Seminary in New York City.

Block, W. "The Limited Nutritional Value of Cannibalism." *American Anthropologist* (1970).

Bodanis, David. *The Secret House.* New York: Simon & Schuster, 1986.

Bonwick, James. *Irish Druid and Old Irish Religions.* London: Griffith, Farran, 1894.

Bordin, Ruth. *Women and Temperance: The Quest for Power and Liberty, 1873–1900.* Philadelphia: Temple University Press, 1981.

Botella, Huguette, and Monique Joannes. *Les feves des rois.* Paris: Editions du Collectionneur, 1994.

Bouton, Cynthia. *The Flour War: Gender, Class and Community in Late Ancien Régime French Society.* State College: Pennsylvania State University Press, 1993.

Bouyer, Christian. *Folklore du Boulanger.* Paris: Maisonneuxe et Larose, 1984.

Briggs, Asa. *William Cobbett.* Oxford, London: Oxford Press, 1967.

Brill, E. J. *Le Repas ritual dans le religion Sud-Arabe.* Leiden/Amsterdam: Simbolaie Biblicae ot Mesopotamicae, 1973.

Brillat-Savarin. *Physiologie du gout (Gastronomy)*. London: Chatto & Windus, 1877.

Briquel, Dominique. *Chrétiens and haruspices: la religion etrusque dernier rempart du paganisme romain*. Paris: Presses de L'Ecole Normale Supérieure, 1997.

Brookes, John. *Gardens of Paradise: The History and Design of the Great Islamic Gardens*. New York: New Amsterdam Press, 1987.

Brothwell, D. R. "Cannibalism in Early Britain." *Antiquity Magazine*, 35:304–7.

Browning, Christopher. *Ordinary Men: Reserve Battalion 101 and the Final Solution in Poland*. New York: HarperCollins, 1992.

Browning, Frank. *Apples*. New York: North Point Press, 1998.

Environmental News Network. *Bushmeat: Logging's Deadly Second Harvest* (April 23, 1999).

Bynum, Caroline Walker. *Holy Feast and Holy Fast*. Los Angeles: University of California Press, 1987.

Camporesi, Piero. *Anatomy of the Senses: Natural Symbols in Medieval and Early Modern Italy*. Cambridge, England: Cambridge Press, 1994.

———. *Exotic Brew*. Cambridge, England: Polity Press, 1990.

———. *The Magic Harvest*. Cambridge, England: Polity Press, 1993.

Capua, Raymond. *The Life of St. Catherine of Siena*. Translated by George Lamb. New York: Kennedy and Sons, 1934 (Originally published mid-1400s).

Carroll, Jon. "Hold the Bird by Its Head." *San Francisco Chronicle* (Jan. 2, 1988).

Cassion, Max. "Une Matiere a Philolgie e Fasgiole." *Carnita du patrimoine ethnologique, no. 22*. Paris: n.p., 1983.

Charan, Bimala. *Heaven and Hell in Buddhist Perspective*. Delhi: Bhartya Publishing House, 1973.

Chavasse, Pye Henry. *Advice to Mothers on the Management of Their Offspring*. London: Royal College of Surgeons, 1844.

Cherici, Peter. *Celtic Sexuality*. London: Duckworth, 1994.

Chesterston, Gilbert. *William Cobbett*. London: Hodder and Stroughton, 1925.

Chetley, Andy. *The Baby Killer Scandal: A War on Want Investigation into the Promotion and Sale of Powdered Milk in the Third World.* London: War on Want, 1979.

Chute, C. *Apples, Apples, Apples.* New York: Doubleday, 1971.

Climent, Don. Head of International Rescue Committee. Personal interview.

Cobbett, William. *William Cobbett's Rural Rides.* London: A. Cobbett, 1853.

———. *Cobbett's Weekly Political Register,* a.k.a. *Two-Penny Trash.* Periodical years 1802–12 and 1825–34.

———. *Cottage Economy,* 18th edition. London: Charles Griffin, 1867.

Codere, Helen. *Fighting with Property: A Study of Kwakiutl Potlaches and Warfare, 1792–1930.* New York: J. J. Augustin Publisher, 1950.

Coe, Sophie. "Iguana, Chocolates, Muskrats, and a Glimpse at Cochineal." *Petit Props Culinaire. 1990,* vol. 65.

———. *America's First Cuisines.* Austin: University of Texas Press, 1994.

———. *True Story of Chocolate.* New York: Thames & Hudson, 1996.

Cohn, Norman. *Europe's Inner Demons.* London: Chatto Heinemann for Sussex University, 1993.

Condamine, M. "Le Pain Mollet: Anecdote Historique" (Tiree du Traite de Police du Commissaire la Maree). *Almanach des muses.* Paris: Chez Delain, n.d.

Condorcet, Marie Jean Antoine Nicolas (Marquis of Condorcet). *The Life of M. Turgot, Comptroller General of the Finances of France in the Years 1774–76.* London: J. Johnson, 1787.

Condren, Mary. *The Serpent and the Goddess.* San Francisco: Harper & Row, 1989.

Conrad III, Barnaby. *Absinthe: History in a Bottle.* San Francisco: Chronicle Books, 1988.

Conrad, Jack Randolph. *The Horn and the Sword: The History of the Bull as Symbol of Power and Fertility.* New York: Dutton, 1957.

Cooper, Joe. *With or Without Beans: Being a Compendium to Perpetuate the Internationally Famous Bowl of Chili Which Occupies Such an Important Place in Modern Civilization.* Dallas, Tex.: W. S. Henson, 1952.

Counihan, Carole M. *The Anthropology of Food and Body: Gender, Meaning and Power.* New York: Routledge, 1999.

Cunnison, Ian. "Giraffe Hunting Among the Humr Tribe." *Sudan Notes and Records: Incorporating Proceedings from the Philosophical Society of the Sudan,* vol. 39 (1958).

Curiae, Amicus. *Food for the Million: Maize Against the Potato.* London: n.p., 1847.

Cushing, Frank Hamilton. "Zuni Breadstuff." *Indian Notes and Monographs,* vol. 8. New York: New York Museum of the American Indian Foundation, 1920.

———. *Zuni Folk Tales.* New York: A. A. Knopf, 1931.

D'Aussy, Legrand. *Histoire de la vie francois.* Paris: N.p., n.d.

Darby, William, et al. *Food: The Gift of Osiris.* San Francisco: Harcourt Brace Jovanovich, 1977.

Darnton, Robert. *The Forbidden Best-Sellers of Pre-Revolutionary France.* New York: W. W. Norton, 1995.

Darrah, Byhelen, "The Basils in Folklore and Biological Science." *Herbarist,* 38 (1972).

David, Elizabeth. "Savour of Ice and of Roses." Oxford: *Petit Propos Culinaire,* vol. 8.

Davidson, Alan (ed). *The Oxford Companion to Food.* Oxford, England: Oxford University Press, 1999.

Delamare. *Traite de la Police.* Paris: N.p., 1710 (and other editions).

Delay, J. *Diethylamide de l'acide d-lysergique et troubles psychiques de l'ergotisme.* Zurich: C. R. Social Biologie, 1951.

Der Meer, L. Bouke. *The Bronze Liver of Piacenza: Analysis of a Polytheistic Structure.* Amsterdam: J. C. Gieben, 1987.

Deslyons, Jean. *Discovrs ecclesiastiques contre le paganisme des roys de la feve.* Paris: Sorbonne, 1664.

Detienne, Marcel. *The Gardens of Adonis: Spices in Greek Mythology.* Hassocks, England: Harvester Press, 1977.

DeWitt, David, and Nancy Gerlach. *The Habanero Book.* Berkeley: Ten Speed Press, 1995.

Diaz del Castillo, B. *The Discovery and Conquest of Mexico 1517–1521.* London: Routledge, 1939.

Diederich, Bernard. "Swine Fever Ironies: The Slaughter of the Haitian Black Pig." *Caribbean Review,* C14, (Winter, 1985).

Donkin, R. A. *Manna: An Historical Geography.* Netherlands: Dr. W. Junk, 1980.

Douglas, Mary. *Purity and Danger: An Analysis of Concepts of Pollution and Taboo.* New York: Frederick A. Praeger, 1966.

Drew, Jesse. "Call Any Vegetable: The Politics of Food in San Francisco." *San Francisco: History, Politics, and Culture.* Edited by James Brook.

Du Bois, Cora. "Attitudes Toward Food and Hunger in Alor." *Language, Culture and Personality: Essays in Memory of Edward Sapir.* Menasaha, Wisc.: Sapir Memorial Publication Fund, 1941.

Dundes, Alan (ed). *The Blood Libel Legend: A Casebook in Anti-Semitic Folklore.* Madison: University of Wisconsin Press, 1991.

Duran, Diego. *Historia de las Indies de Nueva Espana.* Norman: University of Oklahoma, 1971.

Eidlitz, Rabbi E. *Is It Kosher? An Encyclopedia of Kosher Foods, Facts and Fallacies.* Jerusalem: Feldheim Publishing, 1992.

Elias, Norbert. *The Civilizing Process: State Formation and Civilization.* Oxford, England: Oxford Press, 1939.

Epstein, Barbara Leslie. *The Politics of Domesticity: Women, Evangelism and Temperance in Nineteenth-Century America.* Middletown, Conn.: Wesleyan University Press, 1981.

Etheridge, Elizabeth. *The Butterfly Caste.* Westport, Conn.: Greenwood Publications, 1978.

Evans-Pritchard, E. "Azande Historical Texts." *Sudan Notes and Record,* vol 37 (1956).

F. D. Bennet. *Narrative of a Whaling Voyage Around the Globe.* London: n.p., 1840.

Fabre-Vassas, Claudine. *La Bête singulière: les juifs, les chrétiens, le cochon.* Paris: Editions Fallimard, 1994.

Farmer, Paul. *AIDS and Accusation: Haiti and the Geography of Blame*. Los Angeles: University of California Press, 1992.

Fauré, Edgar. *Le disgrace de turgot*. Paris: Gallimard, 1961.

Feeley-Harnik, Gillian. *The Lord's Table: The Meaning of Food in Early Christianity and Judaism*. Washington, D.C.: Smithsonian Institute Press, 1981.

Fildes, Valerie. *Wet Nursing: A History from Antiquity to the Present*. London: Basil Blackwell, 1988.

Flogel, Thomas. "Eating Mushroom in Yunana." *Petit Propos Culinaire* (July 1987).

Forester, Robert (ed). *Food and Drink in History: Selections from the Annales, Economies, Societes, Civilisations. Volume 5*. Baltimore: John Hopkins University, 1979.

Fountain, John. "Crusader Makes a Salsa a Hot Topic." *New York Times* (Oct. 10, 2000).

Franklin, Alfred. *La Vie privée d'autrefois: le café, le thé et le chocolat*. Paris: E. Plon, 1893.

Freedman, Seymour. *The Book of Kashruth*. New York: Freedman, 1970.

Freeman, Sarah. *Mutton and Oysters: The Victorians and Their Food*. London: Victor Gollancz, 1989.

French, Laurence. *Psychocultural Change and the American Indian*. New York: Garland Publishing, 1987.

Frijhoff, Willem, and Dominique Julia. "The Diet in Boarding Schools." *ESC Economies Sociales*.

Furer-Haimendorf, Christoph. *The Sherpas of Nepal*. London: John Murray, 1964.

Fussell, Betty. *The Story of Corn*. New York: A. A. Knopf, 1994.

Gage, Thomas. *The English American, His Travail by Sea and Land, or a New Survy of the West Indies*. London: George Routledge, 1648.

Gajdusek, D. "Kuru." *Transactions of the Royal Society of Tropical Medicine and Hygiene* (1969).

———. "Degenerative Disease of the Central Nervous System in New Guinea." *New England Journal of Medicine* (1978).

Gazette d'un curieux. N.p., n.d.

Gelder, Jan van. *Of Dishes and Discourse: Classical Arabic Literary Representation of Food.* Surrey, England: Curzon Press, 2000.

Ginor, Michael. *Foie Gras: A Passion.* New York: Wiley, 1999.

———. Personal interview.

Glass, James. *Life Unworthy of Life: Racial Phobia and Mass Murder in Hitler's Germany.* New York: Basic Books, 1997.

Goodall, Jane. *The Chimpanzees of Gombe.* Cambridge, Mass.: Harvard University Press, 1986.

Goldziher, I. "Islamisme et Parsisme." *Revue de l'histoire des religions,* no. 43 (1901).

Goody, Jack. *Cooking, Cuisine, and Class.* Cambridge, England: Cambridge University Press, 1982.

Gordon, Bertram M. "Fascism. The Neo Right and Gastronomy." Presented at the 1987 Oxford Symposium on Food and Cookery. London: Prospect Books, 1988.

Gowers, Emily. *The Loaded Table: Representations of Food in Roman Literature.* Oxford, England: Clarendon Press, 1993.

Graetz, H. *History of the Jews,* six volumes. New York: Jewish Parable School of America, 1894.

Graulich, M. "L'Arbre interdit du paradis Azteque" in *Revue de l'histoire des religions,* vol. 27 (1990).

Gray, Francine du Plessix, *At Home with the Marquis de Sade.* New York: Simon & Schuster, 1998.

Grieve, Maud. *A Modern Herbal.* New York: Hafner Publications, 1931.

Grimm, Veronika. *From Feasting to Fasting, the Evolution of a Sin: Attitudes to Food in Late Antiquity.* London/New York: Routledge, 1996.

Grunfeld, Dayan Dr. I. *The Jewish Dietary Laws,* two vols. London: Soncineo, 1972.

Gupta, Shakti. *Plant Myths and Traditions in India.* Delhi: Munshiram Manohailol, 1991.

Hager, Philip. "Asian Refugees Poaching in S.F. Park." *San Francisco Chronicle* (Aug. 1, 1980).

Hale, Edward. *The Life of Christopher Columbus.* Chicago: Howe, 1893.

Hammerer, John. *An Account of a Plan for Civilizing the North American*

Indians, Proposed in the 18th Century. Brooklyn, New York: Historical Printing Club, 1890.

Harris, Lloyd J. *The Book of Garlic.* New York: Aris Books, 1974.

Harris, Marvin. *Cows, Pigs, Wars & Witches.* New York: Random House, 1974.

Harris, Marvin. *Good to Eat: Riddles of Culture and Food.* New York: Simon & Schuster, 1985.

Hart, Keith, and Louise Sperling. "Cattle as Capital." *Ethnos* 52 (1987).

Hartley, Ralph. *The Age of Unreason: Prohibition and Women and What They're Doing.* Boston: Meadow Publishing, 1936.

Heinerman, John. *The Healing Benefits of Garlic.* New York: Random House Value Publishing, 1995.

Heiser, C. C. *Seeds to Civilization: The Story of Food.* Cambridge, Mass.: Harvard University Press, 1973.

Heiser, F. "Systematics and the Origin of Cultivated Plants." *Taxon* 18 (36–45).

Hellbom, Anna-Britta. "The Creation Egg." *Ethnos,* vol. 1 (1963).

Helms, Mary. *Ancient Panama.* Austin: University of Texas Press, 1976.

Herskovits, Melville. "The Cattle Complex of East Africa." *American Anthropologist,* vol. 126.

Hibbert, Christopher. *The Great Mutiny of India 1857.* London: Allen Lane/ Penguin, 1978.

Hilderic, Reverend. *Flower and Flower Lore.* New York: Comumbian Publishing, 1891.

Hill, Christopher. *The World Turned Upside Down: Radical Ideas During the English Revolution.* London: Temple Smith, 1972.

Hill, Malcolm. *Statesman of the Enlightenment: The Life of Anne-Robert Turgot.* London: Othila Press, 1999.

Hirsch, Alan. Neurological Director of Smell & Taste Treatment and Research Center. Personal interview.

Hobhouse, Henry. *Seeds of Change: Five Plants That Transformed Mankind.* London: Sidgwick & Jackson, 1985.

Howey, M. O. *The Cult of the Dog.* Essex, England: C. W. Daniel Company, 1972.

Hunt, Alan. *Governance of the Consuming Passions: A History of Sumptuary Law.* New York: St. Martin's Press, 1996.

Italicus, Silius. *Punica Wars.* Translated by J. D. Duff. Cambridge, Mass.: Harvard University Press, 1934.

Jagchild, Sechin. *Mongolia's Culture and Society.* Boulder, Colo.: Westview Press, 1979.

Janson, Frederic H. *Pomona's Harvest: An Illustrated Chronicle of Antiquarian Fruit Literature.* Portland, Oreg.: Timber Press, 1996.

Jennings, Duffy. "Angry Outcry over Poaching." *San Francisco Chronicle* (Aug. 14, 1980).

Johnston, B. *Eat and Grow Fat.* New York: Sherwood Company, 1917.

Kaplan, Steven. *The Bakers of Paris and the Bread Question, 1700–1775.* Durham, N.C.: Duke University Press, 1996.

Kay-Shuttleworth, James Phillip. *The Moral and Physical Condition of the Working Classes in the Cotton Manufacture in Manchester.* London: J. Ridgeway, 1832.

Kelman, Herbert. "Violence Without Moral Restraint." *Crimes of Obedience.* New Haven, Conn.: Yale University Press, 1989.

Keneally, Thomas. *The Great Shame.* New York: Random House, 1998.

Kennedy, Allison Baily. "Ecce Bufo: The Toad in Nature and in Olmec Iconography." *Current Anthropology,* 23 (1982), 273–90.

Klitzman, Robert. *The Trembling Mountain: A Personal Account of Kuru, Cannibals, and Mad Cow Disease.* New York: Plenum, 1998.

Kobler, John. *Ardent Spirits: The Rise and Fall of Prohibition.* New York: Thrin Press, 1993.

Kryter, Karl. *Physiological, Sociological and Social Effects of Noise.* NASA: NASA Reference Publication 1115, 1984.

La Barre, Weston. *Muelos: A Stone Age Superstition About Sexuality.* New York: Columbia University Press, 1984.

Labnow, Keith. Conservation Program Coordinator at the Arizona-Sonora Desert Museum in Tucson, Arizona. Personal interview.

La Comtesse du Barry. Paris: n.p., 1878.

Lamothe-Langon, Baron Etienne Leon. *Memoirs of the Comtesse du Barry with Minute Details of Her Entire Career as Favorite of Louis XV: Written by Herself.* N.d.

Langercrantz, Angell. "Geophagical Custom." *Studia ethnographica upsaliensia* XVII (1958).

Langercrantz, Sture. "Forbidden Fish." *Orientalia Fuecana* vol. II (1953).
———. *Studia ethnographica upsaliensia.* vol. 1 (1950).

Lanier, Doris. *Absinthe: The Cocaine of the Nineteenth Century, a History of the Hallucinogenic Drug and Its Effect on Artists and Writers in Europe and the United States.* London: n.p., 1995.

Latha, R. E. *Revised Medieval Latin Work List: From British and Irish Sources.* Oxford, England: Oxford University Press, 1965.

Laufer, Berthold. *Geophagy.* Chicago: Field Museum of Natural History, 1930.

Lebeson, Anita Libman. *Jewish Pioneers in America, 1492–1848.* New York: Brentano's Publishers, 1931.

LeClerc, Henri. *Les Legumes de France: leur histoire, usage et vertus therapeutique.* Paris: Legrand, 1927.

Lekatsas, Barbara. "Inside the Pastilles of the Marquis de Sade." *Chocolate: Food of the Gods.* Edited by Alex Szogyi. Westwood, Conn.: Green Wood Press, 1997.

Levin, Harry. *The Myths of the Golden Age in the Renaissance.* Bloomington: Indiana University Press, 1969.

Levine, Renee. *Women in Spanish Crypto-Judau, 1492–1520* (Ph.D. Diss., Brandeis University, 1982).

Lightfoot, J. B. (trans.). *The Epistle of Barnabas.* Athena Data Products, 1990.

Lochhead, Marion, and John Murray. *The First Ten Years: Victorian Childhood.* London: Murray, 1956.

Loi et Actes de government, l'an II, 25 nivoise. French government publication, 1793.

Longstreet, Augustus. "The Fight." *Georgia Scenes.* New York: Harper & Bros., 1851.

Loomis, Stanley. *Du Barry: A Biography.* Philadelphia: Lippincott, 1959.

Love, Theresa. *Dickens and the Seven Deadly Sins.* Danville, Ill.: Interstate Publishers, 1979.

Macalister, R. A. Stewart. "The Vision of Merlino." *Zeitschrift für Celtische*. Tubingen, Germany, 1924.

MacBain, Alexander. *Celtic Mythology and Religion*. Stirling, Scotland: Eneas MacKay, 1917.

MacClancy, Jeremy. *Consuming Culture: Why You Eat and What You Eat*. New York: Henry Holt, 1992.

MacCullough, J. A. *Celtic Mythology*. London: Constable, 1993.

MacDonald, Arthur. *Statistics of Alcoholism and Inebrity*. International Congress of Criminal Anthropology, Hartford, Conn., 1909.

MacDowell, Jim. *Hamasta: The Enigma of Cannibalism on the Pacific Northwest*. Vancouver: Consdall Press, 1997.

Macherel, Claud. *Une vie de pain: faire, penser et dire le pain en Europe*. Bruxelles: Credit Communal, 1994.

Magennis, Hugh. *Food, Drink and Feast in Anglo-Saxon and Germaic Literary Traditions*. Dublin, Ireland: Four Courts Press, 1999.

Malouin, Paul-Jacques. *Descriptions des arts de meunier, du vermicelier et du boulanger*. Paris: n.p., 1771.

Manchester, Sean. *The Grail Church*. Gwynedd, Wales: Holy Grail Press, 1995.

Marriott, Mckin. "Caste Ranking and Food Transactions: A Matrix Analysis." *Structure and Change in Indian Society*. Chicago: Aldine Publishing, 1968.

Marsh, George. *Report on the Artificial Propagation of Fish*. George Perkins Research Center.

Marsh, Peter. *Aggro: The Illusion of Violence*. London: J. M. Dent & Sons, 1978.

Marsh, Thomas. *Roots of Crime: Bio-Physical Approach to Crime Prevention and Rehabilitation*. New York: Nellen Publishing, 1981.

Marsh, William Parker. *Celtic Christianity: Ecology and Holiness*. New York: Lindisfame Press, 2000.

Martinez, Zarela. *The Food and Life of Oaxaca Mexico*. New York: MacMillian. 1997.

———. Personal interview.

Matthews, Thomas. "Culinary Summit." *Wine Spectator* (May 15, 1995).

Maugh, Thomas II. "New Analysis of Breast Feeding Studies Suggests a Boost in IQ of 3 to 5 Points." *Los Angeles Times* (Sept. 23, 1999).

Mazzoni, Cristina. *Saint Hysteria: Neurosis, Mysticism and Gender in European Culture.* Ithaca, N.Y.: Cornell University Press, 1996.

McCance, Robert. *Breads, White and Brown: Their Place in Thought and Social History.* Philadelphia: Lippincott, 1956.

McCulloch, J. R. *A Descriptive and Statistical Account of the British Empire.* London: Longman, Brown, Green and Longmans, 1847.

McIlwaine, Shields. *The Southern Poor White Trash: From Lubberland to Tobacco Road.* Oklahoma City: University of Oklahoma, 1939.

Melchert, Christopher, Director of Regulatory and Technical Affairs for Snack Food. Personal interview.

Mennell, Stephen. *All Manners of Food: Eating and Taste in England and France from the Middle Ages to Present.* Oxford, England: Oxford University Press, 1985.

Mernissi, Fatima. *Women in Moslem Paradise.* New Delhi: Kali for Women Press, 1986.

Miller, Bryan. Craig Claiborne obituary. *New York Times* (Jan. 24, 2000).

Milner, Murray. *Status and Sacredness: A General Theory of Status Relations and an Analysis of Indian Culture.* Oxford, England: Oxford University Press, 1994.

Momigliano, Arnaldo. *Claudius, The Emperor and his Achievement.* London: Clarendon Press, 1934.

Morgan, Arabel. *Total Woman Cookbook.* Old Tappan, New Jersey: H. Revell, 1973.

Morgan, Owen. *The Light of Britannia.* New York: n.p., 1893.

Morton, Marcia, and Frederic Morton. *Chocolate: An Illustrated History.* New York: Crown, 1986.

Moulin, M. *Descriptions des arts et metiers, faites ou approuvess par messieurs de l'Academie Royale des Sciences.* Paris: n.p., 1768.

Murray, Margaret. *The God of the Witches.* Oxford, England: Oxford University Press, 1970.

Naj, Amal. *Peppers: A Story of Hot Pursuits.* New York: A.A. Knopf, 1992.

Neamours, Du Pont (ed.). *Memoirs de la vie et les ouvrages de M. Turgot.* Paris: Guillaumin, 1844.

Neuber, Von Wolf. *Das Holzerne: Lebzeltermodeln Bilder-buch.* Brandstatter: Verlay Christian, n.d.

Newall, Venetia. *An Egg at Easter: A Folklore Study.* London: Routledge, 1971.

Obolensky, Alexander. *Food Notes on Gogol.* Winnipeg, Canada: Trident Press, 1972.

Oldenburg, Don. "On Thin Ground." *Washington Post* (June 23, 1998).

Ortner, Sherry. "Gods' Bodies, Gods' Food: A Symbolic Analysis of a Sherpa Ritual." *The Interpretation of Symbolism.* New York: John Wiley & Sons, 1975.

Orzech, Charles. "Saving the Burning-Mouth Hungry Ghost." *Religions of China in Practice.* Edited by Donald Lopez. Princeton: Readings in Religion, 1996.

Palladin, Jean-Louis. Personal interview.

Panoff, F. "Food and Faeces: A Melanesian Rite." *Man*, vol. 5 (1970).

Parnaik, Eira. "The Succulent Gender: Eat Her Softly." *Literary Gastronomy* (1988).

Pastoureau, Michel. *Bonum, malum, pomum: une historie symbolique de la pomme.*

Paterniti, Michael. "The Last Meal." *Esquire* (May 1998).

Pollock, Nancy. *These Roots Remain: Food Habits in Islands of the Central and Eastern Pacific Since Western Contact.* Honolulu, Hawaii: Institute for Polynesian Studies, 1992. (Distributed for the Institute for Polynesian Studies by the University of Hawaii Press, Laie, Hawaii.)

Probyn, E. "An Ethos with a Bite: Queer Appetites from Sex to Food." *Sexualities,* vol. 2 (1999).

Prucha, Frances Paul (ed.). *Americanizing the American Indians: Writings by the "Friends of the Indians" 1880–1900.* Cambridge: Harvard University Press, 1973.

Pullar, Phillipa. *Consuming Passions: A History of English Food and Appetite.* London: Hamilton, 1970.

Rajshekar, V. T. *Brahminism: Father of Facism, Racism, Nazism.* Bangalore: Dalit Sahitya Academy, 1994.

Rammell, Hal. *Nowhere in America: The Big Rock Candy Mountain and Other Comic Utopias.* Chicago: University of Illinois Press, 1990.

Redcliffe, Salaman. *The History and Social Influence of the Potato.* Cambridge, England: Cambridge University Press, 1949.

Rice, Michael. *The Power of the Bull.* London: Routledge, 1988.

Ridgeway, Jim, and Bill Treger. "Aiding and Abetting Mayhem." *Multinational Monitor* (March 1994).

Robertson, Ritchie. *The Jewish Question in German Literature 1749–1933.* Oxford, England: Oxford University Press, 1999.

Roden, Claudia. *The Book of Jewish Food.* New York: A. A. Knopf, 1997.

Roe, Daphne. *A Plague of Corn: The Social History of Pellagra.* Ithaca, New York: Cornell University Press, 1973.

Rogers, Mara Reid. *Onions: A Celebration of the Onion Through Recipes, Lore and History.* Boston: Addison-Wesley Publishers, 1995.

Rose, Anthony. "Growing Illegal Commerce in African Bushmeat Destroys Great Ape and Threatens Humanity," press statement. Antioch: Institute for Conservation Education and Development, Antioch University.

Ross, Eric. *Food Taboos, Diet and Hunting Strategy: The Adaption to Animals in Amazon.* American Anthropological Institute.

Rozin, Paul. "Effects of Oral Capsaicin in Gustator, Olfactor and Irritant." *Chemical Senses,* 10:579 (1985).

———. Personal communication.

Rudgley, Richard. *Encyclopedia of Psychoactive Substances.* Boston: Little, Brown, 1998.

Rutherford, Ward. *Celtic Lore.* London: Aquarian & Thorsons, 1993.

Rutherford, Ward. *Pythagoras, Lover of Wisdom.* Wellingsborough, Northamptonshire: Aquarian Press, 1984.

Ryckman, Jacques. *Les Confessions publique Sabeennes. Le code Sud-Arabe pureté rituelle.* Annale dell'Istituto Orientale di Napoli, 32 (1972), 1–15.

Sade, Marquis. *The 120 Days of Sodom and Other Writings.* New York: Grove Press, 1966.

Sagar, Sunder Lal. *Hindu Culture and Caste System in India.* New Delhi: Uppal Book Store, 1975.

Sage, Adam. "French Hunters Defy a Ban on Bagging the Bunting." *London Times* (Aug. 14, 1999).

Sahagun, Bernard. *Historia general de la cosas de nueva Espana.* Santa Fe, N.M.: School of American History, 1950.

Saint Germain, Jacques. *La Reynie et las police au grand siècle.* Paris: n.p., 1962.

Saint-Arroman. *Coffee, Tea and Chocolate.* London: n.p., 1852.

Schivelbush, Wolf. *Tastes of Paradise.* New York: Pantheon, 1992.

Schoenthaler, S. J. "The Alabama Diet-Behavior Program: An Empirical Evaluation at the Coosa Valley Regional Detention Center." *International Journal of Biosocial Research,* vol. 5 (1983).

Schoenthaler, Stephen. "Diet and Delinquency: Empirical Testing of Seven Theories." *International Journal of Biosocial Research,* vol. 7 (1985).

Schweid, Richard. *Hot Peppers: Cajuns and Capsicum in New Iberia, Louisiana.* New Berkeley: (1987, reprint, Ten Speed Press), 1989.

Scullard, H. J. *The Etrucscan Cities and Rome.* Ithaca, N.Y.: Cornell, 1967.

Sexton, Regina. "I'd Ate It Like Chocolate! The Disappearing Offal Food Traditions of Cork City." *Oxford Symposium on Food* (1994).

Shankman, Paul. *"Le Roti and Le Boulli:* Levi-Strauss' Theory of Cannabilism." *American Anthropologist Magazine* (1969).

Shapiro, Laura. *Perfection Salad: Women and Cooking at the Turn of the Century.* New York: Farrar, Straus and Giroux, 1986.

Shacher, Isaiah. *The Judensau: A Medieval Anti-Jewish Motif and Its History* (Warburg Institute Surveys #5). London: University of London, 1974.

Shaw, Teresa. *The Burden of the Flesh: Fasting and Sexuality in Early Christianity.* Minneapolis: Fortress Press, 1998.

Shea, George. *The Poems of Alcimus Ecdiscius Avitus,* vol. 172. Tempe, Ariz.: Medieval and Renaissance Texts and Studies, 1997.

Shivley, Donald. "Sumptuary Regulation and Status in Early Toku-
gawa Japan." *Harvard Journal of Asiatic Studies,* vol. 25 (1964–65).

Simoons, Frederick. *Eat Not This Flesh.* Madison: University of Wisconsin Press, 1994.

———. *Plants of Life, Plants of Death.* Madison: University of Wisconsin
Press, 1998.

Singh, Mahedra Pratap. *Life in Ancient India.* Varnasi: Bishwavidyalaya
Prakashan, 1981.

Skinner, Charles. *Myths and Legends of Flowers, Trees, Fruits and Plants in
all Ages and in All Climes.* London: J. B. Lippincott, 1911.

Smith, Andrew. *Pure Ketchup.* Columbia: University of South Carolina
Press, 1996.

———. *The Tomato in America.* Columbia: University of South Carolina
Press, 1994.

Smith, E. N. "Some Middle Georgian Don't Like to Talk About 'Dirty'
Habit" from the Associated Press, April 19, 1999.

Smith, Mahlon. *And Taking Bread: Cerularius and the Azyme Controversy
of 1054* (Theologie Historique #47). Paris: Beauchesne, 1978.

Snellgrove, David. *The Nine Ways of Bon.* London: Oxford University
Press, 1967.

Spencer, Colin. *The Heretic's Feast: A History of Vegetarianism.* London:
Fourth Estate, 1993.

Spielmann, Robert. *You're So Fat: Exploring Ojibwe Discourse.* Toronto:
University of Toronto Press, 1998.

Splaney, L. "Hunting Is Greater Threat to Primates than Destruction of
Habitats." *New Scientist* (March 1998).

Srinvasan, Doris. *Concept of Cow in the Rigveda.* Delhi: Motilal Banarsi-
dass, 1979.

Stearns, Peter. *Fat History: Bodies and Beauty in the Modern West.* New
York: New York University Press, 1997.

Stein, R. *Tibet: Religious Customs.* N.p., n.d.

Steingarten, Jeffrey. *The Man Who Ate Everything.* New York:
A. A. Knopf, 1997.

Stelten, Leo. *Ecclesiastical Latin.* London: Hendrikson, 1995.

Stewart, R. J. *The Mystic Life of Merlin.* New York: Arkana, 1986.

Stoller, Robert, and Gilbert Herdt. "The Development of Masculinity: A Cross-Cultural Contribution." *The Journal of the American Psychoanalytic Association,* vol. 30 (1982).

Szogyi, Alex (ed). *Chocolate: Food of the Gods.* Westford, Conn.: Green Wood Press, 1997.

T. G. Powell. *The Celts.* London: Thames & Hudson, 1958.

Birmingham, Rev. T. M. C. *Prohibition, the Way to National Prosperity.* 1908. Private Printing.

Tannahill, Reay. *Food in History.* New York: Stein and Day, 1973.

———. *Flesh and Blood.* London: Manilton, 1975.

Thiebaux, Marcelle. *The Stag of Love: The Chase in Medieval Literature.* Ithaca, N.Y.: Cornell University Press, 1974.

Thompson, C. J. S. *The Mystic Mandrake.* London: Royal College of Surgeons of London, 1934.

Thornton, Mark. *Alcohol Prohibition Was a Failure.* Washington, D.C.: Cato Institute, 1991.

———. *The Economics of Prohibition.* Salt Lake City: University of Utah Press, 1991.

Thurston, Mary. *The Lost History of the Canine Race: Our 15,000-Year-Long Love Affair with Dogs.* Kansas City, Mo.: Andrews McMeel, 1996.

Titcomb, Margaret, and Mary Kawena Pukui. *Dog and Man in the Ancient Pacific, with Special Attention to Hawaii.* Honolulu, Hawaii: Bernice P. Bishop Museum, 1969.

Tolstoy, Nikolai. *In Quest of Merlin.* London: H. Hamilton, 1985.

Toorn, K. van Der. *Sin and Sanction in Israel and Mesopotamia.* Amsterdam: Studia Semitica Neerlandica 22, 1985.

Trusler. John. *The Honors of the Table.* London: Literary Press, 1791.

Tsao, Hsueh-Chin. *Dream of the Red Chamber.* New York: Doubleday, 1929.

Turgot, Anne-Robert-Jacques. *Oeuvres de Turgot et Documents les Concernant, avec Biographie et Notes,* edited by Gustave Schelle. Five Volumes. Paris: F. Alcon, 1913–23.

Vangaard, Thorkil. *Phallos: A Symbol and Its History in the Male World.* New York: International Universities Press, 1972.

Visser, Margaret. *Moretum: Ancient Roman Pesto.* Oxford Symposium on Food & History, 1992.

———. *Much Depends on Dinner: The Extraordinary History and Mythology, Allure and Obsessions, Perils and Taboos, of an Ordinary Meal.* New York: Grove Press, 1986.

———. *The Rituals of Dinner.* New York: Grove Press, 1991.

Waines, David. *In a Caliph's Kitchen.* Beirut/London: Riad El-Rayyes Books, 1989.

Wasson, Gordon. *Soma.* New York: Harcourt, Brace, Jovanovich, 1968.

———. *Wondrous Mushroom.* New York: McGraw Hill, 1980.

Welsch, Roger L., and Linda K. Welsch. *Cather's Kitchens: Foodways in Literature and Life.* Lincoln and London: University of Nebraska Press, 1987.

Wenzel, Siegfried. *Fasciculus Moru: A Fourteenth-Century Preacher's Handbook.* State College: Pennsylvania State University Press, 1989.

Weston, Jessie L. "The Apple Mystery in Arthurian Romance." *The Bulletin of the John Reylands Library,* vol. 9 (1925).

Wharburton, Clark. *The Economic Results of Prohibition.* New York: Columbia University, 1932.

White, David. *Myths of the Dog-Man.* Chicago: University of Chicago Press, 1991.

Wilson, C. Anne (ed.). *Banquetting Stuffe: The Fare and Social Background of the Tudor and Stuart Banquet.* Edinburgh, England: Edinburgh University Press, 1986.

Wilson, Bee. "Mein Diat." *New Statesman,* London (Oct. 9, 1998).

Wilson, David. *King James VI and I.* London: Jonathan Cape, 1956.

Wilson, Peter. *Ploughing the Clouds: The Search for Irish Soma.* San Francisco: City Lights Books, 1999.

Winkelmann, R. K. *The Erogenous Zones: Their Nerve Supply and Significance,* vol. 34, no. 2 (January 21, 1959).

Woloy, Eleanora. *The Symbol of the Dog in the Human Psyche: A Study of the Human-Dog Bond.* Wilmette, Ill.: Chiron Publications, 1990.

Wright, Clifford. *A Mediterranean Feast.* New York: Morrow, 2000.

Wright, Edward. *The Early History of Heaven.* Oxford, England: Oxford University Press, 2000.

Yalon, Marilyn. *A History of the Breast.* New York: Ballantine, 1997.

Yoder, Stephen. "In This Bully Battle with Japan, the Cry Is 'Toro, Toro, Toro.' " *The Wall Street Journal* (August 7, 2000).

Young, Michael. *Fighting with Food: Leadership, Values and Social Control in a Massi Society.* Cambridge, England: Cambridge University Press, 1971.

Zeuner, F. E. *A History of Domesticated Animals.* London: Hutchinston, 1963.

Zuckerman, Larry. *The Potato: How the Humble Spud Rescued the Western World.* Boston: Faber & Faber, 1998.